T0229863

AI in Wireless for Beyond 5G Networks

Artificial intelligence (AI) is a game changer in many domains, and wireless communication networks are no exception. With the advent of 5G networks, we have witnessed rapid growth in wireless connectivity, which has led to unprecedented opportunities for innovation and new use cases. However, as we move beyond 5G (B5G), the challenges and opportunities are set to become even more significant, offering new, previously unimaginable services.

AI in Wireless for Beyond 5G Networks provides a comprehensive overview of the use of AI in wireless communication for B5G networks. The authors draw on their expertise in the field to explore the latest developments in AI technologies and their applications in B5G wireless communication systems. The book discusses a wide range of topics, including enabling AI technologies, architecture, and applications of AI from smartphones, radio access networks (RANs), edge and core networks, and application service providers. It also discusses the trends in on-device AI for B5G networks.

This book is written in an accessible style, making it an ideal resource for academics, researchers, and industry professionals in wireless communication. It provides valuable insights into the latest field trends and developments and practical possibilities for implementing AI technologies in wireless communication systems.

Above all, this book is a testament to the power of collaboration and innovation in wireless communication. The authors' dedication and expertise have produced a valuable resource for anyone interested in the latest AI and wireless communication developments. This book will inspire and inform readers, and we highly recommend it to scholars interested in the future of AI in wireless communication.

AI in Wireless for Beyond 5G Networks

Edited by
Sukhdeep Singh
Yulei Wu
Mohan Rao GNS
Kaustubh Joshi
Payam Barnaghi
Madhan Raj Kanagarathinam

CRC Press
Taylor & Francis Group
Boca Raton London New York

CRC Press is an imprint of the
Taylor & Francis Group, an **informa** business

Cover image © Shutterstock

First edition published 2024
by CRC Press
2385 NW Executive Center Drive, Suite 320, Boca Raton FL 33431

and by CRC Press
4 Park Square, Milton Park, Abingdon, Oxon, OX14 4RN

CRC Press is an imprint of Taylor & Francis Group, LLC

© 2024 selection and editorial matter, Sukhdeep Singh, Yulei Wu, Mohan Rao GNS, Kaustubh Joshi, Payam Barnaghi, Madhan Raj Kanagarathinam; individual chapters, the contributors

ISBN: 9781032301211 (hbk)
ISBN: 9781032301228 (pbk)
ISBN: 9781003303527 (ebk)

DOI: 10.1201/9781003303527

Typeset in Sabon
by KnowledgeWorks Global Ltd.

Contents

Preface

Artificial intelligence (AI) is a game changer in many domains, and wireless communication networks are no exception. With the advent of 5G networks, we have witnessed rapid growth in wireless connectivity, which has led to unprecedented opportunities for innovation and new use cases. However, as we move beyond 5G (B5G), the challenges and opportunities are set to become even more significant, offering new, previously unimaginable services.

This book provides a comprehensive overview of the use of AI in wireless communication for the B5G networks. The authors draw on their expertise in the field to explore the latest developments in AI technologies and their applications in B5G wireless communication systems. The book discusses a wide range of topics, including enabling AI technologies, architecture, and applications of AI from smartphones, radio access networks (RANs), edge and core networks, and application service providers. It also discusses the trends in on-device AI for the B5G network.

The book is written in an accessible style, making it an ideal resource for academics, researchers, and industry professionals in wireless communication. It provides valuable insights into the latest field trends and developments and practical possibilities for implementing AI technologies in wireless communication systems.

Above all, this book is a testament to the power of collaboration and innovation in wireless communication. The authors' dedication and expertise have produced a valuable resource for anyone interested in the latest AI and wireless communication developments. This book will inspire and inform readers, and we highly recommend it to scholars interested in the future of AI in wireless communication.

TARGETED AUDIENCES

This book targets academics, researchers, and industry professionals in wireless communication. Graduate scholars can select promising research topics from this book suitable for their thesis or dissertation research. Researchers will understand and appreciate AI's challenging issues and opportunities in

B5G wireless networks and can thus quickly find an unsolved research problem to pursue. Research engineers from information technology (IT) companies, service providers, content providers, network operators, and equipment manufacturers can learn the engineering design issues and corresponding solutions after reading some practical schemes described in the chapters. We have required all chapter authors to provide as many technical details as possible. Each chapter also includes references for readers' further studies and investigations. Please contact the editors for more information if you have any comments or questions on specific chapters.

Thank you for reading this book. We hope this book can help you with the scientific research and practical problems of AI in B5G wireless networks.

DISCLAIMER

The ideas and proposals discussed in the chapters are the individual thoughts of the authors and do not reflect any organization's thoughts or information.

About the editors

Sukhdeep Singh received his PhD in computer engineering from Sungkyunkwan University (SKKU) in South Korea in 2016, along with the Superior Research Award from the Electrical and Computer Engineering Department for publishing the maximum number of SCI(E) research papers during his PhD work in 2016. He also received the SKKU Bright Student Scholarship Award. He was part of Brain Korea (BK21) and the National Research Foundation of Korea project during his PhD. He worked in diverse fields during his PhD, such as evolved multimedia broadcast multicast services (eMBMS) scheduling, video delivery architecture for 5G, integrating sociology with next-generation mobile networks, and Digital-to-Digital (D2D) communications. Dr. Singh is currently working with Samsung R&D Institute India–Bangalore in 5G radio access network (RAN) system design, where he is responsible for the research and design of open-standard radio access networks (O-RANs) and network slicing features for 5G networks. He received the Samsung Best Paper Award, conferred by the CEO and president of Samsung Electronics. He received the Samsung annual award in 2023 for breaking a record by publishing the highest number of research papers (in Chief Technology Officer [CTO] list) in 2022, and he has also received the Samsung Citizen Award/ Samsung Excellence Award (quarterly awards) ten times, conferred by the MD of Samsung R&D Institute India–Bangalore. He has published 40+ research articles, 20+ patents, and two books. He has served as guest editor for the *IETE Journal of Research* (Taylor & Francis), and as general chair in workshops hosted at IEEE WCNC 2020 and IEEE Globecom 2020. He also served as technical program chair member for IEEE iNIS 2016, IEEE iNIS 2017, ISRO-ACM ICSE 2017, IEEE iSES 2018, IEEE iSES 2019, IEEE iSES 2020, and IEEE iSES 2021. He has been invited as a guest lecturer by the University of Toronto, San Jose State University, Indian Institutions of Technology (IITs), Indian Institutes of Management (IIMs), and Indian Institutes of Information Technology (IIITs), and as a keynote speaker at Springer's ICIMMI 2019 and the IEEE Virtual Talk Series 2020. He will be serving as a mentor and panelist at Solve for Tomorrow (a flagship event of Samsung) and at Invention Factory (organized by IIT Jammu in conjunction with IIT Bombay and IIT Gandhinagar). He coauthored and edited the world's first book on 6G.

Yulei Wu is a Senior Lecturer with the Department of Computer Science, College of Engineering, Mathematics and Physical Sciences, University of Exeter, United Kingdom. He received his PhD degree in computing and mathematics in 2010 and BSc (1st Class Hons.) degree in computer science in 2006 from the University of Bradford, United Kingdom. His expertise is on intelligent networking, and his main research interests include computer networks, networked systems, software-defined networks and systems, network management, and network security and privacy. His research has been supported by the Engineering and Physical Sciences Research Council, London Mathematical Society, National Natural Science Foundation of China, University's Innovation Platform (Link Fund), and industry. Dr. Wu serves as an associate editor of *IEEE Transactions on Network and Service Management*, *IEEE Transactions on Network Science and Engineering*, and *IEEE Access*, and as an area editor of *Computer Networks* (Elsevier). He also serves as a guest editor for many international journals, including the *IEEE Journal on Selected Areas in Communications*, *IEEE Transactions on Industrial Informatics*, *IEEE Transactions on Cognitive Communications and Networking*, *IEEE Transactions on Sustainable Computing*, and *IEEE Transactions on Computational Social Systems*. He is a senior member of the IEEE and the Association for Computing Machinery (ACM), and a fellow of the HEA.

Mohan Rao GNS is the corporate Vice President at Samsung R&D Institute India–Bangalore (SRI-B) and heads the 5G, 6G, and AI in Wireless R&D teams. Having spent 26 years with Samsung, he has spearheaded all generations of mobile and network protocol R&D, spanning multiple markets and operators. He and his team have been key contributors to wireless protocol standardization, securing multiple essential patents, end-to-end stack development of inter-RAT (radio access technology) protocols, mobility management, protocol systems, the IP Multimedia Subsystem (IMS), Voice over LTE and Voice over New Radio (VoLTE and VoNR), Rich Communication Services (RCS), and many such cutting-edge technologies. After 5G deployment in the U.S. and European markets, they are now driving 6G wireless communication research. Mohan is also a key proponent of the kernel application platform. He also handles and nurtures the global talent pool across Samsung Electronics. Apart from building the Center of Excellence, he also serves as a leader for overall strategy development at SRI-B. He received a BE degree in electronics and communication in Nagarjuna University, Vijayawada, India, in 1995 and stood as University Topper. He also did a management course at the Indian Institute of Management, Bangalore. With 25+ patents in the wireless domain, he has received numerous awards, including the prestigious Best Overseas R&D Employee twice from the president of Samsung Electronics. He was recently conferred Zinnov's Best Global Leader award.

Kaustubh Joshi is currently a Director of Inventive Science with AT&T Labs Research, Bedminster, New Jersey, USA. At AT&T, he has led the creation of a number of research and production systems in the areas of network virtualization, mobility infrastructures, and Internet Protocol (IP) telecommunications, and he has authored more than 100 papers and patents on these topics. His research interests include the intersection of adaptive distributed systems, cloud, and networking.

Payam Barnaghi is the Chairman in Machine Intelligence applied to medicine in the Department of Brain Sciences at Imperial College London. He is deputy director and group lead in the Care Research and Technology Centre at the UK Dementia Research Institute. He is an associate editor of *IEEE Transactions on Big Data* and vice chair of the IEEE Special Interest Groups (SIG) on Big Data Intelligent Networking. His main research goal is to develop AI and machine learning solutions for healthcare and create affordable and scalable digital systems that can be applied across a range of health conditions. He works on machine learning, internet of things (IoT), semantic computing, adaptive algorithms, and computational neuroscience to solve problems and develop new technologies for future healthcare systems.

Madhan Raj Kanagarathinam received a BE degree in computer science and engineering from Anna University, Chennai, India, in 2012. He is currently pursuing his PhD at the Indian Institute of Technology (IIT) Madras. He has nine years of working experience in design and development of TCP/IP protocols, Multipath TCP, and UNIX-flavored operating systems. Currently, he is working as a senior chief engineer for Samsung R&D Institute India–Bangalore. Previously, he worked as an engineer with Aricent Technology (India) Private Limited. He is the author of 15 articles and more than 25 inventions. His current research interests include communication and networks, which include pre-6G/beyond 5G, next-generation mobile networks, software-defined network architecture, wireless transport-layer protocols, and cross-layer optimization techniques. He is also the winner of the IEEE Bangalore Young Technologist of the Year 2020 award. He is a senior member of the IEEE and a member of the ACM.

Contributors

Sharan Kumar Allur
Samsung R&D Institute
    India-Bangalore
Bangalore, India

Ashok Kumar Reddy Chavva
Samsung R&D Institute
    India-Bangalore
Bangalore, India

Jiasi Chen
University of California
Riverside, California

Ankit Dixit
Pune, India

Marten Fischer
University of Applied Science
Osnabrück, Germany

Prash Goel
Pune, India

Anusha Gunturu
Samsung R&D Institute
    India-Bangalore
Bangalore, India

Kaustubh Joshi
AT&T Labs Research
Bedminster, New Jersey

Sripada Kadambar
Samsung R&D Institute
    India-Bangalore
Bangalore, India

Vasanth Kanakaraj
Samsung R&D Institute
    India-Bangalore
Bangalore, India

Shubham Khunteta
Samsung R&D Institute
    India-Bangalore
Bangalore, India

Issaac Kommineni
Samsung R&D Institute
    India-Bangalore
Bangalore, India

Mahantesh Kothiwale
Samsung R&D Institute
    India-Bangalore
Bangalore, India

Vishal Murgai
Samsung R&D Institute
    India-Bangalore
Bangalore, India

Frank Nordemann
University of Applied Science
Osnabrück, Germany

Saikrishna Pedamalli
Samsung R&D Institute
    India-Bangalore
Bangalore, India

Manikantan Srinivasan
NEC Corporation India
and
Indian Institute of Technology
    Madras
Chennai, India

Prabhu Kaliyammal Thiruvasagam
NEC Corporation India
and
Indian Institute of Technology
    Madras
Chennai, India

Ralf Tönjes
University of Applied Science
Osnabrück, Germany

Tuyen X. Tran
AT&T Labs Research
Bedminster, New Jersey

Caglar Tunc
AT&T Labs Research
Bedminster, New Jersey

Introduction

Sukhdeep Singh, Mohan Rao GNS,
and Madhan Raj Kanagarathinam
Samsung R&D Institute India-Bangalore
Bangalore, Karnataka

Artificial intelligence (AI) and wireless communication are two of the most rapidly developing technologies transforming industries worldwide. AI is revolutionizing how we interact with technology by enabling machines to process vast amounts of data, learn from it, and make decisions that emulate human intelligence. On the other hand, wireless communication has enabled people to connect to the internet anytime and anywhere. The next generation of wireless networks, beyond 5G (B5G), promises to deliver faster speeds, lower latency, and better reliability. With AI as one of the core pillars, the next-generation wireless experience has been enhanced from the smartphone, radio access network (RAN), edge, and core all the way up to the application service provider.

AI increasingly integrates into 5G smartphones, enabling advanced capabilities and improving the overall user experience. Here are some ways that AI is being used in 5G smartphones:

1. *Camera*: AI algorithms are used to enhance camera performance in 5G smartphones. These algorithms enable features such as facial recognition, object detection, and image segmentation, which improve the quality of photos and videos taken by the camera.
2. *Voice assistants*: Many 5G smartphones have built-in voice assistants, such as Siri, Bixby, and Google Assistant, which use AI to understand natural language and respond to user commands.
3. *Personalization*: AI algorithms are used to personalize the user experience of 5G smartphones. This includes suggesting apps, customizing the user interface, and predicting the user's behavior.
4. *Gaming*: AI is being used to enhance gaming performance in 5G smartphones. For example, AI algorithms can predict the movements of other players in multiplayer games, improving the player's reaction time.
5. *Network optimization*: AI is being used to optimize the performance of 5G networks. This includes predicting congestion and adjusting real-time network settings to ensure the best possible connection.

In a nutshell, AI is playing an increasingly important role in 5G smartphones.

DOI: 10.1201/9781003303527-1

1

AI is also being integrated into B5G RANs, enabling a wide range of advanced capabilities. Here are some ways that AI is being used in B5G RANs:

1. *Network optimization*: AI algorithms are being used to optimize B5G RANs, ensuring that data is delivered efficiently and reliably. This includes things like load balancing, traffic routing, and congestion control.
2. *Resource allocation*: AI algorithms can be used to allocate network resources, such as bandwidth and power, in real time. This can improve network performance and efficiency, particularly in dynamic environments.
3. *Self-healing networks*: AI algorithms can be used to detect and resolve network faults automatically. This can reduce the need for manual intervention and improve network availability and reliability.
4. *Intelligent beamforming*: AI algorithms can be used to optimize the direction and shape of radio beams, improving signal quality and reducing interference in B5G RANs.
5. *Predictive analytics*: AI algorithms can be used to analyze data from a wide range of sources to predict network performance and identify potential issues before they occur. This can help operators proactively optimize their networks and improve the quality of service for end users.

Overall, AI is playing an essential role in B5G RANs, improving network performance and reliability. By leveraging AI, operators can unlock new use cases and improve the overall user experience.

AI plays a vital role in 5G edge networks. AI is being integrated into 5G edge networks, enabling a wide range of advanced capabilities. Here are some ways that AI is being used in 5G edge networks:

1. *Network optimization*: AI algorithms are used to optimize 5G edge networks, ensuring that data is delivered efficiently and reliably. This includes things like load balancing, traffic routing, and congestion control.
2. *Predictive maintenance*: AI algorithms can analyze data from sensors and other sources to predict when 5G edge network equipment may fail. This allows for proactive maintenance, reducing downtime and improving network reliability.
3. *Security*: AI algorithms are being used to enhance the security of 5G edge networks. This includes things like identifying and mitigating potential security threats, as well as detecting and preventing unauthorized access to the network.
4. *Edge computing*: AI algorithms can be used to analyze data at the edge of the network, reducing the amount of data that needs to be sent back to the cloud for processing. This can improve performance and reduce latency.
5. *Service automation*: AI algorithms can automate many tasks involved in managing 5G edge networks, such as service provisioning, configuration management, and performance monitoring.

AI is also being integrated into the 5G core network, enabling advanced capabilities and improving network performance and efficiency. Here are some ways that AI is being used in the B5G core network:

1. *Network orchestration and automation*: AI algorithms can be used to automate many of the tasks involved in managing the B5G core network, such as network planning, deployment, and operation. This can reduce the time and cost involved in network management and improve the overall efficiency of the network.
2. *Intelligent traffic routing*: AI algorithms can be used to route traffic in real time based on network conditions and user demands. This can improve network performance and efficiency, particularly in dynamic environments with high traffic volumes.
3. *Predictive analytics*: AI algorithms can be used to analyze data from a wide range of sources to predict network performance and identify potential issues before they occur. This can help operators proactively optimize their networks and improve the quality of service for end users.
4. *Intelligent network slicing*: AI algorithms can be used to optimize network slicing, allowing operators to create virtual networks tailored to specific use cases and user demands. This can improve the network's overall efficiency and enable new use cases.
5. *Security*: AI algorithms can be used to enhance the security of the B5G core network, identifying and mitigating potential security threats in real time.

To summarize, AI is increasingly important in the B5G core network. By leveraging AI, operators can unlock new use cases and improve the overall user experience.

AI is being integrated into 5G application service providers, enabling advanced capabilities and improving the user experience. Here are some ways that AI is being used in 5G application service providers:

1. *Personalization*: AI algorithms can be used to personalize the user experience based on user preferences and behavior. This can improve user engagement and satisfaction.
2. *Content recommendation*: AI algorithms can be used to recommend content to users based on their interests and behavior. This can improve user engagement and satisfaction.
3. *Real-time analytics*: AI algorithms can be used to analyze data in real time, enabling real-time insights and decision making. This can be particularly useful in applications like the internet of things (IoT), where real-time analytics are critical.
4. *Intelligent automation*: AI algorithms can automate many tasks involved in managing and delivering applications, improving efficiency and reducing costs.

5. *Natural language processing*: AI algorithms can be used to enable natural language processing in applications, allowing users to interact with applications using natural language. This can improve the user experience and reduce the learning curve for new applications.

To conclude, AI is increasingly important in 5G application service providers. By leveraging AI, application service providers can unlock new use cases and improve the overall user experience.

AI can enable new applications and services that were impossible with previous generations of wireless networks. For example, AI-powered drones can be used for aerial surveillance and delivery services, while autonomous vehicles can be used for transportation. These applications require high-speed, low-latency, and reliable wireless communication, which B5G networks can provide. AI can also be used to develop intelligent healthcare systems that remotely monitor patients and provide personalized treatment, improving the quality of care and reducing healthcare costs. In conclusion, AI has the potential to revolutionize the way we use wireless communication and enable new applications and services in 5G and B5G networks. AI has the potential to transform wireless communication in many ways, from optimizing network performance to improving antenna design, enhancing security, and enabling new applications and services. As B5G networks continue to evolve, we can expect AI to play an increasingly important role in shaping the future of wireless communication.

This book explores the potential technologies and applications of AI in wireless for B5G networks from an end-to-end perspective. We aim to discuss challenges, enabling technologies, architecture, and applications of AI from smartphones, RANs, edge and core networks, and application service provider perspectives. This detailed end-to-end perspective is expected to pave the way for innovative research and solutions for empowering the next generation of wireless AI. The following is an overview of the chapters:

Chapter 1 discusses the evolution of deep learning and the need to have on-device AI. It further presents the optimization techniques for efficiently providing AI on devices. It proposes the generic hardware-tailored deep learning architectures and how they can be utilized for on-device learning. The chapter concludes by presenting thoughts on advancements in AI in the wireless domain to accommodate the future prospects of on-device AI.

Chapter 2 delineates the importance of on-device AI. It presents details about the applications of on-device AI to enhance the mobile camera experience. Furthermore, it depicts the advancements in on-device AI with respect to personal assistants and the role of AI in making them more proficient. The chapter concludes with a presentation of hardware augmentation on smart devices to enable faster neural network computations, which have opened up tremendous opportunities for AI-based application developers.

Chapter 3 discusses different schemes and the feasibility of hosting machine learning (ML) models on modem chipsets, including traditional NodeB, user equipment (UE; on smartphone devices), and virtual RAN (vRAN) environments. Furthermore, the advancements and contemporary methods of realizing the execution of ML models in open-standard radio access networks (O-RANs) and the role of smart network switches are presented.

Chapter 4 provides a brief introduction to research works in the field of AI/ML-based B5G communication systems from RAN and UE perspectives. It discusses various channel estimation techniques, various training mechanisms, related mathematical analysis, and simulation results. Furthermore, it presents channel state information (CSI) estimation and prediction techniques on the RAN and UE side, its system model, and deep learning–based CSI prediction techniques, followed by numerical results. It then presents decoder optimization methods providing decoding metrics for turbo and low-density parity-check (LDPC) codes, early termination using ML, followed by related simulation results. It discusses power amplifier nonlinearity correction methods along with the respective system model, deep learning architecture for digital predistortion (DPD), and a presentation of the simulation results. Finally, the chapter covers the beam prediction methods and algorithms in detail, followed by their performance analysis with the help of simulation experiments.

Chapter 5 provides a brief background on deep learning, including frameworks and measurements. The authors then discuss AI on the edge, that is, how to carry out the entire process of building AI models, starting with application domains where deep learning on the network edge can be useful, different architectures and methods to speed up deep learning inference, and training deep learning models on edge devices. Following this, they discuss AI for the edge, where critical problems in edge computing (EC) are addressed with the help of popular and effective AI technologies, including resource management, network functions, and B5G. Finally, they conclude with open research challenges and conclusions.

In Chapter 6, we discuss the role of EC and AI/ML techniques in B5G networks to enable ultra-low-latency services and self-learning, respectively, to ensure service continuity and enhance the service quality and experience of users. Furthermore, this chapter presents EC architectures and how EC can be integrated with the B5G system from a standardization point of view. It also discusses some of the key technology enablers for EC in B5G networks, then presents the role of AI/ML in B5G edge networks. The chapter ends with some of the future research directions in the area of AI/ML at B5G edge networks.

Chapter 7 discusses the challenges in the 5G core (5GC) network due to the rapid increase in data-intensive applications, bursty traffic conditions, and the problems of buffer bloat and congestion in the 5GC. The user plane function (UPF) in the 5GC network is the backbone node, and most data flows are download flows from internet servers to 5G UE. This chapter proposes using AI to mitigate congestion in the downlink, and flow classification using AI to manage resources in the core network efficiently. The chapter further discusses the challenges that transport-layer protocols face due to high intermittence, handovers from high-BDP (bandwidth-delay product) to low-BDP cells, and radio link control (RLC) configurations with large buffers. The chapter proposes using ML-based predictions for optimal bandwidth regulation in the UPF to determine the optimal maximum receive window (maxRWND) for Transmission Control Protocol (TCP) flow in the UPF. The proposed ML model can be trained on an external node and deployed on the session management function (SMF) to predict maxRWND per the UPF.

Chapter 8 delineates the benefits of AI as a service (AIaaS), followed by a brief classification of AI, related technologies, and usage in terms of AIaaS. Thereafter, it presents the principles of AIaaS, providing a glimpse of the AIaaS stack. It briefs different vendors in the market providing AIaaS based on different service types and application areas. It also gives a picture of the energy consumption aspects of AIaaS and an overview of carbon emissions produced in different data centers globally, followed by the ways to tackle them. Finally, it sheds some light on data protection and privacy aspects of AIaaS with some concluding remarks and a way forward.

Chapter 9 overviews digital twins and their role in B5G networks. It presents the envisioned architecture of the digital twin framework, which consists of three main components: the physical domain or subsystem of interest, the RAN digital twin, and the digital twin engine. It discusses the applications of digital twins, emphasizing their capabilities and the performance metrics that digital twins can gauge. It also introduces exemplary use cases from different domains with diverse performance requirements. It describes the design objectives to be considered while building digital twins. Finally, it discusses different players in the digital twin ecosystem. It proposes strategies for collaboration to overcome the challenges of building a unified digital twin ecosystem, along with some conclusory remarks.

Chapter 1

On-device AI

Sharan Kumar Allur

Samsung R&D Institute India-Bangalore
Bangalore, India

1.1 BACKGROUND

With artificial intelligence (AI) being part of our everyday lives, we are already witnessing exponential growth in the application of AI in several fields. Advancements in AI and deep learning in vision, voice, sound, and other domains have drastically influenced AI's reach and attachment rates. From the beginning of deep learning to various research breakthroughs, AI outcomes have significantly influenced business outcomes on a large scale in several organizations, both big and small. It has become evident that embracing AI will help industries by augmenting human capabilities with AI advancements. For example, with the growing power and capabilities of smartphone devices and faster wireless communication capabilities, smartphone users make up around 75% of the world population. Optimizing AI for on-device AI features so that user data remains on the device is critical for the growth of users using these embedded devices. Taking this as a cue, this chapter talks about the innovations and changes that have emerged with deep learning evolution to accommodate wireless networks as a domain.

The next wave of 6G is blooming with AI-based differentiations that drive AI in wireless.

1.2 EVOLUTION OF DEEP LEARNING

More than 150 years ago, nobody would have imagined that machines would develop human-level intelligence. Today, most AI-based automation has replaced mundane jobs like initial customer support, package scanning, and many more with the help of machine intelligence.

1.2.1 How and when did things change?

Perception turns images and sounds into concepts in the human mind. Our mind starts building perception as early as a few months of age, when it starts building predictive models of the real world and starts creating new concepts. It was in the early 1900s that neuroscientists started to understand more

DOI: 10.1201/9781003303527-2

about the anatomy of the human brain. Nobel Prize winner Santiago Ramón y Cajal was one of the first neuroanatomists who discovered the anatomy of neurons [1] and the science behind human learning.

Five decades later, in the 1950s, Alan Turing proposed the Imitation Game, popularly known as the Turing test, which is a test to identify if intelligent behavior that is exhibited is that of a human or a machine. This is one of the first important steps toward quantifying a machine's intelligence.

Geoffrey Hinton, often referred to as one of the "godfathers" of AI and deep learning, proposed in 1986 that representations can be learned by backpropagating errors in a network of neuron-like units. Yann Le Cun, also known as the father of convolutional neural networks, in 1990 proposed and demonstrated the workings of handwritten digit recognition with backpropagation. He is the one who also proposed gradient-based learning, which revolutionized deep learning in computer vision. In 2012, Alex Krizhevsky proposed a new convolutional neural network (AlexNet) that surpassed state-of-the-art accuracy on the ImageNet dataset. He also talked about speeding up training time by utilizing graphics processing units (GPUs). In 2017, Ashish Vaswani introduced the power of attention in transformer architectures for natural language tasks.

The four main categories of machine learning (ML) are supervised learning, unsupervised learning, self-supervised learning, and reinforcement learning. Supervised learning is all about mapping input to an output. ML models have a labeled dataset used to learn and map input representations to outputs. Examples include logistic regression, support vector machines, decision trees, and random forests. In the case of unsupervised learning, models match patterns to form clusters with an unlabeled dataset. Example include K-means clustering, principal component analysis, and hierarchical clustering. Self-supervised learning is a combination of labeled and unlabeled datasets. In all previous categories, there is no way to get feedback in the form of a reward, which is the case with reinforcement learning. Deep learning is a class of techniques that can be either supervised, unsupervised, self-supervised, or reinforced, where a model consists of multiple hidden layers in between the input and output layers. Popular types include convolutional neural networks and recurrent neural networks.

1.2.2 Why is AI possible now?

The manifestations of AI such as ML and deep learning have become industry go-to standards in solving large-scale problems in the areas of vision, natural language, speech, sound, and text. AI has caused massive disruption and has transformed nearly every industry, from healthcare to automotive, manufacturing, industrial inspections, and retail, among others. These changes are accredited to the exponential growth in algorithms for AI, the availability of voluminous data, the rise in computational power, and interactions with the domain expertise.

AI is mainly more computations, more formulas, and more algorithms that are complex. These are growing exponentially. Algorithms are maturing in several areas. For example, in the case of vision, this includes complex scene understanding in cluttered or occluded situations, depth mapping for every frame in a 4K video, emotion understanding, and so on. These algorithms will drive the next-generation user experience.

Data, of course, is the key ingredient for the rapid growth of AI. For example, there is so much data generated by users that is useful for personalization, suggestions, recommendations, and so on. According to an International Data Corporation (IDC) report from 2017, annual data creation is forecasted to reach 180 zettabytes in 2025—which translates to an astounding 180 trillion gigabytes! With more algorithms to apply to huge data, we need more computational power. In 2018, OpenAI found that the amount of computational power used to train the largest AI models had doubled every 3.4 months since 2012. We are already witnessing this trend, as there has been a significant increase in the on-device capabilities of mobile devices. All of this, when combined with domain expertise, will help solve major problems in domains like voice, vision, and text.

1.3 NEED FOR ON-DEVICE AI

Data has shown that if the application can provide a smooth experience for an end user with no frame drops or jitter, it is most likely that the user is going to come back to use the application again and again. With limited hardware capabilities in edge devices, it is essential to give a better user experience. With the demand to run concurrent-use cases, it is more evident that efficiency in these neural networks is essential for a better user experience.

Real-time requirements of a given use case need to be catered to at a given performance boundary. For example, for a video playback or video recording, it is extremely essential to meet the framerate requirements of that particular scenario. This poses a unique challenge for AI models to have deterministic real-time responses, which can be achieved with on-device computing of these AI models.

ML models specifically are very heavy and extremely power hungry, clocking high frequencies with heavy load. Developers really have to ensure optimal usage of battery power. For many decades, the focus was to solve a problem using AI to get things done in the first place, rather than worrying about speed and efficiency due to cloud-based AI capabilities. Over the past 5–6 years, however, the focus has largely shifted to the efficiency of a given AI feature on the edge.

The AI community has done a fantastic job in terms of democratizing AI. Tools, frameworks, and software development kits (SDKs) required to build and develop AI models are now easily available and extremely efficient. Some of these ecosystems are TensorFlow, Pytorch, and others. These ecosystems have really helped researchers (ML model developers) focus more on the new algorithms to push research boundaries in the area of new deep learning architectures. In addition to these ecosystems, the support for implementation of AI on edge devices is also ever increasing. Similar to TensorFlow, TensorFlow Lite is a mobile library for deploying models on mobiles, microcontrollers, and other edge devices. Developers who deploy these heavy deep learning models on edge devices have incorporated many techniques related to performance, memory, and power optimization.

While an enormous amount of data is generated by users that can serve as a potential source for improving AI models on embedded devices, issues such as privacy and data breaching prevent the utilization of such data for refining the trained deep neural networks (DNNs). Federated learning has emerged as an ideal solution that enables encrypting of user-specific data and transferring only the encryptions to central servers, followed by aggregation and subsequently refinement of the AI model. On-device learning lies at the core of federated learning. Therefore, it is extremely critical to ensure the privacy of user data, which in recent times has become an issue of major concern for the users of AI.

1.4 OPTIMIZATIONS FOR EFFICIENT ON-DEVICE AI

Performance optimization starts with good knowledge of compute-intensive operations in these mathematical models (see Figure 1.1). There are several ways to get layer-wise profiling done to collect these statistics for a given network.

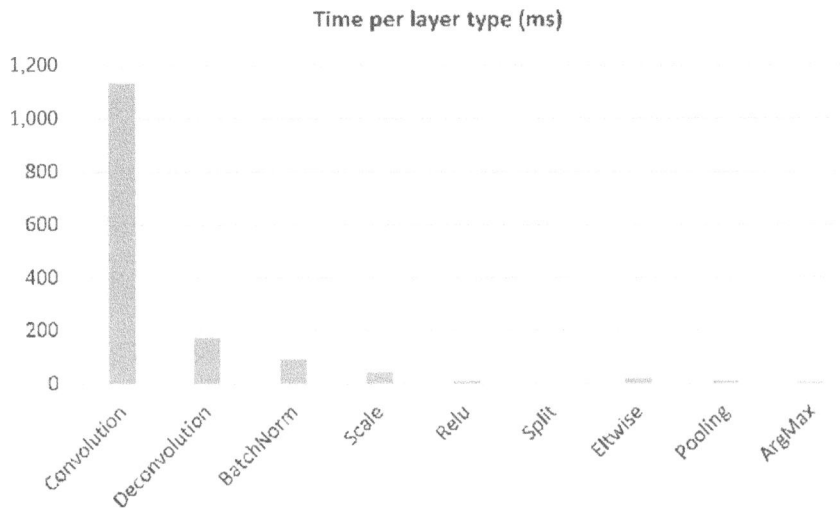

Figure 1.1 Time taken for inference of DNNs: in this example, convolution, deconvolution, batch normalization and scaling, relu, split, and eltwise.

1.4.1 Generic matrix multiplication

Figure 1.1 represents the time spent by various layers in sample DNN architecture, where layers that represent convolution are implemented using generic matrix-to-matrix multiplication (GEMM). Deep understanding of the optimal way to load these matrices onto the processor cache and execute vectorized instructions to perform matrix multiplication defines the degree of optimization one can achieve.

This optimization, along with parallelizing given the workload with multiple threads on multiple compute cores in an embedded system-on-a-chip (SoC), could lead to significant improvements in performance. Typically, GPU architectures meant for parallel execution of workloads help improve the performance drastically. With an OpenCL implementation for optimized code (kernel), performance improvement could be in the range of 10×. With a dedicated AI accelerator, a compute element where these computations are implemented in the hardware, performance improvements could increase up to 100×, depending on the operations-per-second capability of such hardware blocks.

1.4.2 Operator fusion

Apart from vectorization, operator fusion is another technique that helps improve effective cache utilization. Operator fusion (or kernel/layer fusion) is a key optimization in many state-of-the-art DNN execution frameworks, such as TensorFlow, Apache TVM, and mobile neural networks (MNNs), which aim to improve the efficiency of DNN inference.

Operator fusion is a technique to combine multiple operations together into a superset to optimally execute on a given compute element. Figure 1.2 shows an example of combining convolution, batch normalization, and scaling into a single superset of operation. Without the operator fusion, each of these operations would have to fetch the memory into central processing unit (CPU) registers, perform the operation, and store the results back into the memory. For three operations, load and store must execute three times. With operator fusion, we could optimize the round trip to the memory by loading, doing multiple operations on the loaded data, and then storing data back at once.

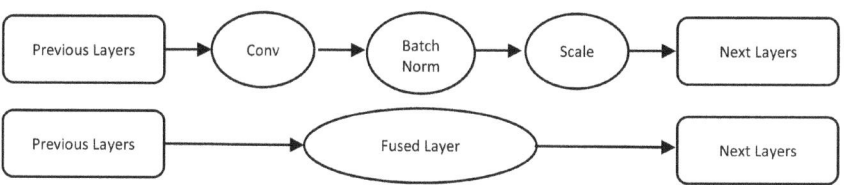

Figure 1.2 Pictorial representation of operator fusion (convolution, batch normalization, and scaling in this example).

1.4.3 Low-precision computing

To optimize mathematical calculations, it is important to understand how precise these calculations need to be and whether we can reduce the precision to speed up computations. Low-precision computations for deep learning networks are the new paradigm shift for efficient execution of these AI algorithms. How accurately we can represent numbers used for various mathematical calculations depends on how many bits we use. A 32-bit floating point is the default representation used while training deep learning networks; however, to reduce training time, some prior work has shown that a 16-bit floating point could be sufficient for training deep learning networks. For inference, performance benefits are directly proportional to the reduction in the number of bits used to represent these numbers. Arithmetic with lower bit depth is faster, assuming that the hardware supports it. Lower bit width also means a reduction in the memory used to store these models: FP32 $\rightarrow x$ amount of savings, FP16 $\rightarrow 2x$ savings, and IN8 $\rightarrow 4x$ savings, respectively. Lower bit width also means we can squeeze more data into the same cache/registers. This means that the number of times that random-access memory (RAM) is accessed to load the data is reduced, which saves power. While the exact benefit depends on the underlying implementation in the software and hardware, it has become a norm to do the inference for complex deep learning models, such as classification and object detection, giving huge performance benefits. So how does this translation happen from FP32 or FP16 to IN8 or INT4? This happens through quantization. Many different algorithms have been used to apply several quantization schemes to these DNNs, such as channel-wise, per tensor, data-free quantization, and quantization-friendly MobileNet, to name a few. For floating-point numbers, typically, the IEEE754 floating-point standard acts as a guide for all representations. Mostly, the quantization loss is insignificant compared to floating-point precision; however, in some cases, the precision loss is significant when compared to floating-point precision. This is where two broad methods of quantization mechanisms help largely. These are (a) Post-training. (b) Quantization aware training. In case of post training quantization, model training happened in 32 bit floating point representation and after training these weights are quantized to 8 bit integer values. In case on quantization aware training, fake quantization nodes with integer 8 bit weights are added along side 32 bit weights during training to simulate the behaviour of quantization in forward pass.

1.4.4 Memory optimization

Until now, we have looked at performance optimizations critical to meet use-case key performance indicators (KPIs) for the realization of use cases such as object detection, classification, and many more. When deep learning algorithms are applied to high-resolution input images in which every pixel has to update to generate a new pixel, for scenarios such as low light, super resolution, and so on, it is challenging to manage runtime memory requirements for such intensive workloads. Runtime memory utilization optimization becomes critical for loading and executing these algorithms on mobile devices and other edge devices that have limited memory.

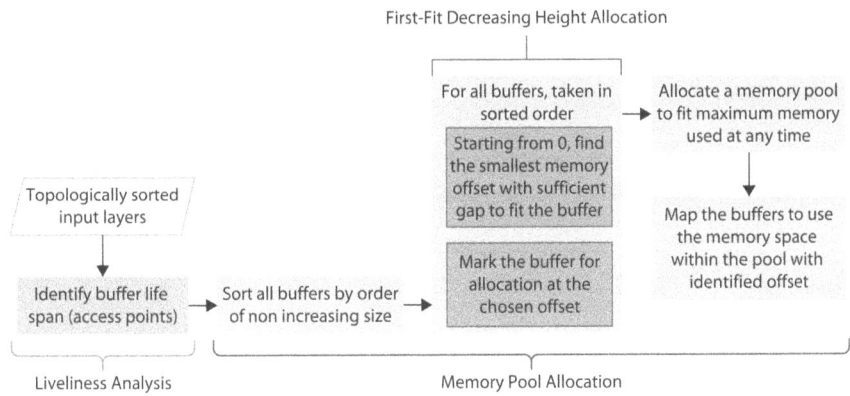

First-Fit Decreasing Height Allocation

For all buffers, taken in sorted order

Starting from 0, find the smallest memory offset with sufficient gap to fit the buffer

Mark the buffer for allocation at the chosen offset

Allocate a memory pool to fit maximum memory used at any time

Map the buffers to use the memory space within the pool with identified offset

Topologically sorted input layers

Identify buffer life span (access points)

Sort all buffers by order of non increasing size

Liveliness Analysis

Memory Pool Allocation

Figure 1.3 Efficient memory pool allocation algorithm for CNN inference [2].

A fine-grained liveness analysis, followed by memory pool allocation (Figure 1.3) by calculating the lifetime of each required buffer (including internal buffers) of a network and assigning an offset to each buffer for sharing a common memory pool, results in efficient reuse of memory across buffers [2].

1.5 HARDWARE TAILORED ARCHITECTURES [6]

Recently, machines have started playing a role in designing the architectures of DNNs. Automated machine learning (AutoML) provides methods and processes to make ML available for non-ML experts, improve the efficiency of ML, and accelerate research on ML. Neural architecture search (NAS), a subfield of AutoML, helps automate most of the design choices for a given task. For example, EfficientNet designed by Google is an outcome of NAS. To understand this more, one has to look at the evolution of the deep learning architectures ResNet, DenseNet, and InceptionNet.

ResNet: The accuracy of deep learning architectures started increasing by increasing the depth of the network with networks like VGG and others. There came a point where it started becoming difficult to train deeper networks due to the problem of vanishing gradients. Initially, normalized initialization and intermediate normalization layers addressed this problem for smaller networks. However, with the increasing depth of the networks, the problem of deteriorating gradients resulted in inefficient training of DNNs. With residual [4] mapping, the shortcut connections that simply perform identity mapping and the outputs of previous layers added to the outputs of the stacked layers (Figure 1.4) helped resolve this issue for deeper networks. Identity shortcut connections add neither extra parameters nor computational complexity but remain efficient when it comes to minimizing the problem of vanishing gradients.

DenseNet: ResNet architecture helps ensure an increase in information flow during forward and backpropagation with the skip connections. DenseNet

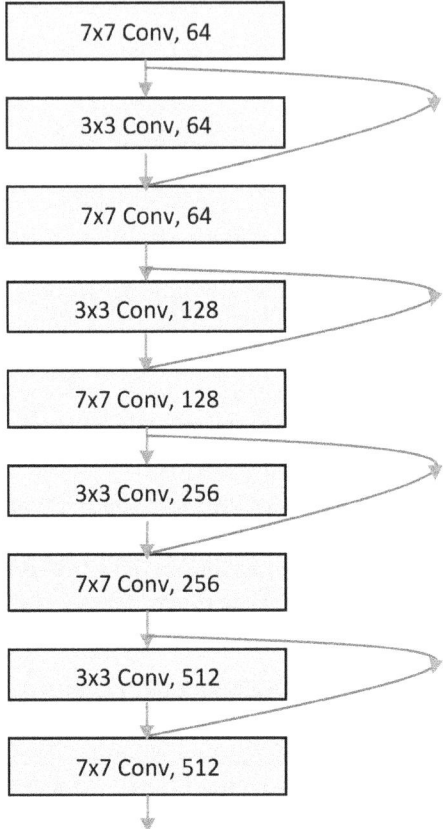

Figure 1.4 Skip connections in residual networks [3].

takes inspiration from ResNet to further increase the connectivity in the network to maximize the information flow (Figure 1.5). In DenseNet [5], for each layer, the feature maps of all preceding layers act as input to all the subsequent layers. DenseNets have several compelling advantages: They (1) significantly reduce the complexity in terms of the number of parameters, (2) strengthen feature propagation, and (3) enable feature reuse.

InceptionNet: InceptionNet introduced several low-level changes to the architecture, such as:

a. *Smaller convolutions*: Replace 5×5 filters with 3×3 filters.
b. *Asymmetric convolutions*: Replace 3×3 convolutions with 1×3 followed by 3×1.

These changes (Figure 1.6) not only helped improve accuracy but also significantly reduced complexity and time to infer. This is one of the most commonly used DNN architectures as backbone even today.

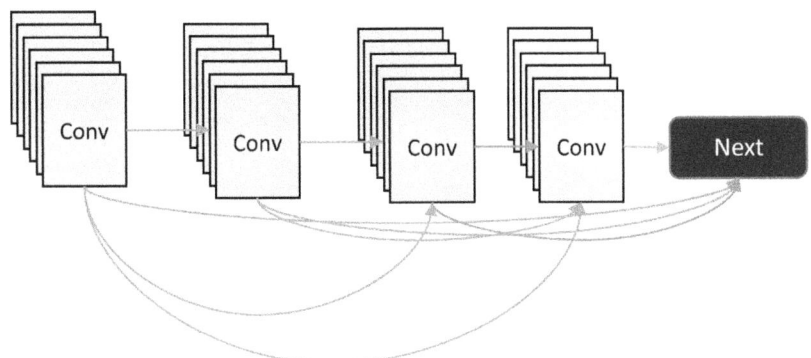

Figure 1.5 Dense connections in DenseNet.

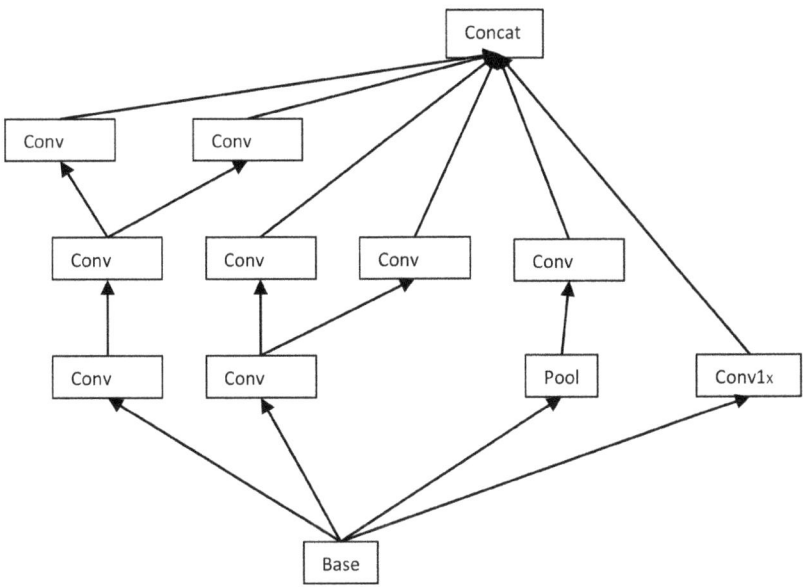

Figure 1.6 Functioning of the inception module.

While these state-of-the-art backbone networks have been extremely successful in many tasks, it is clear that designing a deep learning architecture needs skilled expertise to experiment with various ideas to come up with an optimal desired architecture.

Hyperparameter search is a field of ML that automates searching of efficient architectural parameters such as number of nodes per layer, number of layers, type of activation functions, and so on, as well as non-architectural parameters such as batch size, learning rate, regularization, and so on. NAS (Figure 1.7) is a subfield of hyperparameter search that mainly focuses on

Figure 1.7 Neural architecture search.

architectural parameter search automation. There are three main phases in NAS: search space design; search strategy, and evaluation strategy.

1.5.1 Search space design

There are two fundamental types of search spaces (Figure 1.8). Global search space covers deep learning graphs that represent an entire neural network architecture, and cell search space focuses on discovering granular submodules called cells that build an entire neural network.

1.5.2 Search strategy

The search strategies comprise a set of algorithms to navigate through the search space intelligently and converge on the best possible design while realizing only a minimal number of function evaluations (training the entire network). Broadly, the search strategies, classified in terms of the optimization methodology, implemented to obtain the design of the network are evolutionary search, Bayesian optimization, gradient-based optimization, and reinforcement learning (RL). In evolutionary strategies, the search space is navigated based on recombination and mutation strategies that help the optimizers to escape the local minima. Bayesian optimization implements a surrogate model to navigate the search

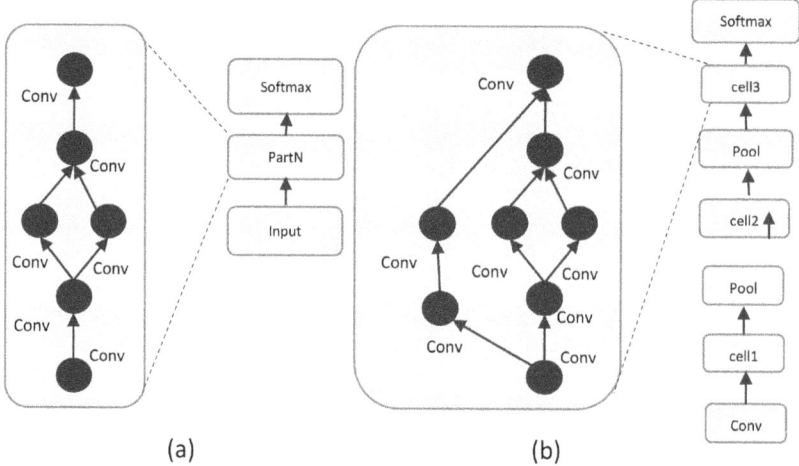

Figure 1.8 Search space (neural architecture search). (a) Global search space. (b) Cell-based search space.

space and thus minimizes the number of function evaluations required during the optimization. The gradient-based search strategy approximates the integral space into a continuous representation and aims to perform the NAS simultaneously with the training of the network, thus leading to a one-shot search strategy. Finally, RL-based methodology observes the accuracy of a given network as a reward and aims to optimize the network to maximize the reward.

1.5.3 Evaluation strategy

A trained network is evaluated for generalizability, and several evaluation strategies are implemented to test the networks during the NAS. These metrics are set as the objective function/rewards during the NAS, as depicted in Figure 1.7. There are several search evaluation strategies in the literature: weight sharing, hypernetworks, network morphisms, partial training, and full training.

Most of the latest optimized deep learning architectures are machine-generated architectures, as machines can explore many more combinations automatically compared to manual handcrafting of a deep learning architecture by an expert. New methods of optimizing the search space, search time, and evaluation strategy are currently being explored.

1.6 ON-DEVICE TRAINING

On-device training has been the focus of several companies in the mobile world, as it enables the processing of data closest to the source, ensuring privacy, reliability, real-time responses, and efficient use of network bandwidth. Generally, the neural networks are trained offline with a predefined dataset specifically to solve a problem. Once deployed on the device, this model works on new data with new attributes that are unseen during training with a training dataset. Thus, with on-device training of neural networks that are enabled with the new data, these models will adapt on device and perform tasks such as continuous learning and personalization. However, there are challenges associated with achieving on-device training, such as limited unlabeled data available on device, problems with overfitting and catastrophic forgetting, and limited compute and storage capabilities on device. On-device training would also need significant computing power and will consume sufficient energy in terms of battery usage. Careful scheduling on training workloads needs to be planned and processed. Data collected on the device is also susceptible to adversarial attacks. Careful designing of such on-device learning features, with additional inputs from the way a given feature is expected to behave, would address these challenges.

1.6.1 Transfer learning

ML models rely on a large set of training data to solve problems such as image recognition, object detection, speech recognition, and language so that they can be as generic and unbiased as possible. Instead of training the model from scratch, we could train the model on a large dataset like ImageNet (pretrain)

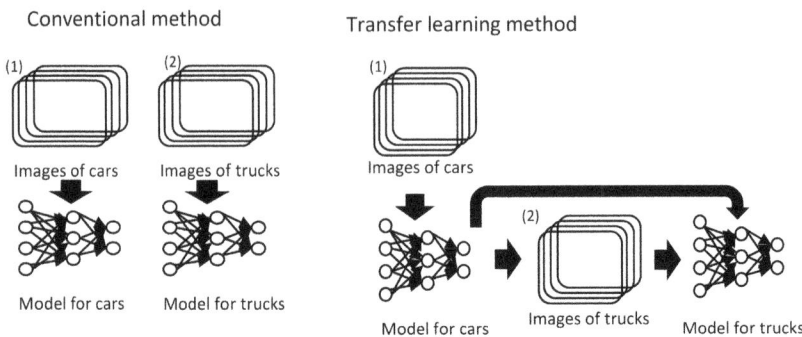

Figure 1.9 Transfer learning.

and then fine-tune it for custom tasks. Figure 1.9 shows this process, known as transfer learning.

1.7 FUTURE RESEARCH DIRECTIONS

Current advances of AI in wireless can pave the way for new-generation communication systems that are reliable and intelligent. New algorithms could solve various wireless communication system challenges, especially with transformer-based architectures that can be context aware.

Generative networks can be explored to augment various areas of communication system design. When optimizing the next generation of deep learning algorithms to utilize the on-device capabilities of GPUs, dedicated accelerators could be another area to study. As networks are growing larger with increasing numbers of parameters and complexity, there is a continuous need for either increased on-device computing or new ways of optimizing the on-device execution of these deep learning algorithms.

REFERENCES

1. https://neuroscientificallychallenged.com/posts/history-of-neuroscience-ramon-y-cajal
2. Arun Abraham, Manas Sahni, Akshay Parashar – https://ieeexplore.ieee.org/document/8990427
3. Kaiming He, Xiangyu Zhang, Shaoqing Ren – Deep residual Learning for Image Recognition. https://arxiv.org/abs/1512.03385
4. Gao Huang, Zhuang Liu, Laurens Van Der Maaten – Densely Connected Convolutional Networks. https://arxiv.org/abs/1608.06993
5. Christian Szegedy, Wei Liu, Yangqing Jia, Pierre Sermanet – Going Deeper with Convolutions. https://arxiv.org/pdf/1409.4842.pdf
6. Hadjer Benmeziane, Kaoutar El Meghraoui, Hamza Ouarnoughi – A Comprehensive Survey on Hardware-Aware Neural Archicture Search. https://arxiv.org/pdf/2101.09336.pdf

Chapter 2

Introduction to on-device AI and its applications in mobile phones and personal assistants

Prash Goel and Ankit Dixit
Pune, India

Scenario 1:

ME: Hey Google! Can you book a meeting appointment on my calendar at 4 PM today with Alex?
GOOGLE: Yeah sure! Do you also want to send a notification to Alex?

Scenario 2:

ME: Okay Google! Can you record and caption this talk for me?
GOOGLE: Yeah sure!

Do you see what is happening? These are two examples of conversations between a human and a machine! Isn't this exciting? When you call out for your phone, and it responds back to you? And this also works when your phone is offline or has no active internet connection. So, what exactly is this?

ON-DEVICE PERSONAL ASSISTANT: This heavily relies on speech processing. It is a subfield of natural language processing, which is in fact another subdomain under a huge umbrella of what we today call *artificial intelligence* (AI). Let's learn about this.

2.1 INTRODUCTION TO ON-DEVICE AI

We are witnessing tremendous advances in technology, and now next-generation technology is available for commercial use in an economical and easy-to-carry footprint. Such technologies make our lives easier, and the rise of AI is helping to bring this change faster. An emerging subfield of AI is on-device AI, which harnesses the power of small computers. It powers modern-day mobile camera systems by enhancing their power to shoot in any condition: bright sunlight, deep shadows, or both. Modern phone cameras have tremendous capability to shoot every detail present in the scene using high dynamic range (HDR) computed on the device. Another application of on-device AI mobile camera systems is advanced facial recognition systems to unlock phones. We have powerful language translators right inside our pocket. Advanced on-device AI solutions are present in not just smartphones but also smart watches. These

DOI: 10.1201/9781003303527-3

can now detect a disease before it occurs; for example, these can detect atrial fibrillation (AFib) and notify you about your current health conditions. With the rise in the development of edge-based devices, surveillance of remote locations becomes far easier. Now your surveillance camera can not only record video but also notify you if something suspicious is happening on the scene. Figure 2.1 shows various application and benefits of on device AI.

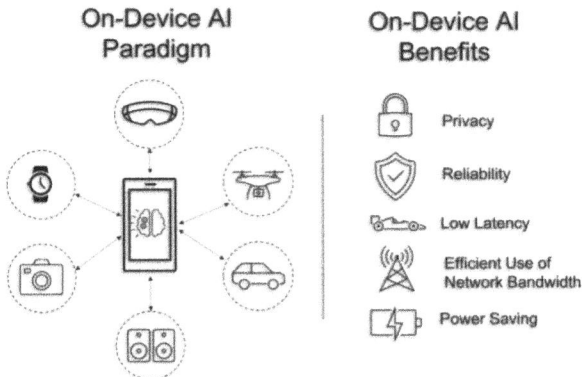

Figure 2.1 An overview of different applications and benefits of on-device AI.

With growing advancements in technology and the rise of its involvement in our lives, concerns about user privacy are increasing. On-device processing solves this problem quite efficiently, as it significantly cuts down on the need for data transmissions to powerful servers. It is also cost-effective, as it reduces the need for powerful computers and thus saves on their maintenance too, so there is no need to create big data centers. This chapter will present details about applications of on-device AI to enhance the mobile camera experience. Also, it will show how advancements in on-device AI are shaping up the future-ready personal assistant (PA).

2.2 ON-DEVICE AI TO IMPROVE THE MOBILE CAMERA EXPERIENCE

Mobile cameras have seen major transformations in the past decade, and on-device AI has played a big role in this. Today's smartphones function more as cameras than as phones. Coupled with the advancements in lens optics and multi-lens camera setups making their way to the phones, on-device AI has improved the mobile camera experience so much that the photos taken with mobile cameras can compete with the photos taken with expensive DSLR (digital single-lens reflex) cameras. On-device AI is being used to automatically adjust camera settings, such as white balancing, shutter speed, and exposure. Highly complex algorithms enabling HDR and night photography can also run on these devices. All of these technologies are empowering common people to shoot some amazing pictures with a tiny DSLR-like camera that they can carry anywhere in their pockets.

2.2.1 HDR photography on mobile devices

Dynamic range means the amount of variation in bright and dark areas in a particular scene. A scene with just bright areas or just dark areas has low dynamic range and is easy to capture. On the other hand, a scene that has both bright and dark areas is difficult to capture.

It is not possible to capture such a scene in a single shot. One of the most common ways to do this is by capturing multiple images at various exposures and then combining them to get a clear HDR image. The merging of images involves more than just averaging, and all of the processing happens locally on the device.

2.2.2 Night photography on mobile devices

Capturing low-light scenes such as a glorious landscape or the sky at night has always been challenging. Due to the low amount of light, the signal-to-noise ratio (SNR) drops in such scenes, and thus the shutter needs to be exposed for long durations to capture enough light. However, this requires specialized setup so that the camera remains still during the process of capturing the scene. Computational photography and on-device AI have made this possible, even on a smartphone.

All of the top-of-the-line smartphones currently in use come with a Night Mode. They rely on niche algorithms that capture 30–40 images within a few seconds, and then perform various operations to merge these images together to produce a clear photo of a dark scene. Some of these operations include scene optimization to adjust camera settings, such as ISO and shutter speed, bundle adjustment, gamma correction, sharpening, white balancing, tone mapping, and so on. Furthermore, since users are not expected to be completely still, optical image stabilization (OIS) is used throughout the scene capture to reduce the blur effect. However, even OIS is unable to yield a perfectly stable image, and thus optical flow is used to set an exposure time according to the scene motion.

2.2.3 On-device AI for XR applications

AI-enabled cameras are a big enabling factor for the development of useful extended-reality (XR) applications. XR includes augmented reality (AR), virtual reality (VR), and mixed reality (MR) (Figure 2.2). Various technology companies are betting big on all of these applications, and these are regarded as the future of human–computer interaction. On-device AI is being applied to the data gathered through infrared (IR), time-of-flight (ToF), and light detection and ranging (LiDAR) sensors in conjunction with RGB (red-green-blue) cameras to infer a three-dimensional (3D) map of the surroundings and use that for various XR applications. Detection of ground plane and surfaces such as tabletops, walls, and so on plays a key role in successful AR applications, and

 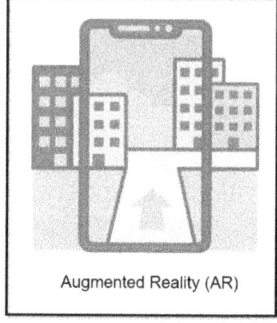 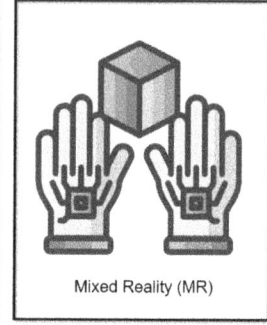

| Virtual Reality (VR) | Augmented Reality (AR) | Mixed Reality (MR) |

Figure 2.2 Different types of extended realities.

simultaneous localization and mapping (SLAM) is applied to achieve this. Due to advanced hardware and AI algorithms, this complex algorithm currently can be run on devices. Various companies are bundling these algorithms in their own software development kits, such as ARCore by Google [1] and ARKit by Apple [2], so that they can utilize their proprietary hardware such as neural processing units (NPUs) and tensor processing units (TPUs) to the full extent.

2.2.4 Biometric applications

On-device AI scores a big win over server-based computation because of growing privacy concerns. Since all of the computation can happen on the device, there is no need to send data to a server, and thus user privacy is not compromised. This is helpful for applications like face recognition, fingerprint matching, and iris scanners to lock and unlock the devices. All of the user biometric data can reside on the device, and complex algorithms to identify the user can run on the device itself. Apple has implemented such systems for their Face ID and Touch ID in their iPhones [3] (Figure 2.3).

 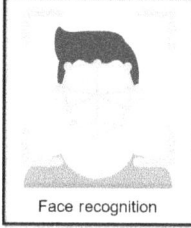  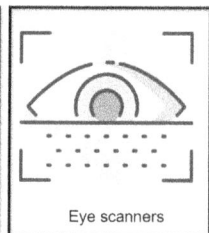

| Fingerprint scanners | Face recognition | Voice recognition | Eye scanners |

Figure 2.3 Biometric authentication types.

2.3 ON-DEVICE AI IN PERSONAL ASSISTANTS

Currently, almost every tech giant has some sort of AI-based PA, like Google's Assistant, Apple's Siri, Microsoft's Cortana, Samsung's Bixby, and Amazon's

Alexa. All of these assistants work in a similar way: You ask them a question or command a job, and they answer back or run the job on the device.

These devices use microphones (most of the time, more than one) to hear your voice signal and then process it using ML model(s) to identify what you are asking. Based on the query and the device response, there are basically four stages to performing this task.

1. *Wake word detection*: Your PA continuously hears its surroundings and processes them using a very simple neural network, as soon as it hears its wake command (Figure 2.4); for example, "Hey Google!" or "Hey Siri!" or "Alexa!"

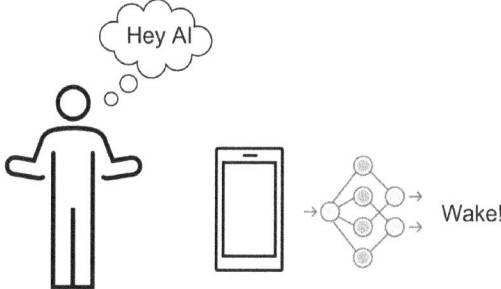

Figure 2.4 Wake word detection.

2. *Speech recognition*: After detection of the wake word, the device hears the command. Now a larger and more powerful neural network is used to recognize the voice command; for example, "Please call Alex on mobile." Still, the device has no idea what you have asked; it has just converted the voice signal into meaningful text form (Figure 2.5).

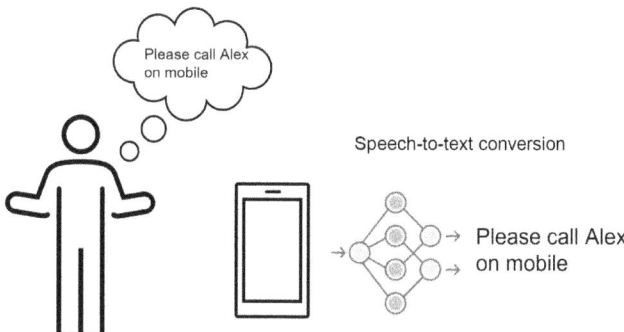

Figure 2.5 Speech recognition.

3. *Natural language understanding*: This is the crucial stage where natural language processing kicks in and your device tries to make

meaning out of your command. Remember that this is different from speech recognition. In this stage, with the help of an advanced neural network, the device tries to understand the command/action you have asked for. For example, when you ask it to schedule an appointment, the device will try to figure out the action in the command—in this case, calling. Once identified, the device will perform the action (Figure 2.6). Now, what if it requires more information to fulfill the action? That's stage 4.

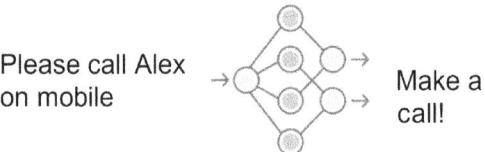

Figure 2.6 Natural language understanding.

4. *Speech synthesis*: In the final stage, the device responds to the user. For this, it uses speech synthesis to talk like a human. This is known as text to speech. Another neural network will be used for this. These kinds of neural networks are known as generative adversarial networks. The device synthesizes the human voice and responds to the user for either gathering more information or acknowledging the given task (Figure 2.7).

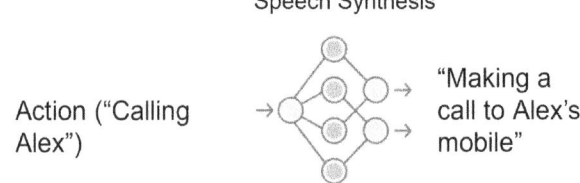

Figure 2.7 Speech synthesis.

Now, based on the action to be performed, the device may require access to the internet for information gathering. For example, if a user has asked for weather information, the device will search the query on the internet to provide the information. Figure 2.8 summarizes this process.

On-device PAs are quite popular and useful. You can multitask better with the help of such applications, and as the technology moves forward, it is getting more mature with time. And now, when the smart home devices market is at its peak, PAs are becoming a need rather than just a technological demonstration.

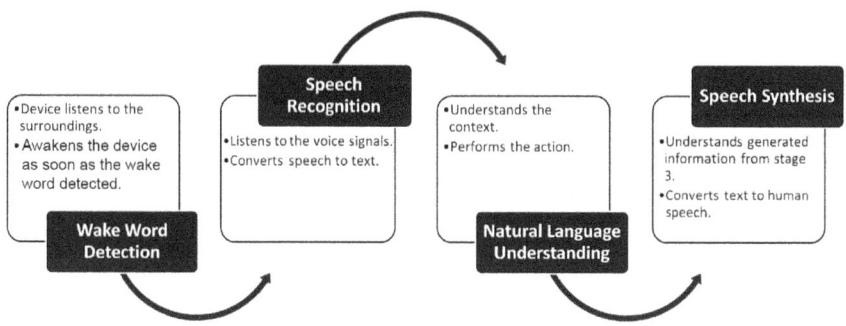

Figure 2.8 On-device PA process flow.

2.4 HARDWARE AUGMENTING THE SOFTWARE ADVANCEMENTS

Running such complex algorithms on mobile devices requires specialized processors so that the accuracy and latency are not compromised. Various phone manufacturers have been innovating in this direction and rolling out mobile processors that are designed specifically to enable faster neural network computations. Such processors are called NPUs, and they are designed to be power efficient and accurate in AI computations. The Samsung Neural Processing Unit and Apple Neural Engine are two examples of such processors [4, 5].

In the earlier days of smartphones, their main function was to run a few applications in parallel and provide a basic, colorful user interface. These devices did not have a very powerful processor. You could open a few applications at once and then switch between them, but that was all.

Nowadays, mobile devices are equipped with quite powerful microprocessors or, rather, a network of multiple powerful processors. Thanks to the gaming industry, it forces the chip manufacturers to make a system-on-a-chip that can run high-end graphical games on such tiny devices. Now, since the reemergence of AI, developers have started using the same computational power to run large ML models on such systems, which opened up tremendous opportunities for AI-based application developers.

Figure 2.9 shows the capability of a ML toolkit for mobile app development. This shows how far mobile devices have come, and how they can be utilized to achieve different day-to-day works in the blink of an eye.

CREDITS

Figures 2.2 and 2.3 have been designed using images from flaticon.com.

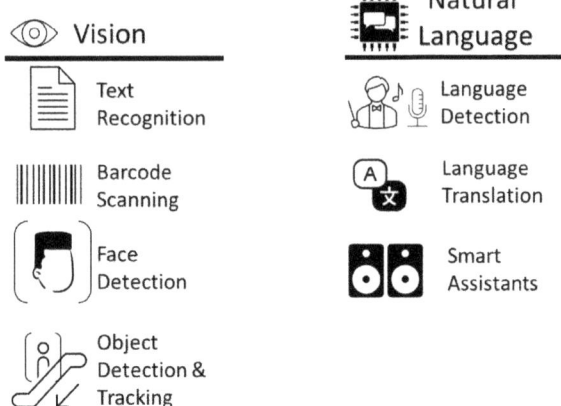

Figure 2.9 Google's ML Kit applications [6].

REFERENCES

1. Google AR Core: https://developers.google.com/ar
2. Apple ARKit: https://developer.apple.com/augmented-reality/arkit/
3. Apple Face ID and Touch ID: https://support.apple.com/en-in/HT208108
4. Samsung Neural Processing Unit: https://semiconductor.samsung.com/support/tools-resources/dictionary/the-neural-processing-unit-npu-a-brainy-next-generation-semiconductor/
5. Apple Neural Engine: https://machinelearning.apple.com/research/neural-engine-transformers
6. https://developers.googleblog.com/2019/05/new-ml-kit-features-easily-bring.html

Chapter 3

AI computation on RAN and User Equipment (UE)

Mahantesh Kothiwale
Samsung R&D Institute India-Bangalore, Bangalore, India

3.1 INTRODUCTION

While artificial intelligence (AI) and machine learning (ML) use cases on cellular wireless networks are being significantly emphasized, this raises another vital topic, the realization of neural network (NN) training and execution on compute platforms of radio access networks (RANs), core networks (CNs), and end-user equipment. Wireless modem chipsets, offered in the telecommunications (telecom) industry before 5G commercialization, have not necessarily achieved the compute capabilities needed for executing ML models, hence the NN libraries. Traditional modem chipsets, integrated on RAN and in smartphone devices, have less to offer for AI computation. Once a specific use case of AI in wireless is identified, training and executing the corresponding ML model can be a challenge due to a scarcity of computational resources. On the other hand, containerized RAN deployed under a virtual cloud environment has the opportunity to utilize abundantly available computational power on commercial off-the-shelf (COTS) servers. Such virtualized RAN on the cloud also can potentially offload AI computation to various compute machines, such as graphics processing units (GPUs), data processing units (DPUs), and other AI accelerators. Hardware and software architects of wireless modems need to consider different schemes of AI computation, along with primary compute-intensive operations such as high-speed packet processing and modem physical-layer operations.

In this chapter, we will discuss different schemes and the feasibility of hosting ML models on modem chipsets, including traditional NodeB, UE (user equipment; on smartphone devices), and virtual RAN environments. Furthermore, the advancements and contemporary methods of realizing the execution of ML models in open-standard RAN (O-RAN) and role of smart network switches will be discussed.

3.2 REALIZATION ON USER EQUIPMENT

For a discussion of compute capabilities, let us pick smartphone devices, as they are the most widely accomplished UE. The latest configurations of smartphone devices are equipped with varied computation capabilities, such

DOI: 10.1201/9781003303527-4

27

as 4G and 5G modem chipsets; WiFi chipsets; chipsets for user application processing that host the operating system, such as Android; and even AI accelerators in the latest devices. To execute AI models on such devices, there are interesting research trends in industry to optimize the core NN libraries [1, 2], customize the training of ML models [3], and split the computation of ML models across the available compute engines [4].

3.2.1 Current computing capabilities of smartphone devices

3.2.1.1 Modem chipsets and application chipsets

The aggregated maximum-throughput requirements of LTE and the 5GNR (New Radio) connected mode in the case of the E-UTRAN New Radio dual-connectivity (ENDC) mode can define the number of central processing units (CPUs) and their clocking speed in a modem chipset. In the current market, smartphones with 5G modems offer Quad-core to Octa-core reduced-instruction-set computer (RISC) CPUs with maximum clocking rates of up to 1.5 GHz. The number of tensor operations that a typical Octa-core can perform is a few giga-operations per second (GOPs). Typical AI accelerators on the application processors of smartphone devices can perform a few trillion tensor operations per second (TOPs).

Considering the maximum radio resource utilization of 800 MHz in the millimeter-wave (mmW) band, the downlink throughput supported by a 5G modem chipset can be up to 5 Gbps, which can be achieved well within the capacity of an Octa-core ARM Cortex A series with a 1.5 GHz clock. The maximum compute capacity of 5G modem chipsets can be a few GOPs. This indicates that modem chipsets from before the 5G era may not support heavy NN execution of a given ML model. Execution of ML models locally within current modem chipsets can also be a challenge.

At the same time, recent application processor chipsets within smartphone devices are equipped with the compute capabilities of enough TOPs. An ML model representing a wireless use case from modem space can be delegated to an application processor within the device. Such delegation comes at the cost of latency of communication between the modem and application processors. A radio access protocol stack within a modem generates inference parameters, whereas output from an ML model needs to be generated at the application processor. Such a round-trip time delay can be the vital parameter to decide the delegation. A typical round-trip delay of this sort can range between 2 and 5 ms on recent 5G-enabled smartphones. The most stringent AI use cases come from the physical layer and involve asking for inference execution latencies within the range of 1–5 transmission time intervals (TTIs), which range from 125 μs (mmW band) to 0.5 ms (LTE/Sub6). Such physical-layer AI use cases can be (but are not limited to) channel state information (CSI) prediction, best-beam prediction as part of beam management, and AI-based CSI compression.

3.2.2 Lightweight AI

In light of the stringent requirements of AI use cases in a device's modem protocol stack, one must establish an optimized and lightweight AI framework to execute ML models locally within the device's modem chipsets. Interesting initiatives have been taken for lightweight AI. In this section, we delve into the key integral features of such lightweight AI.

3.2.2.1 Optimization of ML models

3.2.2.1.1 Acceleration of kernels (core NN libraries)

Core NN operations such as (but not limited to) *feedforward*, *backpropagation*, and different activation functions (e.g., *softmax*) [5] need to be optimized, and they need custom kernels for different targeted compute platforms. The majority of these mathematical operations need vector processing and require the best utilization of SIMD/Vector operations of processors in an embedded system's world. *TensorFlow Lite* offers such custom optimized kernels for GPUs, for DSPs, and most importantly for the CPU category of ARM utilizing ARM Neon architecture. The TensorFlow Lite framework has addressed (and is still addressing) necessary challenges to enable on-device ML by helping developers run their models on mobile, embedded, and edge devices, and hence it is an appropriate framework for modem chipsets on a smartphone device [6]. TensorFlow Lite refers to accelerated kernel packages as *Delegates* [7].

3.2.2.1.2 Quantization

The most apparent method of accelerating an ML model is quantization. *Quantization* is about fine-tuning and reducing the width of operands (e.g., *weights*) of vector operations, without compromising on the accuracy of the model. Eight-bit quantization is the most optimized way for running models quicker while maintaining accuracy [1]. It is interesting to see that optimizations with quantization at the sub-8-bit level can also be beneficial in certain cases of low-accuracy ML models [2]. The great news is that the TensorFlow Lite framework provides an accelerated kernel and post-training quantization [8] for widely used modem chipsets.

3.2.2.1.3 Parallelize ML model training

Another important method of accelerating the execution of ML models is by disaggregating the training by each layer. Model parallelism is achieved by distributing the layers of the model to different computing entities in close vicinity (necessarily on the same system-on-a-chip [SoC]). The benefit of one such work is discussed in Refs. [2, 3].

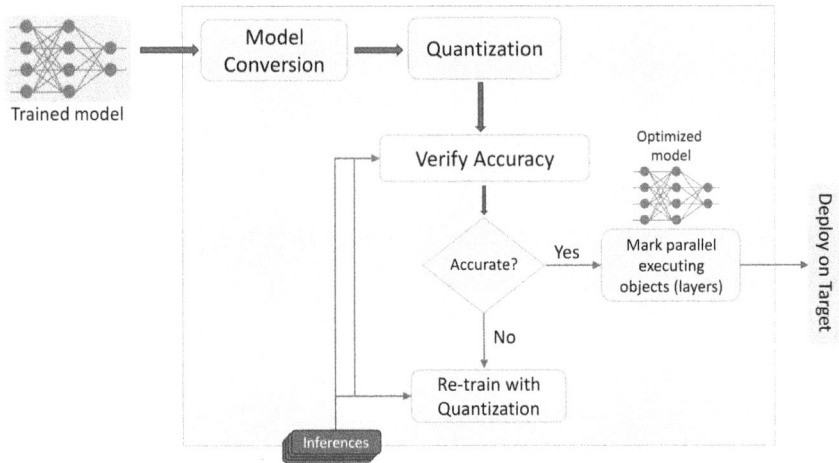

Figure 3.1 Typical workflow of a lightweight AI framework.

3.2.2.1.4 *Model conversion*

As discussed, a lightweight AI framework needs accelerated kernels, optimiza-tion (e.g., quantization) of the model during training, post-training of models, and identification of parallel executing objects. The lightweight AI framework will have the capability to accelerate and optimize an ML model generated via any training environment, such as Caffe, TensorFlow, Pytorch, Keras, and so on. This requires the need of *model conversion* as a key feature, which converts any model to a common format, which can be interpreted successfully by lightweight AI. A typical workflow of a lightweight AI framework is given in Figure 3.1.

3.3 REALIZATION ON vRAN AND O-RAN

Thanks to the growth of cloud-based services, and an availability of abundant computational power on COTS servers, we see that RAN deployment is shift-ing from custom hardware–based solutions to web-based services. This shift (to virtual RAN, or vRAN) has unlocked bigger opportunities to telecom operators to make radio access technology into an open standard (O-RAN) that can be implemented by any new players in the telecom domain.

Unlike the challenges of computational-resource crunch on modem chip-sets in UE, compute platforms on COTS offer sufficient TOPs. It can be eas-ier, from a resource availability aspect, to realize an ML model training and execute it on vRAN. At the same time, latencies of communication between the computing nodes are the major challenge to address.

Before discussing the methods used to address the challenges of latencies, let us have a look at current proposals in O-RAN standards to train and execute ML models.

The O-RAN WG (Working Group) 2 [9] defines the ML model hosting configurations. A RAN Intelligent Controller (RIC) is a logical function that enables non-real-time control (NRT-RIC) and real-time control (RT-RIC) to optimize RAN elements and resources, and AI/ML workflow including model training, execution, and updates. Figure 3.2 explains the different logical functional entities in which ML models can be trained and executed.

3.3.1 O-RAN control loops

Control loops, defined in the O-RAN specification of Workgroup 2 (WG2) [9], cover the different possibilities in which an ML model can execute and an inference engine (an AI/ML use case application in which inferences are generated) can execute.

3.3.1.1 Real-time control loops (Loop1)

In real-time control loops, the use case applications and ML model are hosted within an O-RAN distributed unit (O-DU) or O-RAN remote radio unit (O-RU). This provides minimal round-trip delay of inference input to the ML model and output of the ML model for use case applications; the delay is estimated to be around 10 ms.

3.3.1.2 Near-real-time control loops (Loop2)

In near-real-time control loops, the use case applications are hosted within an O-DU or O-RU, and ML models are hosted and executed within a near-real-time RIC. The round-trip delay in this case is estimated to be between 10 ms and 1 s.

3.3.1.3 Non-real-time control loops (Loop3)

In non-real-time control loops, the use case applications run within an O-DU or O-RU, and ML models are executed at a non-real-time RIC. The round-trip delay estimated in this case is >1 s.

3.3.2 Role of federated learning

In the virtualized environment, distributed training and distributed execution of ML models are obvious, rather inevitable choices for the best utilization of computational resources available nearby.

However, O-RAN talks about federated learning. To date [9], RT-RIC and NRT-RIC are the only logical entities considered for the training and execution of ML models. Other entities, such as the O-DU, O-RAN centralized unit (O-CU), and O-RU, are not considered for executing ML models. However, AI/ML deployment scenario 1.5 from O-RAN Work Group 2 (WG2) [10], which is a future study, mentions that O-DU, O-CU, and O-RU can also

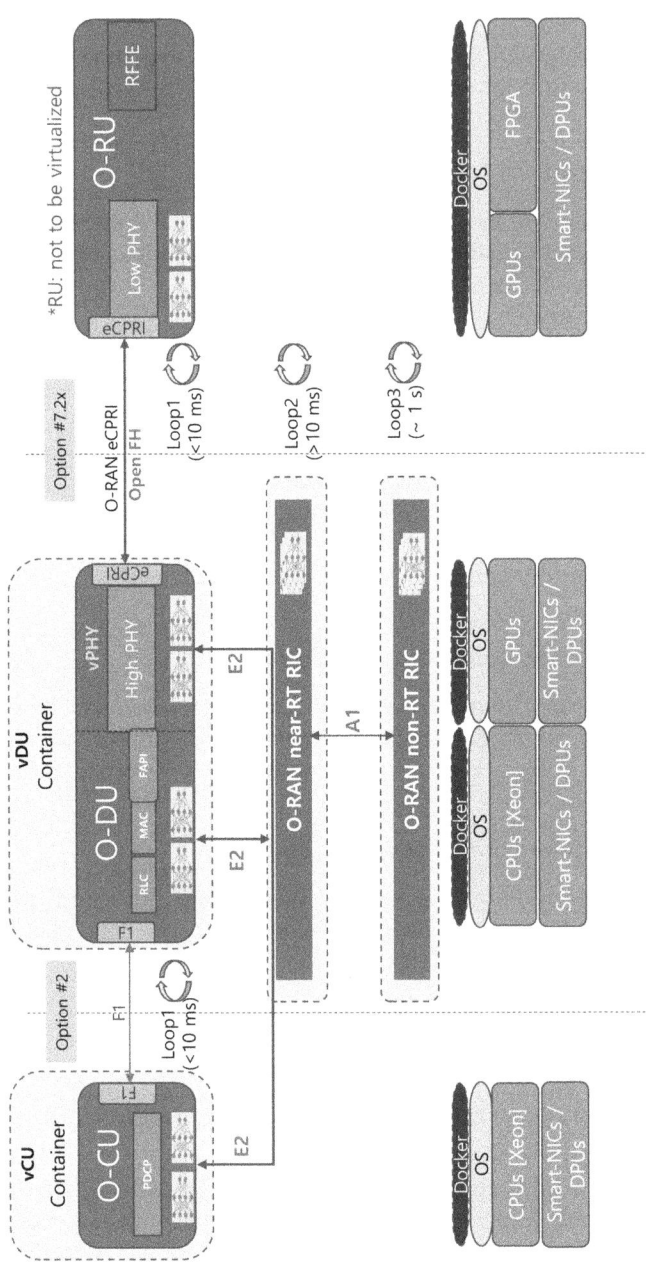

Figure 3.2 Logical functions and control loops in an O-RAN.

host ML models. Deployment scenario 1.5 is essential for Beyond 5G and 6G AI/ML use cases, where control loop execution needs to be faster.

3.3.3 AI-native approach

For the Beyond 5G and 6G latency requirements for the execution of ML models, we envision that each logical node of O-RAN is required to have the capability to host ML models. Several AI-native nodes need to work together to complete the execution of ML models in the fastest possible time. Figure 3.3 depicts an O-RAN model with a 7.2x split [11], where each logical and functional unit is a smart AI-native node.

Vital features that a typical AI-native node will support are explained in the remainder of this section.

3.3.3.1 Inference routing

All AI-native nodes together will form a custom network in which the common database of resource availability at each node is maintained. Such a database is synchronized and mirrored at each node. Any given AI-native node, when running an AI/ML use case and having inference to be passed to an ML model, runs *inference-routing* logic and chooses the best, nearest, and free AI-native node, based on the synchronized database. Inference routing also essentially leads to choosing the best control loop for the execution of inferences. In Ref. [12], the inferences of the deep NN (DNN) model are routed for performance improvement.

3.3.3.2 Load balancing

By the virtue of inference routing based on the synchronized database, each of the nodes is balanced to share the load and together achieve the best performance.

3.3.3.3 Split computing

Two or more AI-native nodes together can split and execute the ML models. One such mechanism can be passing a series of inference inputs to different nodes and executing them in parallel. Another trending and well-known mechanism is training the ML model across the computing nodes, where one of the AI-native nodes can act as a parameter server [13] and the remaining nodes share the load of training and synchronize the training process via a parameter server.

3.3.3.4 Local AI acceleration

Each AI-native node applies the optimization techniques that have been discussed already in the context of realizing ML models on UE. AI-native nodes can apply methods such as quantization [1] and parallelizing ML model execution [3, 4].

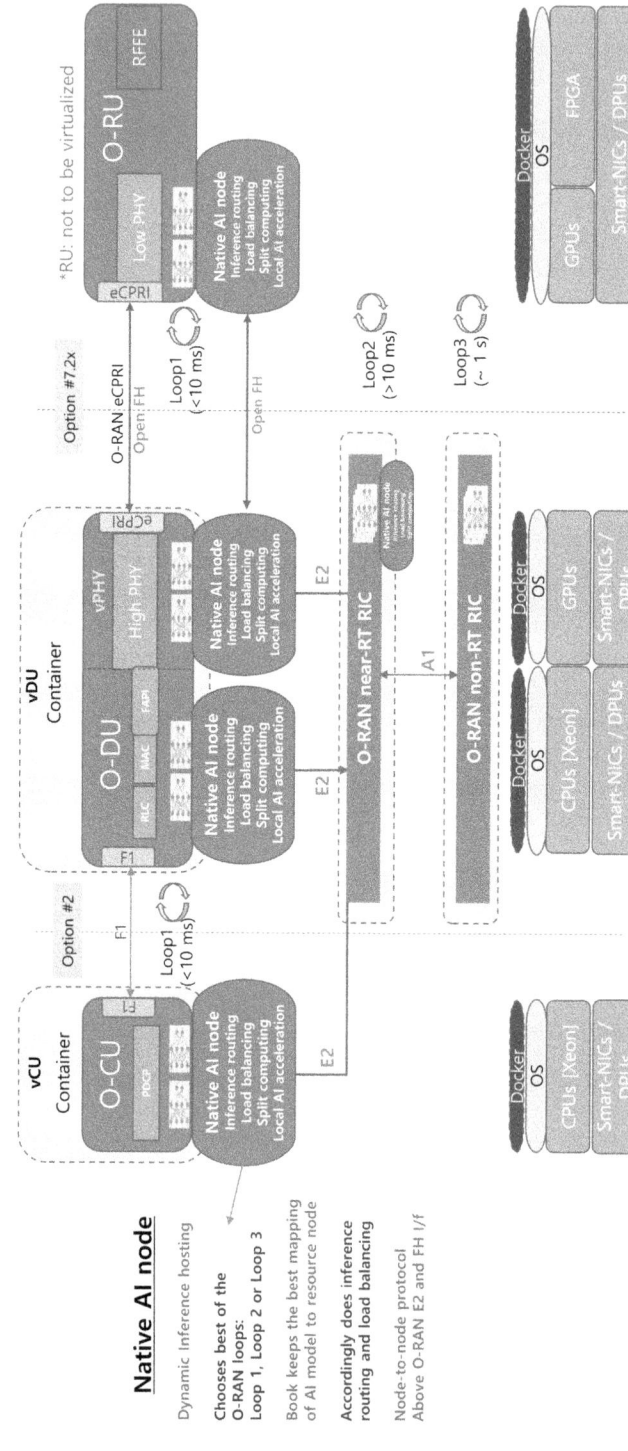

Figure 3.3 Visualization of native AI in O-RAN.

3.4 IN-NETWORK COMPUTING FOR ML

Distributed training of DNN models is a major choice for training from larger datasets [14]. The deeper the model, the more accuracy it offers. When training is done via distributed compute nodes, two challenges need to be addressed to reduce the training time of the DNN models. One is the compute latency itself, and another is the communication cost between computing nodes of a distributed network. Compute latency can be addressed by scaling the compute nodes. However, reducing the communication latency between the nodes needs special techniques. In this section, we will discuss one of the important techniques, which is leveraging smart switches or smart-NICs.

3.4.1 Smart switches or smart network interface cards (smartNICs)

Smart network interface cards (smartNICs) and DPUs are programmable network peripherals [15, 16] with which the user can program packet-processing logic. These devices offer high-speed packet processing due to their customized silicon infrastructure. Stateless packet parsing and packet header preparation are done at the line rate of communication. Although smartNICs are primarily designed for high-speed packet processing at the line rate, they motivate ML practitioners to utilize the moderate compute capabilities offered to reduce the communication costs of distributed training. One such method of leveraging smartNICs to improve the performance of communication costs of distributed ML is via a network aggregation of model updates and sharing the updates to different nodes at the line rate [17].

3.5 CONCLUSION

In this chapter, we presented the aspects of realizing the AI/ML model for learning and inference executions, on different platforms ranging from smartphone devices to RAN servers on a typical O-RAN deployment and also on smart networks' switches. The potential approaches are explained to realize AI/ML use cases on computationally constrained smartphone devices. Necessary methods to apply on an O-RAN deployment, such as federated learning and native AI, are presented with appropriate references. Opportunities for in-network computing of ML via smartNICs and DPUs are presented. Overall, the chapter stands as a collective reference of compute platform selections and deployment on contemporary end-user devices, RANs, and core network environments.

REFERENCES

1. https://arxiv.org/pdf/1803.03383.pdf High-Accuracy Low-Precision Training, Christopher De Sa, Megan Leszczynski, Jian Zhang, Alana Marzoev, Christopher R. Aberger, Kunle Olukotun, Christopher Re

2. Ulppack: Fast Sub-8-Bit Matrix Multiply on Commodity Simd Hardware, Jaeyeon Won, Jeyeon Si, Sam Son, Tae Jun Ham, Jae W. Lee
3. Hydrozoa: Dynamic Hybrid-Parallel DNN Training on Serverless Containers, Runsheng Benson Guo, Victor Guo, Antonio Kim, Joshua Hildred, Khuzaima Daudjee
4. https://arxiv.org/pdf/1809.02839.pdf Efficient and Robust Parallel DNN Training Through Model Parallelism on Multi-GPU Platform, Chi-Chung Chen, Chia-Lin Yang, Hsiang-Yun Cheng
5. https://souryadey.github.io/teaching/material/Basic_Operations_of_Neural_ Networks.pdf Basic Operations of Neural Networks, Sourya Dey
6. https://www.tensorflow.org/lite/guide Tensor Flow Lite Overview and Key Features
7. https://www.tensorflow.org/lite/performance/delegates Tensor Flow Lite Delegates: Hardware Acceleration of TensorFlow Lite Models by Leveraging on-Device Accelerators
8. https://www.tensorflow.org/lite/android/delegates/hexagon TensorFlow Lite Hexagon Delegate: Qualcomm Hexagon Library to Execute Quantized Kernels on the DSP
9. https://orandownloadsweb.azurewebsites.net/specifications WG2: O-RAN AI/ ML Workflow Description and Requirements 1.03 [O-RAN.WG2.AIML-v01.03]
10. https://orandownloadsweb.azurewebsites.net/specifications WG2: Chapter 5. Deployment Scenarios., Scenario 1.5 from Table 2 - AI/ML Deployment Scenarios [O-RAN.WG2.AIML-v01.03]
11. https://orandownloadsweb.azurewebsites.net/specifications Section 4.3.6 O-RU., 7-2x split: WG1: O-RAN Architecture Description 7.0 [O-RAN.WG1. O-RAN-Architecture-Description-v07.00]
12. https://deepai.org/publication/a-framework-for-routing-dnn-inference-jobs-over-distributed-computing-networks A Framework for Routing DNN Inference Jobs over Distributed Computing Networks, Sehun Jung, et al. KONKUK UNIVERSITY
13. https://www.cs.cmu.edu/~muli/file/ps.pdf Parameter Server for Distributed Machine Learning, Mu Li1, Li Zhou, Zichao Yang, Aaron Li, Fei Xia, David G. Andersen, and Alexander Smola
14. https://papers.nips.cc/paper/2012/file/6aca97005c68f1206823815f66102863-Paper.pdf Large Scale Distributed Deep Networks, Jeffrey Dean, Greg S. Corrado, Rajat Monga, Kai Chen, Matthieu Devin, Quoc V. Le, Mark Z. Mao, Marc'Aurelio Ranzato, Andrew Senior, Paul Tucker, Ke Yang, Andrew Y. Ng
15. https://www.xilinx.com/content/dam/xilinx/publications/product-briefs/ xilinx-alveo-sn1000-product-brief.pdf Xilinx Alveo SN1000 Smart-NIC
16. https://resources.nvidia.com/en-us-accelerated-networking-resource-library/ datasheet-nvidia-bluefield?lx=LbHvpR&topic=networking-cloud   NVIDIA® Bluefield®-3 data processing unit (DPU)
17. https://www.usenix.org/system/files/nsdi21-sapio.pdf   Scaling   Distributed Machine Learning with In-Network Aggregation, Amedeo Sapio, Marco Canini, and Chen-Yu Ho, KAUST; Jacob Nelson, Microsoft, Panos Kalnis, KAUST; Changhoon Kim, Barefoot Networks; Arvind Krishnamurthy, University of Washington; Masoud Moshref, Barefoot Networks, Dan Ports, Microsoft; Peter Richtarik, KAUST

Chapter 4

AI/ML-based design principles of transceivers for wireless systems

Ashok Kumar Reddy Chavva, Saikrishna Pedamalli, Sripada Kadambar, Anusha Gunturu, and Shubham Khunteta

Samsung R&D Institute India-Bangalore, Bangalore, India

4.1 INTRODUCTION

In beyond-5G (B5G) systems, we see the influence of artificial intelligence (AI) and machine learning (ML) on the physical layer and beyond. Initial AI/ML-influenced systems will not be a complete replacement of the end-to-end system with AI-based transceivers, but a carefully curated usage of AI in the modules that take advantage of AI. In this chapter, we describe related works in AI in wireless communications and describe AI-based system designs, highlighting the interactions between the communication layers.

AI in wireless communications [1–5] is an emerging technique that is expected to play a crucial role in achieving the expected and required key performance indicators (KPIs) of the next-generation communication networks. The future wireless networks will be highly complex, heterogeneous, and ubiquitous. This paves the path for intelligent techniques to analyze the wireless communication systems and make them seamless for some of the difficult challenges, such as estimating channel characteristics, network topology, and placement of devices. AI will play an important role in applications like channel estimation, resource allocation, equalization, channel decoding, and complex system computations in next-generation communication networks. In Ref. [6], the authors give an introduction to ML and its applications to communication systems. AI-based channel estimation techniques using deep learning (DL) applied to wireless communication systems are presented in Ref. [7]. The 3rd Generation Partnership Project (3GPP) has also started a study item on using AI/ML applications for the 5G New Radio (NR) air interface [8]. This involves various use cases. Some of the use cases shortlisted for further study involve channel state information (CSI) compression, CSI prediction, beam prediction, and positioning enhancements [9–11]. Furthermore, to enable and encourage usage of AI/ML for wireless systems, the International Telecommunication Union (ITU) has been organizing challenges with the help of various research institutes across the world.

DOI: 10.1201/9781003303527-5

4.1.1 AI-based B5G communication systems

AI-based communication system blocks are known to perform well in cases where the system model is not perfect [12]. In Figure 4.1, we illustrate typical baseband modules for user equipment (UE) that can have AI influence in a 4G or 5G communication system. In the receive path, radiofrequency (RF) impairments, automatic gain controllers (AGCs), and time and frequency acquisition can be trained to perform the conventional job. For the case of RF impairment compensation, when the assumed impairment model is accurate, conventional mitigation schemes perform very well. For cases with an inaccurate system model, it is difficult to find a conventional optimal mitigation method. In such cases, with sufficient training, AI can perform better than the conventional compensation schemes. Modules like channel estimation [7] and log-likelihood ratio (LLR) estimation [13] may find complete AI replacements. These methods either try to perform very similarly to conventional optimal schemes at reduced complexity or perform better than the conventional schemes in cases where conventional optimal schemes do not exist in the literature. Other blocks like channel decoders may not need complete replacement in the immediate future, but even in modules that do not need replacement, we can fine-tune the parameters using AI. For example, using an AI-based approach, it is possible to predict, using the LLR statistics, the status of a transport block (TB) or code block (CB) cyclic redundancy check (CRC) well before the completion of a set of fixed numbers of iterations run in conventional channel decoders like turbo or low-density parity check (LDPC) [14]. Similarly, we can ignore decoding the TB with a hybrid automatic repeat request (HARQ) until we are confident of decoding it successfully. In the uplink path, the transmit power control algorithm for a physical random access channel (PRACH), sounding reference signal (SRS), physical uplink control channel (PUCCH), and physical uplink shared channel (PUSCH) can use AI approaches to improve its efficiency.

For millimeter-wave systems, AI can be used to efficiently select the beam. An AI-based beam selection method can be shown to perform better than conventional beam selection schemes. In conventional beam selection schemes, the next beam pair is selected based on the available beam pair measurements, while the AI-based method can be trained to predict the future beam given that the present beam is known along with environmental parameters. In Ref. [15], a DL method that uses environmental data such as GPS, traffic simulator, and LIDAR (light detection and ranging) data is proposed to shortlist the beam pairs. In Ref. [16], sensor data on UE is used to predict and shortlist the beam pairs that are more relevant to measure using recurrent neural networks (RNNs). Along similar lines, a CSI reporting function at UE can use AI to improve the system throughput by reporting the predicted CSI [17, 18]. Such a method will have considerable gains, as it overcomes the effects of channel aging, resulting from the delay in the usage of CSI from the time it is reported by UE, to a good extent.

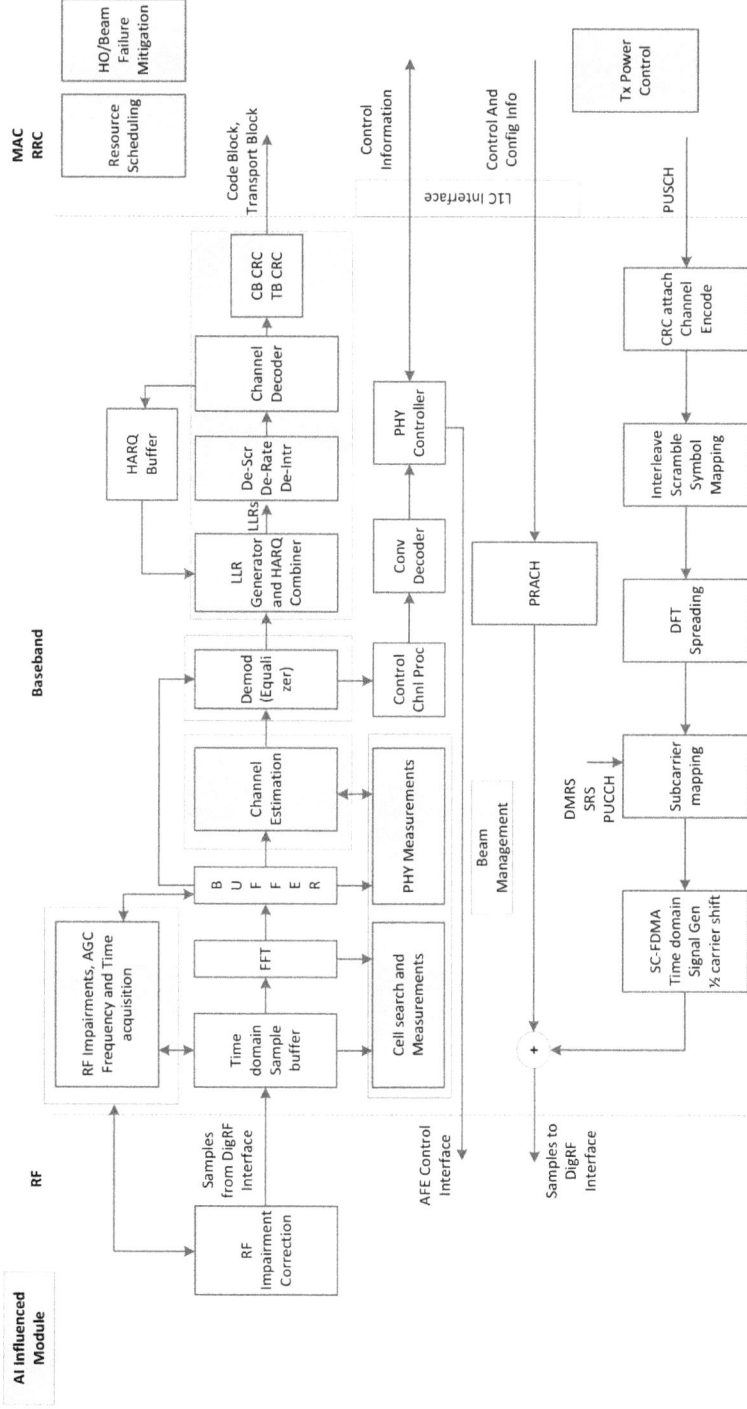

Figure 4.1 Block diagram of a baseband system with AI-influenced modules.

The first systems that use AI will use it to optimize wireless systems at the module level; the interactions between the modules and layers will continue to be conventional, as discussed above. Figure 4.2 illustrates the conventional layer-based interactions between multiple layers at the transmitter and receiver. In later realizations of B5G or 6G, we expect the interactions between the layers to facilitate AI-enabled modules in an efficient way. We show an end-to-end AI-enabled modular communication system in Figure 4.3; different layers at the transmitter and receiver will exchange the AI states, which represent the present state of the system at that layer. For example, SCI feedback like the channel quality indicator (CQI), precoding matrix indicator (PMI), and rank indicator (RI) in a conventional scheme can be replaced by a representation of the channel in an AI-enabled module as a state exchange that is decoded at the base station (BS) with a matching AI-enabled module. This state exchange may not have a physical meaning and might be difficult to interpret by humans, unlike conventional systems.

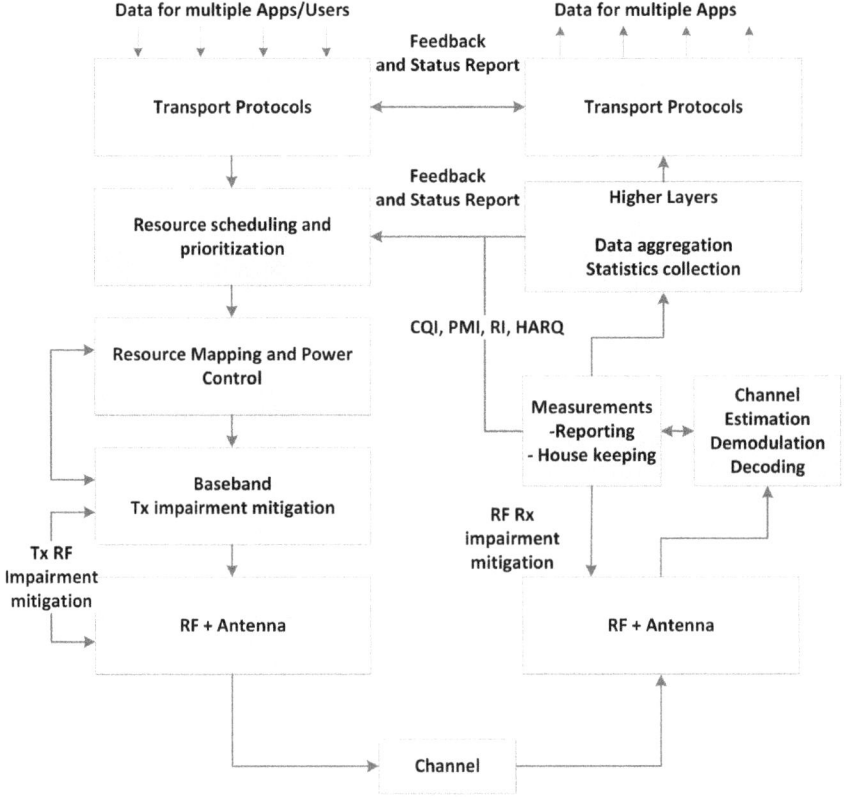

Figure 4.2 Interactions between multiple layers at the transmitter and receiver in a conventional communication system.

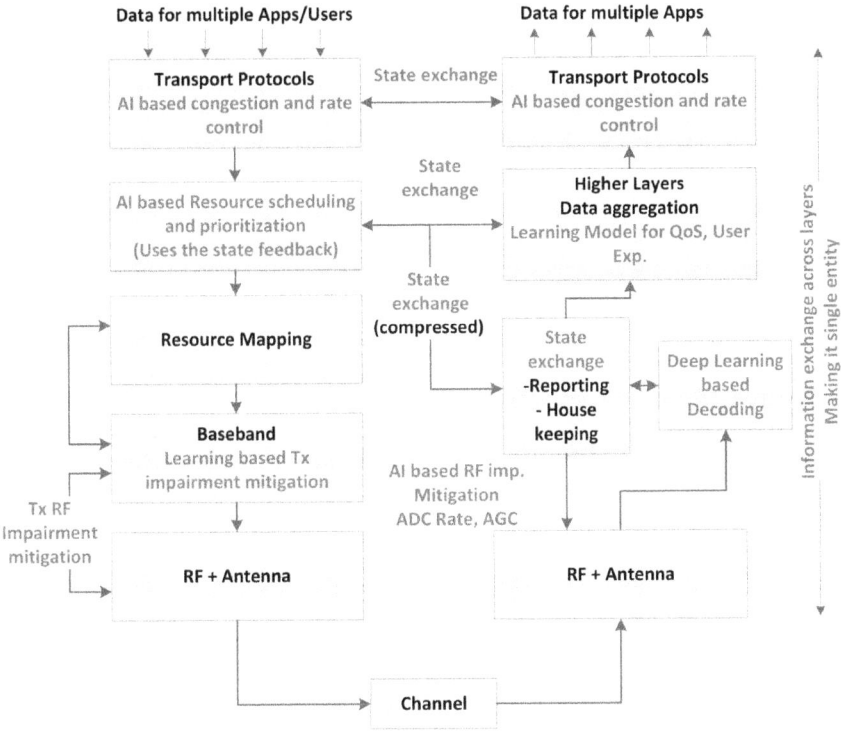

Figure 4.3 Interactions between multiple layers at the transmitter and receiver in an envisioned communication system based on AI.

In Figure 4.3, we further summarize typical applications of AI in multiple layers. For example, the transport layer can use AI for congestion control that responds to fading channels efficiently compared to conventional transport protocols. The feedback schemes can now report tailored information to suit the needs of AI-based components. Unlike the conventional system where each layer communicates with neighboring layers, in the AI-based system, we envision interactions between multiple layers with no specific restrictions. This will enhance the trainability to various channel conditions and the system's response to it. Systems with end-to-end AI-enabled modules will need an efficient mechanism for debugging system failures and will need to cover such cases in training future systems. Another important challenge with end-to-end AI-enabled communication systems is data for training covering the numerous scenarios that arise in wireless systems. Even if we are prepared to generate such data, it takes an enormous amount of time to train. The proposed AI-enabled modular communication system, as shown in Figure 4.3, with state exchanges that efficiently represent the system can overcome these challenges with its modular trainability.

The application of AI in wireless systems has begun, however, at a slow pace. We will see its application in higher layers first, mainly on the network side of communication systems. At the lower layers, specifically at the physical layer, the system is designed based on specific system models handling specific scenarios. Typically these models are quite accurate, resulting in good performance of the algorithms designed based on these models. So, at the physical layer, conventional algorithms will give strong competition to AI-based algorithms. Even here, in the initial stages, AI is expected to be used to estimate a few specific parameters driving the conventional algorithms. It is imperative to design AI schemes that allow continuous enhancement and efficient failure detection. Creating an end-to-end system based on AI will be long-drawn and take more research effort to become practically realizable.

In the rest of this chapter, we cover a few AI/ML applications in the physical layer of either the UE or RAN, also known as the BS. Namely, in Section 4.2, we discuss the aspects of channel estimation, and how such a critical block in the receiver can be replaced by a DL-based method and where it can be useful. In Section 4.3, CSI estimation and prediction are discussed. This is one of the three use cases that the 3GPP working group has decided to study in detail as part of Release 18 [8]. These parts of the system enable the cellular system to use the assigned frequency bands efficiently, by adapting to each user and to the time-varing and frequency-selective channels. In Section 4.4, we cover an intricate use case of choosing the number of iterations in iterative channel decoders that are typically used in 4G and 5G systems. This will establish the use of learning methods in decisions that are otherwise very finely handcrafted by experts. In Section 4.5, we cover an important module called digital predistortion (DPD) in the transmitter, which helps mitigate the nonlinearities of the power amplifier (PA). This is a use case where the model for nonlinearities in the PA is not accurate, and where an AI-based method is able to perform better than the conventional methods. Finally, in Section 4.6, we discuss the problem of beam selection and prediction in millimeter-wave systems. This is the second of the three use cases that the 3GPP working group planned to study as part of Release 18 [8]. The use cases covered in this chapter provide directions to apply AI-based methods for replacing the conventional methods or making them more efficient in transceiver design.

4.2 CHANNEL ESTIMATION

The traditional methods for channel estimation, like least squares (LS) and minimum mean square error (MMSE) [19], are studied in great detail and optimized for channel estimation. The LS estimation method does not involve any prior knowledge of channel statistics. The MMSE method performs better in various channel conditions compared to LS using the second-order channel statistics but is computationally complex to implement for practical wireless channels, whose statistics can change with time.

The application of DL in the physical layer for channel estimation is discussed in Ref. [20, 21], which adopts a data-driven DL approach to model all modules of an orthogonal frequency-division multiplexing (OFDM) receiver using a fully connected deep neural network (FC-DNN). It demonstrates that deep neural networks (DNNs) can learn various wireless channels subjected to nonlinear distortion and frequency selectivity and achieve performance comparable to that of traditional methods with a limited number of pilots. An approach that avoids offline training by fitting the parameters on the fly for channel estimation is described in Ref. [22]. In ChannelNet [7], the time–frequency response of a fast-fading channel is treated as a two-dimensional (2D) image with a known channel at the pilot position. It poses the problem of channel estimation as a super-resolution problem, considering the channel response at the pilot position as a low-resolution image. It is implemented by using convolutional neural network (CNN)-based super-resolution (SRCNN) [23] and image restoration (denoising CNNs [DnCNN]) [24] networks.

In practical wireless communication systems, the channel parameters' delay spread (DS), Doppler spread (DoS), and signal-to-noise ratio (SNR) vary with time. The DS manifests as the coherence bandwidth of a channel in the frequency domain. The channel exhibits correlation within the coherence bandwidth. The DoS manifests as the coherence duration of the channel, within which the channel is correlated. We observe that the channel estimation depends on these parameters [25]. In the following part of this section, we cover a DL-based channel estimation method that considers the channel properties in the design and training of the network [26].

In an OFDM system, the received signal at i^{th} subcarrier and j^{th} symbol can be represented as:

$$Y_{i,j} = H_{i,j}X_{i,j} + N_{i,j}, \tag{4.1}$$

where $H_{i,j}$, $X_{i,j}$, and $N_{i,j}$ denote the channel coefficient, transmitted signal, and noise at i^{th} subcarrier and j^{th} symbol, respectively.

To estimate the channel we transmit reference signals, called *pilots* in this section, at predefined pilot locations. Using these, the channel coefficients at the pilot positions are estimated. In this section, we propose a DL-based channel estimation method for time-varying and frequency-selective channels that consists of three components, namely, the noise filter (NF), frequency domain interpolator (FDI), and time domain interpolator (TDI), as shown in Figure 4.4. The proposed DL-based channel estimation is further described below.

The NF network is used to denoise the channel coefficients at the pilot positions. The output of the NF network $\hat{\mathbf{H}}_p$ is given by:

$$\hat{\mathbf{H}}_p = f_{NF}(\tilde{\mathbf{H}}_p), \tag{4.2}$$

where $\hat{\mathbf{H}}_p$, f_{NF}, and $\tilde{\mathbf{H}}_p$ denote the denoised pilots, noise filter function, and noisy pilots, respectively.

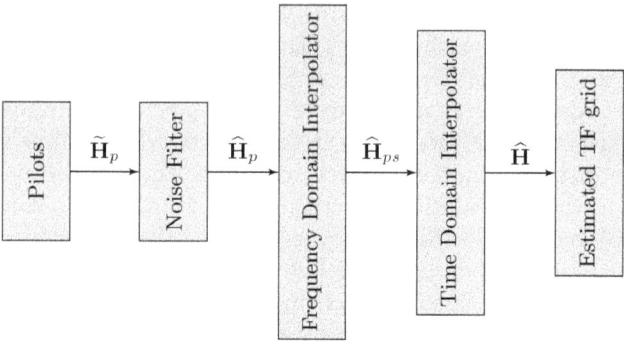

Figure 4.4 Block diagram of DL-based channel estimation with flexible delay and Doppler networks.

The NF network is a two-layer CNN. The first layer consists of eight filters of size $(4N_{NF} - 1) \times 1$, followed by the rectified linear unit (ReLU) activation function. The last layer consists of two filters of size $(4N_{NF} - 1) \times 1$, where N_{NF} corresponds to the number of resource blocks (RBs) available.

The FDI network is used to estimate the channel coefficients of the OFDM symbols with pilots. The output of the FDI network $\hat{\mathbf{H}}_{ps}$ is given by:

$$\hat{\mathbf{H}}_{ps} = f_{FDI}(R_{FDI}(\hat{\mathbf{H}}_p)), \tag{4.3}$$

where $\hat{\mathbf{H}}_{ps}$, R_{FDI}, and f_{FDI} denote the estimated channel coefficients of the pilot symbols, the mapping function that maps the denoised pilots to their respective positions in the pilot symbols, and the FDI function.

The FDI network is a two-layer CNN. The first layer consists of eight filters of size 5×1, followed by the ReLU activation function. The last layer consists of two filters of size 7×1.

The TDI network is used to estimate the channel coefficients of the entire time–frequency (TF) grid. The output of the TDI network $\hat{\mathbf{H}}$ is given by:

$$\hat{\mathbf{H}} = f_{TDI}(R_{TDI}(\hat{\mathbf{H}}_{ps})), \tag{4.4}$$

where $\hat{\mathbf{H}}$, R_{TDI}, and f_{TDI} denote the estimated channel coefficients of the entire TF grid, the mapping function that maps the estimated pilot symbols to their respective positions in the TF grid, and the TDI function.

The TDI network is a two-layer CNN. The first layer consists of eight filters of size 1×11, followed by the ReLU activation function. The last layer consists of two filters of size 1×11.

Together, for estimating the channel coefficients of the TF grid from the noisy pilots, we have:

$$\hat{\mathbf{H}} = f_{TDI}(R_{TDI}(f_{FDI}(R_{FDI}(f_{NF}(\tilde{\mathbf{H}}_p))))). \tag{4.5}$$

The size of the kernels for the NF network is based on the maximum number of pilots per OFDM symbol. The sizes of the kernels for the FDI and TDI networks are chosen in such a way that at least two pilots are present in the kernel to obtain the unknown values lying between the pilots.

4.2.1 Training mechanism

We observe that the channel estimation depends on the parameters DS, DoS, and SNR. These parameters vary with time. To cover a wide range of these parameters, we propose to train the networks on a grid of values for each one. In the proposed method, we use multiple pilots within a symbol to filter noise in the NF network. So, to factor in the dependency of the coherence bandwidth in NF network training, we choose to train the NF network for multiple combinations of the SNR and DS. The FDI and TDI networks solely depend on the DS and DoS, respectively. In this way, if any one of the variables among the SNR, DS, and DoS is changed, then the network corresponding to that variable alone can be replaced to obtain the desired result. The input, output, and loss function of each of the networks are discussed next.

The input for the NF network is the vector of noisy channel coefficients at the pilot positions $\tilde{\mathbf{H}}_p$, and the output is a vector of denoised channel coefficients at the pilot positions $\hat{\mathbf{H}}_p$. Let $\mathbf{H}_{ps}$ denote the vector of pilot symbols, then the input for the FDI network is the vector of partially filled channel coefficients of the pilot symbols $\tilde{\mathbf{H}}_{ps}$:

$$\tilde{\mathbf{H}}_{ps} = \left(\begin{array}{ll} \mathbf{H}_{ps} & \text{at pilot frequency tones} \\ 0 & \text{at other frequency tones.} \end{array} \right. \tag{4.6}$$

The output is a vector of estimated channel coefficients of the pilot symbols in the TF grid $\tilde{\mathbf{H}}_{ps}$. Let $\mathbf{H}$ denote the vector of the entire TF grid, then the input for the TDI network is the vector of the partially filled TF grid with the pilot symbols $\tilde{\mathbf{H}}$:

$$\tilde{\mathbf{H}} = \left(\begin{array}{ll} \mathbf{H} & \text{at pilot symbols} \\ 0 & \text{at other symbols.} \end{array} \right. \tag{4.7}$$

The output is the vector of estimated channel coefficients of the entire TF grid $\hat{\mathbf{H}}$.

Let Θ_{NF}, Θ_{FDI}, and Θ_{TDI} be the vectors of NF, FDI, and TDI network parameters, respectively, so that $\hat{\mathbf{H}}_p = f(\Theta_{\text{NF}}; \tilde{\mathbf{H}}_p)$, $\hat{\mathbf{H}}_{ps} = f(\Theta_{\text{FDI}}; \tilde{\mathbf{H}}_{ps})$, and $\hat{\mathbf{H}} = f(\Theta_{\text{TDI}}; \tilde{\mathbf{H}})$. Then, the parameters Θ_{NF}, Θ_{FDI}, and Θ_{TDI} will be trained to minimize the loss functions L_{NF}, L_{FDI}, and L_{TDI}, respectively. The loss functions are given by the mean square error (MSE) between the estimated channel coefficients and the ideal channel coefficients. For N training samples, the loss functions L_{NF}, L_{FDI}, and L_{TDI} are given by:

$$L_{NF} = \frac{1}{N}\sum_{i=0}^{N-1}\left\|\hat{\mathbf{H}}_p^{(i)} - \mathbf{H}_p^{(i)}\right\|_2^2, \tag{4.8}$$

$$L_{FDI} = \frac{1}{N}\sum_{i=0}^{N-1}\left\|\hat{\mathbf{H}}_{ps}^{(i)} - \mathbf{H}_{ps}^{(i)}\right\|_2^2, \tag{4.9}$$

$$L_{TDI} = \frac{1}{N}\sum_{i=0}^{N-1}\left\|\hat{\mathbf{H}}^{(i)} - \mathbf{H}^{(i)}\right\|_2^2. \tag{4.10}$$

4.2.2 Simulation results

We benchmark the proposed algorithm with an ideal linear minimum mean square error (LMMSE) and ChannelNet [7]. Here, the LMMSE method assumes the availability of ideal second-order statistics for estimation purposes. We consider clustered delay line, type A (CDL-A) and type D (CDL-D), for performance evaluation. Here, CDL-A is the non-line-of-sight (NLoS) channel and CDL-D is the line-of-sight (LoS) channel.

Figure 4.5 plots the channel estimation error E as a function of the SNR for the proposed solution, ChannelNet and the ideal LMMSE, with the DS

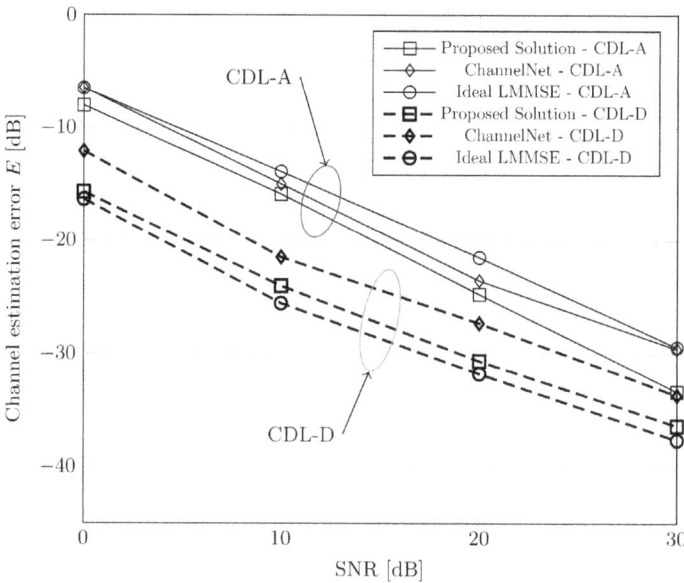

Figure 4.5 Channel estimation error E as a function of the SNR for different methods (DS = 1,000 ns and DoS = 150 Hz.

and DoS fixed to 1,000 ns and 150 Hz, respectively. We observe that the estimation error goes down with an increase in SNR as expected. For the CDL-A channel, the proposed method performs the best with a gain of 4 dB at an SNR of 30 dB compared to the ideal LMMSE and ChannelNet. An ideal LMMSE performs best on the CDL-D channel with a gain of 1 dB compared to the proposed method, and 4 dB compared to the ChannelNet at an SNR of 30 dB. We observe that the ideal second-order statistics used for the LMMSE method are accurate and consistent for CDL-D because of the LoS component, whereas for CDL-A, which is the NLoS channel, these averaged ideal statistics do not correspond per RB statistics. This difference in ideal statistics results in a performance difference of the LMMSE. The channel estimation error of the proposed method and ChannelNet saturates beyond a 40 dB SNR. We further observe improved performance at low SNR values when we use more RBs for the NF network. This is because of the availability of more pilots for noise filtering.

To study the robustness of the proposed algorithm, we evaluate its performance with mismatched parameters. Here, we study the robustness of the proposed method with a mismatch in both the DS and DoS. For estimating the channel (2,000 ns, 100 Hz) with the LMMSE, we used the channel characteristics of (1,500 ns, 150 Hz) (mismatch) and (2,000 ns, 100 Hz) (matched). For estimating the channel with the proposed method, we trained the NF and FDI networks with a DS value of 1,500 ns and the TDI network with a DoS value of 150 Hz (Proposed$_{mismatch}$), the NF and FDI networks with a DS value of 2,000 ns and the TDI network with a DoS value of 100 Hz (Proposed$_{matched}$), and the NF and FDI networks with a combination of channels with DS values of (1,000, 1,500, and 2,000 ns) and the TDI network with a combination of channels with DoS values of (100 and 150 Hz) (Proposed$_{combined}$). For estimating the channel with the ChannelNet, we trained the network with channel (1,500 ns, 150 Hz) (ChNet$_{mismatch}$) and with channel (2,000 ns, 100 Hz) (ChNet$_{matched}$), and channels with all combinations of DS values of (1,000, 1,500, and 2,000 ns) and DoS values of (100 and 150 Hz) (ChNet$_{combined}$).

Figure 4.6 plots the channel estimation error E as a function of the SNR for channel CDL-A with a mismatch in DS and DoS values. The performance drop observed when using Proposed$_{combined}$ is less than 2 dB for all SNR points compared to Proposed$_{matched}$.

4.3 CSI ESTIMATION AND PREDICTION

CSI estimation and reporting comprise one of the important blocks in wireless communication systems, as they help the transmitter decide the best-suited modulation scheme, the spatial rate, and the corresponding precoding schemes. With the recent interest in ML applications to wireless communications, 3GPP has started to study AI/ML applications for the air interface. One of the important use cases being studied is CSI prediction [9].

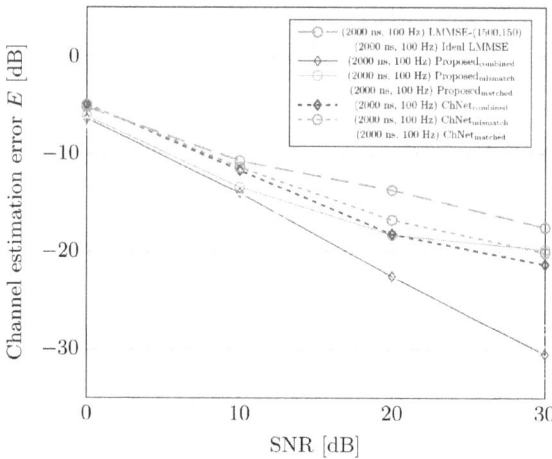

Figure 4.6 Effect of DS and DoS mismatch together: Channel estimation error E as a function of the SNR for the proposed method, ChannelNet and the LMMSE.

Obtaining precise and up-to-date CSI at the transmitter is challenging due to several factors such as estimation accuracy and reporting overhead. Furthermore, delayed usage of the reported CSI at the transmitter also deteriorates the link capacity. This is due to the variations in the channel between the times that it is estimated and used, known as the channel aging problem [27].

Channel properties change over the duration of channel coherence time which is largely caused due to user motion. Thus, the receiver is expected to share multiple CSI reports during this period, which otherwise results in significant degradation of the achievable data rate [27]. However, frequent CSI sharing causes higher reporting overhead, which may degrade the performance of the system. Hence, in general, this is regulated by the network. For example, in the case of 5G NR, the UE CSI reporting periodicity is configured by the BS. Thus, generating accurate CSI reports while compensating for the aging effects is instrumental for UE to achieve efficient link adaptation.

A number of studies have characterized the effects of channel aging both at the UE and at the system level. In Ref. [28], CSI reporting using prediction is studied for BS power consumption reduction. Furthermore, in Ref. [29], channel aging is addressed by designing an optimal CSI reporting pattern for the UEs to maximize the achievable system capacity. Also, studies have shown that channel prediction using Kalman [30] and Weiner filtering [27] can improve the aging effects. Nonetheless, their application remains challenging due to their feasibility and the complexity aspects.

CSI reporting in NR mainly consists of three parameters for link adaptation: the precoding matrix indicator (PMI), rank indicator (RI), and channel quality indicator (CQI). The PMI and RI jointly determine the preferred transmit precoder configuration, whereas the CQI indicates the modulation and coding rate (MCS) preference [31]. Figure 4.7 shows the high-level view

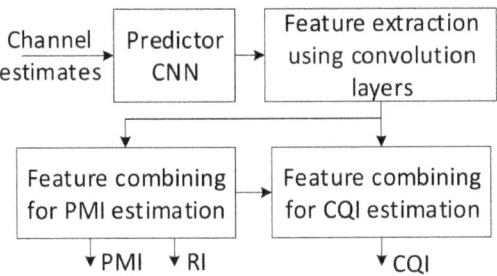

Figure 4.7 High-level flow diagram of deep learning-based CSI prediction (DCP).

of deep learning-based CSI prediction (DCP). Typically, a UE estimates and shares the CSI metrics with the BS periodically or upon receiving a request from the BS. Furthermore, algorithms proposed for long-term evolution (LTE) [32] are also applicable to NR due to their CSI framework similarities. But the conventional methods are effective at smaller bandwidths and CQIs, as the estimation accuracy deteriorates with the scaling [33]. Hence, in Ref. [34], the authors employ ML to improve the CQI selection accuracy. Moreover, conventional methods incur greater estimation complexity at higher transmission ranks; thus, generally, approximations are used [35]. In addition, the NR CSI also includes parameters to support beamforming, such as the CSI reference signal resource indicator.

4.3.1 System model

We consider a BS communicating with UE using OFDM transmissions. The BS schedules data to the UE in transmission time units of a duration T_s, known as a slot, and let n denote its index. Furthermore, a subcarrier to which data is mapped in an OFDM symbol is known as a resource element (RE) k. We denote the number of transmit and receive antennas as N^t and N^r, respectively, and define $N^t \times N^r$ as the port configuration used. Let $H \in \mathbb{C}^{N^r \times N^t}$ denote the baseband channel between the BS and UE. Thus, the vector Y_k received on the RE k in slot n is:

$$Y_k(n) = H_k(n)X_k(n) + Z_k(n), \tag{4.11}$$

where $X_k \in \mathbb{C}^{N^t \times 1}$ denotes the transmitted symbol, and $Z = N(0, \sigma^2 I) \in \mathbb{C}^{N^r \times 1}$ is the additive white Gaussian noise. Furthermore, let $P \in \mathcal{P}$ denote the L rank precoder used for the transmission. We assume that the same precoder is used across a frequency sub-band spanned by $\mathcal{K}$ REs for the data transmission. After the combining operation, we denote the precoded signal of rank L received at the UE as:

$$R_k(n) = C_k(n)Y_k(n) = C_k(n)(H_k(n)P\dot{X}_k(n) + Z_k(n)), \tag{4.12}$$

where R_k is the post-equalization symbol received, C_k denotes the combining vector used at the UE, and $\dot{X}_k \in C^{L \times 1}$ represents the codeword transmitted at the BS. Moreover, we denote $\dot{H}_k^P = C_k H_k P \in \mathbb{C}^{L \times L}$ as the effective layer-wise channel matrix corresponding to the precoder P used. Furthermore, we represent $\dot{b}_k^{ij,P}$ as its corresponding entry in the ith row and j^{th} column. Generally, the combiner matrix C_k is chosen based on either the maximum likelihood or MMSE criterion. For example, in the case of the MMSE, the combining vector is given by $C_k = ((H_k P)^{\dagger}(H_k P) + \sigma^2 I)^{-1}(H_k P)^{\dagger}$. Moreover, the optimal PMI $\hat{P}$ for the frequency band can be chosen based on the sum rate maximization (SRM) [32] given by:

$$\hat{P} = \arg\max_{P \in \mathcal{P}} R_P, \tag{4.13}$$

$$R_P = \sum_{k \in \mathcal{K}} \sum_{l=1}^{L} \log_2(1 + \gamma_k^{l,P}), \tag{4.14}$$

where $\gamma_k^{l,P}$ denotes the signal-to-interference-plus-noise ratio (SINR) of layer l in slot n, given by:

$$\gamma_k^{l,P} = \frac{\left|\dot{b}_k^{ll,P}(n)\right|^2}{\sum_{u \neq l}\left|\dot{b}_k^{lu,P}(n)\right|^2 + \sigma^2 \sum_v \left|c_k^{lv}(n)\right|^2}. \tag{4.15}$$

For feedback, $\hat{P}$ is communicated to BS by assigning its index and rank to PMI and RI, respectively. Furthermore, for CQI selection corresponding to $\hat{P}$, nonlinear combining techniques such as effective exponential SINR mapping (EESM) or mutual information effective SINR mapping are used. For example, in the case of EESM [34], the effective SINR $\bar{\gamma}_q^{\hat{P}}$ is given as:

$$\bar{\gamma}_q^{\hat{P}} = -\alpha_q^{(1)} \ln\left(\frac{1}{|\mathcal{K}|L}\sum_{k \in \mathcal{K}}\sum_{l=1}^{L}\exp\left(-\frac{\gamma_k^{l,\hat{P}}}{\alpha_q^{(2)}}\right)\right), \tag{4.16}$$

where $q \in \mathcal{Q}$ denotes the CQI corresponding to which effective SINR is computed. Furthermore, the parameters $\alpha_q^{(1)}$ and $\alpha_q^{(2)}$ are pretuned per the CQI. $\bar{\gamma}_q^{\hat{P}}$ is then mapped to an equivalent block error rate (BLER) value, and the CQI $\hat{q}$ with the highest spectral efficiency (SE) meeting the target BLER is chosen for reporting. We assume that the UE indicates its CSI preference to the BS with a periodicity of T_{RP} slots. Furthermore, for a CSI preference received in slot n, the BS uses it for transmissions in slots $n+1$ to $n+T_{RP}$, assuming a full buffer traffic model [36].

4.3.2 Deep learning–based CSI prediction

In this section [17], we describe the DCP, which is based on the CNN. Figure 4.8 shows the DCP design consisting of the following subblocks:

- *Channel prediction module* (CPM), which is trained for predicting the channel with $\hat{d} = \lceil T_{RP}/2 \rceil$. Furthermore, we enable CPM only for SNR $> \beta$.
- *Feature generation module* (FGM) for computing the common features to be used for PMI and CQI estimation.
- *PMI estimation module* (PEM) for computing the precoder preference using SNR and FGM features.
- *CQI estimation module* (QEM) for computing the CQI preference using SNR, FGM features, and PEM output.
- *DL-based channel estimator* (DCE), which is an ensemble of FGM, PEM, and QEM performing CSI computation.

Furthermore, we set the stride of CNN layers to 1 unless specified otherwise.

4.3.2.1 Channel prediction module

Figure 4.8 shows the CNN-based channel predictor. It consists of three convolutional layers with 16, 4, and 2 kernels, respectively, all using linear activation. For each RE $k \in \mathcal{K}$ per transmit and receive port, the network is trained to predict the channel for $\hat{d} = \lceil T_{RP}/2 \rceil$. Furthermore, the most recent $M = 8$ respective channel estimates are used as inputs to the first convolutional layer. Note that the prediction for each RE is generated independent of the others; hence, only the temporal correlation is exploited, which reduces the complexity. Furthermore, the last dimension of kernel size of the first layer and the

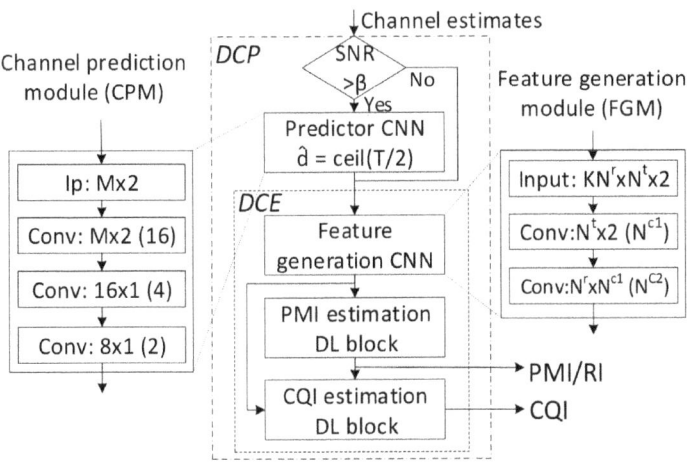

Figure 4.8 Deep learning–based CSI prediction (DCP).

number of kernels in the third layer are set to two. These correspond to the real and imaginary parts of the input and predicted channel data, respectively. Furthermore, we train the model by minimizing the MSE loss function between the predicted and actual channel estimates.

4.3.2.2 DL-based CSI estimation block

The DCE is a learning-based model trained to estimate the precoder and CQI using the channel estimates. As shown in Figure 4.9, it consists of three components: the FGM, PEM, and QEM. The first stage, the FGM, as shown in Figure 4.8, consists of only the convolutional layers and is used for generating the features common for both the PMI and CQI estimation. It consists of an input layer to receive the channel estimates, followed by three convolutional layers. The input layer reshapes the received channel estimates into $I \in \mathbb{R}^{|\mathcal{K}|N^r \times N^t \times 2}$, which is then processed by the subsequent two layers using linear activation. The stride of the second convolutional layer is set to $N^r \times 1$. The number of kernels in the first and second layers are N^{c1} and N^{c2}, respectively, which are tuned depending on the port configuration $N^t \times N^r$. Note that the FGM output should be optimal for both PMI and CQI generation. Thus, the FGM is trained to generate $|\mathcal{K}|N^{c2}$ features using an inductive feature-learning method, which is generally used in multitask learning problems [37]. The approach improves the estimation complexity of the CQI by avoiding reprocessing of the channel estimates after PMI computation, as the generated features can be reused for CQI estimation.

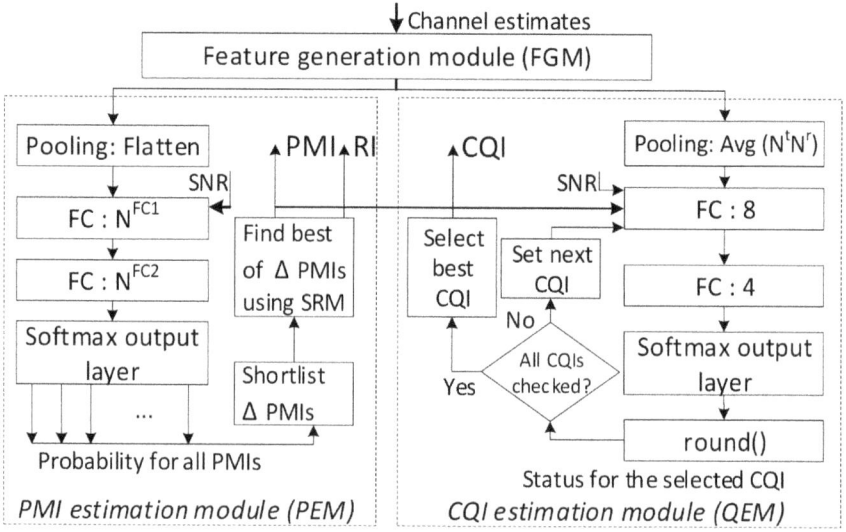

Figure 4.9 Deep learning–based CSI estimation (DCE) and its detailed flowchart.

Figure 4.9 shows the structure of the PEM and QEM. The PEM DL block consists of a pooling layer for flattening, followed by two fully connected (FC) layers with N^{FC1} and N^{FC2} nodes, respectively. Similar to the FGM, the number of nodes in each FC layer is tuned based on the port configuration. Furthermore, the structure of the QEM DL block is the same as that of the PEM. But the pooling layer generates $N^t N^r$ outputs by averaging the inputs from the FGM. The number of nodes in the first and second FC layers is set to 8 and 4, respectively. In both the PEM and QEM, the first FC layer uses ReLU activation, and the second layer uses a custom activation function $\log_2(1 + \text{ReLU}(x))$, where x denotes the weighted sum of inputs to the node. Furthermore, the first FC layer of both the PEM and QEM receives additional inputs. In the case of the PEM, the SNR is fed along with the common features. Furthermore, the SNR, PEM output, and CQI class index are passed as additional inputs to the QEM. Corresponding to the QEM inputs, the output layer generates the probability of successful transmission from the BS to the UE. Furthermore, this is rounded off to its closest integer to indicate transmission success or failure status. Hence, the QEM block is executed $|\mathcal{Q}|$ times (i.e., once per CQI class index), and we choose the CQI candidate with the highest SE predicted to be successful for reporting.

For the PEM, the number of output classes equals the number of PMI candidates $|\mathcal{P}|$ for the configuration. Using softmax activation, the PEM output vector indicates the probability of each PMI being the SRM candidate, as in Equation (4.13). For the smaller port configurations such as 2×2, we select the output PMI with the highest probability for reporting. But with this approach, the PEM SE loss incurred compared to the SRM increases for larger port configurations. Hence, to limit the loss, for a higher number of ports, we treat the PEM output as a priority list for the SRM evaluation, as in Equation (4.13), considering their probabilities. Furthermore, the number of such candidates for SRM evaluation Δ is chosen depending on the upper bound on the percentage of SE loss incurred δ, compared to the SRM. For example, to maintain $\delta \leq 1\%$ for 4×4, $\Delta = 5$ (i.e., the top-five PEM candidates out of 96 are evaluated using the SRM). In Table 4.1, we summarize the PEM parameters for $\delta \leq 1\%$ for the multiple port configurations.

Table 4.1 PMI Estimation Module (PEM) layer dimensions and number of SRM candidates Δ, for evaluation

$N^t \times N^r$	N^{C1}	N^{C2}	N^{FC1}	N^{FC2}	$|\mathcal{P}|$	Δ
2×2	56	6	128	64	6	1
4×4	128	16	256	128	96	5
8×8	192	16	256	128	384	50
16×16	256	16	256	192	640	74

Note: $|\mathcal{P}|$ = The number of candidate PMIs (up to four layers); PMI, precoding matrix indicator.

4.3.3 Numerical results

For dataset generation, we used a 3GPP NR link-level simulator in MATLAB with a CDL-A channel model [38]. Furthermore, for the training and testing of models, we used the Keras library with a Tensorflow backend. We trained separate PMI estimation models for up to a 16×16 port configuration, as shown in Table 4.1. A channel DS of 10 ns is used, and the DoS is set to $f_D = 100$ Hz, corresponding to a low-mobility scenario of 3.6 km/hr at 30 GHz. We set the subcarrier spacing to 120 kHz; hence, each slot is of duration $T_s = 0.125$ ms with 14 OFDM symbols. Hence, the channel coherence time, $1 / (4f_D) = 2.5$ ms, consists of 20 slots [39]. Furthermore, we used the cross-polarized antennas at the BS and UE, and considered up to rank-4 MIMO (multiple-input and multiple-output) transmissions. We used a frequency band size of 16 RBs (i.e., 192 REs per OFDM symbol in frequency). The CSI pilot density is set to two REs per RB per slot [40]; thus, $|\mathcal{K}| = 32$. The precoder set is chosen as per the NR Type-1 single-panel codebook with *codebookMode = 1* [31]. Furthermore, for EESM, we simulated CQI mapping as in Ref. [34]. We summarize the schemes used for benchmarking as follows:

- *Ideal*: Ideal PMI, RI, and CQI selection.
- *SRM-EESM*: The SRM PMI as in Equation (4.13), and the EESM CQI as in Equation (4.16).
- *DCE*: DL-based CSI estimation. as in Section 4.3.2.2.

For these methods, two variants—namely, first variant with no channel aging effect referred as NCA and second variant with the effect of channel aging referred as CA—are defined as follows:

- *Ideal-NCA, SRM-EESM-NCA, and DCE-NCA*: For scheduling in slot n, the channel estimates are assumed to be known a priori. For method X-NCA, the CSI of slot n is estimated using the method X.
- *Ideal-CA, SRM-EESM-CA, and DCE-CA*: For method X-CA, the CSI is reported once every T_{RP} slots, which is used in slots $n + 1$ to $n + T_{RP}$ for scheduling. Furthermore, the report in slot n is estimated using the method X using the channel estimates of slot n.
- *DCP-CA*: The DCE CSI is reported once every T_{RP} slots. For estimation in slot n, the DCE uses the slot $n + \lceil T_{RP}/2 \rceil$ channel predicted by the CPM. The CSI is used in slots $n + 1$ to $n + T_{RP}$.

4.3.3.1 CSI estimation performance

Figure 4.10 shows the CSI performance of Ideal-NCA, DCE-NCA, and SRM-EESM-NCA for 4×4 ports under a NCA scenario. Note that the SE increases with the SNR for all of the methods, and Ideal-NCA outperforms the rest. At the higher SNRs, SRM-EESM-NCA SE loss increases compared to that of Ideal-NCA. This is attributed to the lower mapping accuracy of the

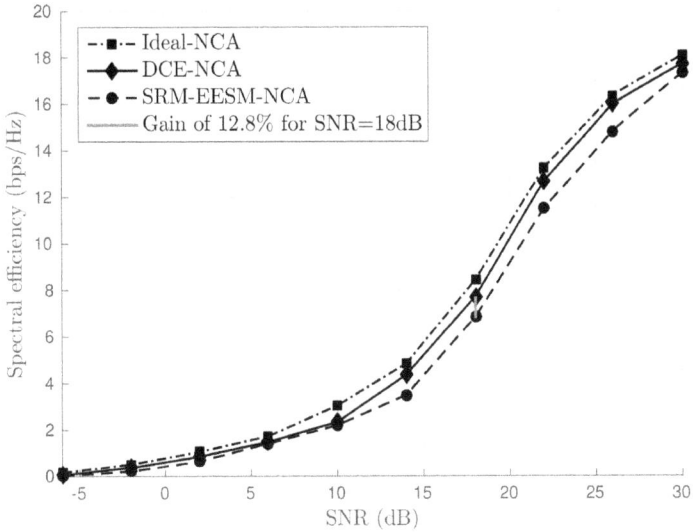

Figure 4.10 DCE estimation performance under no channel aging: SE as a function of the SNR (4 × 4 ports, CDL-A).

EESM due to the increased averaging across layers, as in Equation (4.16), for higher rank transmissions [33]. Unlike SRM-EESM-NCA, DCE-NCA SE loss remains almost the same; thus, it outperforms SRM-EESM-NCA, particularly at higher SNRs. For example, at 18 dB, the SNR SE achieved by DCE-NCA is 12.8% higher than that of SRM-EESM-NCA. Overall, DCE-NCA achieves a 15.4% higher average SE than SRM-EESM-NCA for SNR > 10 dB.

4.3.3.2 CSI prediction performance

Figure 4.11 plots the SE achieved as a function of the SNR for DCP-CA, Ideal-CA, and Ideal-NCA. For all of the methods, SE performance improves with the SNR, but deteriorates with the CSI reporting periodicity T_{RP} due to the CA. The degradation is due to the increase in overall estimation error with T_{RP}, with respect to the channel used for CSI estimation. At the higher SNRs, note that the DCP-CA achieves a better SE due to the usage of prediction with $\hat{d} = \lceil T_{RP}/2 \rceil$, compared to the Ideal-CA. For example, for $T_{RP} = 16$ at an SNR of 18 dB, the DCP-CA SE is 17.8% higher than that of Ideal-CA. Overall, for an SNR > 10 dB, DCP-CA shows an average SE gain of 20.6% and 11.2% at $T_{RP} = 16$ and $T_{RP} = 8$, respectively. Furthermore, for an SNR ≤ 10 dB, prediction gains are marginal. Thus, for a 4 × 4 configuration, $\beta = 10$ dB can be used for the model in Figure 4.8. Note that the DCP-CA achieves almost the same SE at half the reporting periodicity compared tp the Ideal-CA.

Figure 4.12 plots the SE performance of the DCP-CA and other benchmarking methods as a function of T_{RP}. As expected, the DCP-CA achieves the

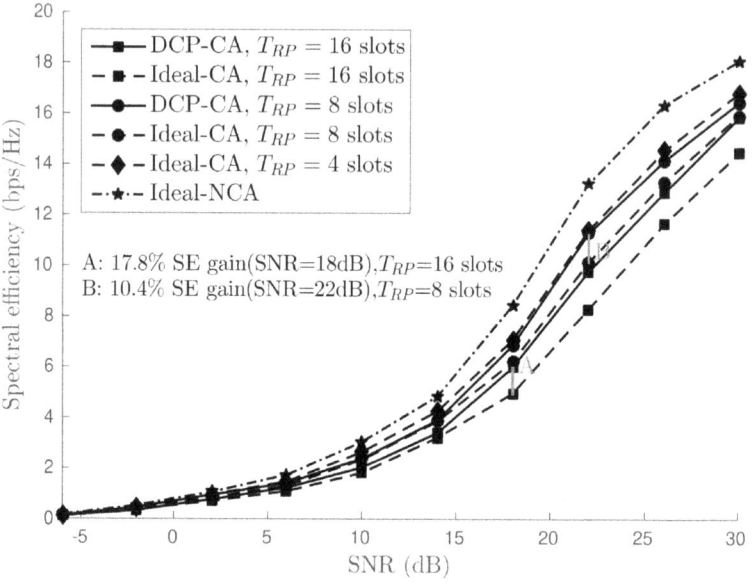

Figure 4.11 DCP prediction performance: SE as a function of the SNR (4 × 4 ports, CDL-A; coherence time: 20 slots).

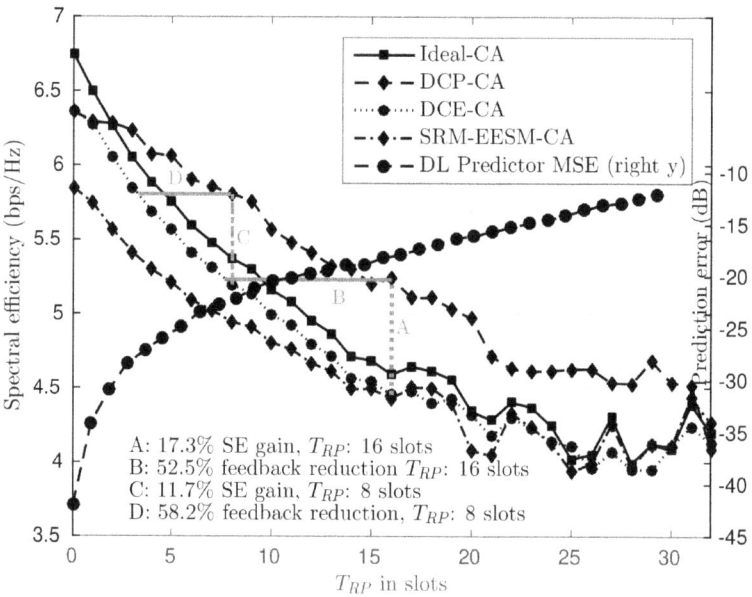

Figure 4.12 DCP aging performance: SE as a function of reporting periodicity T_{RP} (4 × 4 ports, CDL-A; coherence time: 20 slots).

same SE performance as that of the DCE-CA and Ideal-CA at a higher T_{RP} due to the prediction. Note that the SE achieved by the DCE-CA for $T_{RP} = 8$ is achieved by DCP-CA at $T_{RP} = 16$. A similar observation can be made for DCE-CA at $T_{RP} = 4$ and DCP-CA at $T_{RP} = 8$. Hence, prediction usage results in an overhead reduction of 50%. Furthermore, the DCP-CA SE at $T_{RP} = 8$ is higher by 6.5% compared to SRM-EESM-CA at $T_{RP} = 4$. Thus, even at 50% of the reporting overhead, DCP-CA achieves a 6.5% higher SE than SRM-EESM-CA. Furthermore, the plot also shows the prediction MSE $\tilde{\sigma}_d^2$ of the CPM as a function of the delay d. Note that the MSE of the CPM increases with delay due to a reduction in the channel correlation.

Overall, we summarize the DCP-CA benefits as twofold. DCP-CA can improve the SE at a given T_{RP} due to aging compensation. Furthermore, at the system level, the DCP-CA can be used to reduce the CSI reporting overhead by half, while causing no SE degradation at the UE over conventional methods.

4.4 DECODER OPTIMIZATIONS

Another example worth noting is channel decoder optimization. Channel decoders that are practically implemented like the turbo decoder and LDPC decoder involve iterative procedures that refine the LLRs of the information bits over the iterations. The decoding procedure of the turbo codes involves two decoders passing the extrinsic information of the coded bits to each other, and thereby reaching convergence in an iterative manner [41]. Similarly, an LDPC decoder exchanges soft information iteratively between variable and check nodes, which correspond to the parity constraints and data symbols of an LDPC codeword, respectively [42–44]. Reducing the number of iterations in these decoders is of significant interest, given their complexity and the time taken to process each iteration.

Multiple early termination (ET) techniques have been proposed and proven to be efficient in solving the trade-off between desirable performance and complexity reduction for iterative decoders. ET techniques use two types of metrics as the evaluation criteria. One is soft decision based, which uses LLRs of the bits as metrics, and the other is hard decision based, which uses hard bit outputs of the decoder as metrics. Some of the well-known ET techniques, including both soft and hard decision outputs used for turbo decoders, are the sign change ratio (SCR), hard decision aided (HDA) [45], sign difference ratio (SDR) [46], improved HDA (IHDA) [47], and LLR histogram [48]. Similarly for LDPC decoders, the parity check equation (PCE) is the most standard ET technique used, with others being the convergence of mean magnitude (CMM), variable node reliability (VNR), and so on [49–51]. As can be observed, multiple methods have been proposed for turbo and LDPC decoders independently. Also, ET techniques for turbo decoders are evaluated for binary phase-shift keying (BPSK) modulation in most of the available literature [45–48], and results with 16 quadrature amplitude modulation (16-QAM) are presented in Ref. [52].

Similarly, ET techniques for the LDPC are evaluated up to 64-QAM in Ref. [53], while most of the other literature covers BPSK modulation [49–51]. In addition, it can be noted that all of these ET techniques are evaluated for the additive white Gaussian noise (AWGN) channel.

In this section, we show an ET method for the iterative decoder using an ML-based algorithm [14]. The proposed ML algorithm takes the soft decision (LLR)-based metric as the input at an iteration, and predicts the decoding status of the received codeword at that iteration.

4.4.1 Decoding metric for turbo and LDPC codes

We consider turbo and LDPC encoder structures, defined by 3GPP, for LTE and 5G NR technologies, respectively [54, 55]. Let I_{MAX} be the maximum number of iterations for the decoder used in the implementation of a standard fixed-iteration decoder for turbo and LDPC codes.

4.4.1.1 Turbo codes

A turbo encoder consists of two parallel concatenated convolutional codes and an interleaver. The decoder has two component decoders, and each of them uses the Bahl–Cocke–Jelinek–Raviv (BCJR) algorithm that estimates the maximum a posteriori (MAP) probabilities of the LLRs [56]. The two decoders exchange the extrinsic LLRs with each other iteratively until the configured I_{MAX} is reached, and finally give the hard outputs as the decoded bits [41]. Typically, updating the LLRs through both the decoders is considered as one iteration for the turbo decoder. In the remainder of this section, we consider each component decoder operation as one iteration to determine the ET, similar to Ref. [57].

4.4.1.2 LDPC codes

LDPC encoders are the set of linear block codes defined by a sparse parity check matrix (PCM), $\mathbf{H}_{M \times N}$ [42]. The number of columns N in the matrix is defined by the codeword (c) length, and the number of rows M is defined by the number of parity check constraints of the codeword. An LDPC decoder uses the belief-propagation method [43], in which the variable nodes representing the columns of the PCM, and the check nodes representing the rows, iteratively exchange the reliability of each bit and update the LLRs of the bits at every iteration. The decoding stops when either the decoder reaches I_{MAX} or all of the parity constraints are satisfied as $\mathbf{H}.\mathbf{c}^T = 0$.

4.4.1.3 Decoding metric

In Ref. [48], an LLR histogram obtained from each iteration is used as a metric in evaluating the early stopping criterion of a decoder. This metric achieves a reasonable trade-off between performance and complexity by reducing the

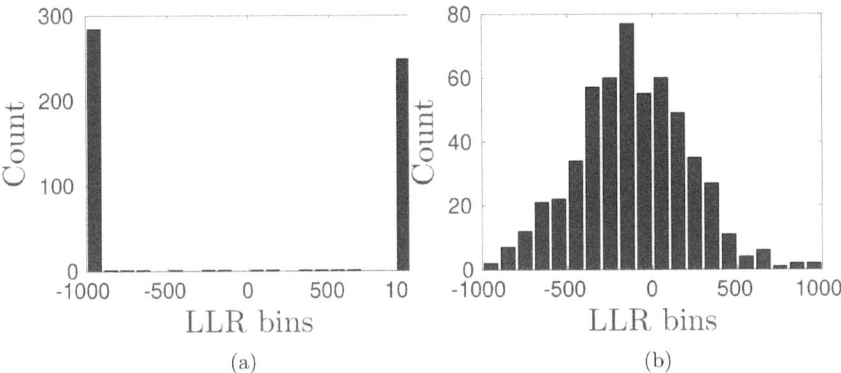

Figure 4.13 Example patterns of pre-normalized LLR histograms: (a) CRC-success; (b) CRC-failure. LLRs correspond to the LTE turbo decoder at $I_{MAX} = 12$, $N = 544$ bits.

average number of iterations significantly, with negligible loss in performance. Also, this metric is independent of the length of the codeword, which makes it more efficient in terms of complexity while evaluating large codewords. We use the same metric in the proposed ML-based ET method. We limit the range of LLRs to $[-M, M]$ before obtaining the histogram. This achieves a single network ML model that works for all of the codewords having different ranges of LLRs. Furthermore, the histogram values are normalized by the total number of bits in the codeword N. We use a cyclic redundancy check (CRC) to determine if the codeword is decoded successfully at the predicted iteration [51]. *CRC-success* indicates that the codeword is decoded successfully, and *CRC-failure* indicates otherwise. From now on, we use CRC status to indicate the decoding process as a success or a failure. Figure 4.13a and 4.13b show the example patterns of pre-normalized LLR histograms limited to $M = 1000$, for the codewords with CRC-success and CRC-failure, respectively, at iteration I_{MAX}. We observe that the LLR histogram with CRC-success has a wide separation between the positive and negative LLRs, indicating that they are clearly distinguishable and can be decoded; whereas the LLR histogram with CRC-failure resembles a Gaussian shape, with positive and negative LLRs merging toward zero, and cannot be decoded.

4.4.2 Early termination using ML

DNN-based ML models implement a learning process based on the previous data and the corresponding experience associated with it. We propose to use one such DNN-based ML model in the ET of an iterative channel-decoding procedure [14]. In the proposed ET method, a DNN-based ML model is embedded in the decoder architecture, as shown in Figure 4.14. In this algorithm, the decoder updates the normalized LLR histogram at each iteration and feeds it to the DNN. Based on the normalized LLR histogram, the DNN sends a prediction on the

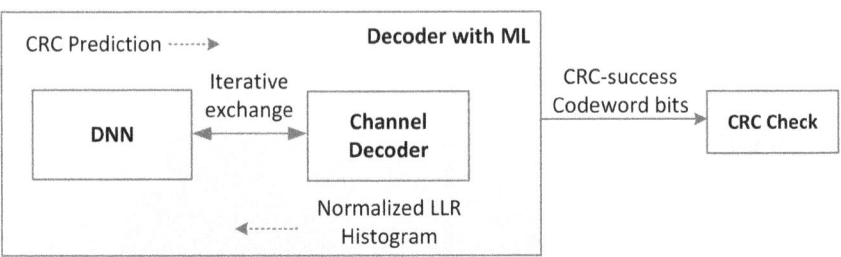

Figure 4.14 Block diagram of an early termination of an iterative channel decoder using a DNN-based ML model.

decoding status of the codeword in the form of a CRC. From Figure 4.14, it can be seen that the CRC check is run only for the codeword with a CRC-success prediction, whereas CRC-failure predictions are terminated immediately.

We choose a fully connected DNN with an input layer of length K; three hidden layers of lengths L_1, L_2, and L_3, respectively; and an output layer of length 3. All of the hidden layers use leaky rectified linear units (LReLUs) as activation units, and the output layer uses a softmax classifier, as represented in Figure 4.15. Let $x_0, x_1, ..., x_K$ denote the normalized LLR histogram values of a codeword at the input layer. The softmax classifier at the output layer generates the probabilities p_0, p_1, and p_2 from the outputs y_0, y_1, and y_2, respectively, as shown in Figure 4.15. Each of these probabilities corresponds to a class of CRC prediction. The probability p_i corresponding to the ith output class can be obtained using softmax as [58]:

$$p_i = \frac{e^{y_i}}{\sum_j e^{y_j}}. \tag{4.17}$$

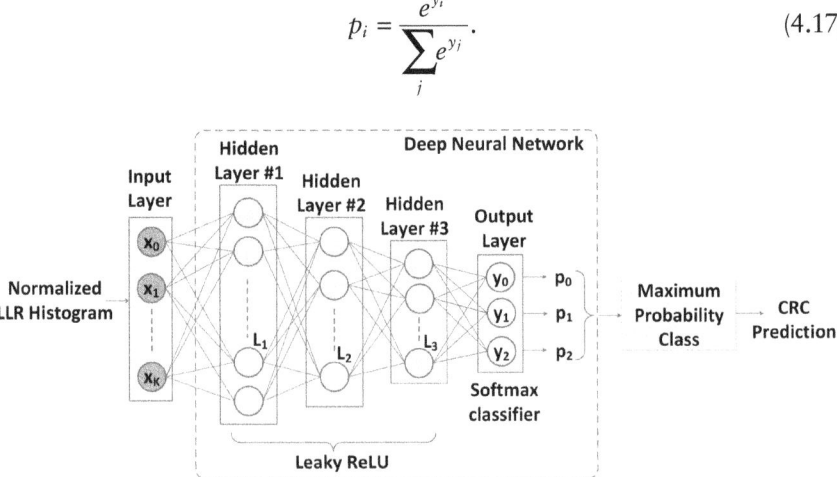

Figure 4.15 Fully connected DNN-based ML model with a normalized LLR histogram of K bins as the input layer; three hidden layers with leaky ReLU activation functions and L_i neurons in each layer, $i \in \{1, 2, 3\}$; and an output layer with a softmax classifier for three classes of CRC prediction.

The final output, the CRC prediction shown in Figure 4.15, is the class corresponding to the maximum of probabilities obtained from the softmax classifier, as given in Equation (4.17).

$$\text{CRC Prediction Class} = \arg \max_{i \in \{0,1,2\}} p_i. \tag{4.18}$$

4.4.3 Simulation results

We evaluate the performance of the ET methods in terms of the BLER and the average number of iterations (ANI). We use $I_{MAX} = 12$ for the turbo decoder, and $I_{MAX} = 15$ for the LDPC decoder. We compare the performance of the proposed algorithm with fixed iterations implemented with I_{MAX}, IHDA (implemented as given in Ref. [49] for the LDPC and Ref. [57] for turbo decoders), and genie methods for the turbo decoder. We use the PCE method [53] for the LDPC decoder in addition to these methods. The genie method is noncasual, assumes knowledge of the transmitted codeword at the receiver, and knows the exact iteration number at which to terminate. It is shown in the literature as the limit of any possible ET method.

Figure 4.16 shows ANI as a function of the MCS index for turbo and LDPC decoders. Each point in the graph is simulated at the SNR corresponding to a 10% BLER, which is the typical operating region for LTE and 5G NR users. From Figure 4.16, we observe that the ANI increases with the MCS index within a modulation scheme. This pattern is consistent for all of the methods except for the fixed iteration, as it is set to be a constant value. Furthermore, all of the ET methods outperform the fixed iteration method. We also observe that the proposed ML-based ET method for the turbo decoder outperforms the IHDA and fixed iteration methods consistently for all modulation schemes in terms of ANI reduction. The ANI of the proposed scheme is 44.65%, 37.39%, and 30.36% lower than that of the IHDA method, at MCS indices 6 (QPSK), 12 (16-QAM), and 17 (64-QAM), respectively. Overall, the proposed method requires 25–57% lower ANI for the turbo decoder, compared to the IHDA method, considered across all MCS indices, as shown in Figure 4.16a.

From Figure 4.16b, we observe that the ANI of the LDPC decoder doesn't have an increasing pattern with respect to the MCS index, like that of the turbo decoder in Figure 4.16a. However, we notice that all of the ET methods follow a similar pattern. The proposed ML-based ET method for the LDPC decoder outperforms the PCE, IHDA, and fixed iteration methods for all modulation schemes in terms of ANI reduction. The ANI of the proposed scheme is 34.52%, 32.04%, and 35.87% lower than that of the PCE method, and 25.77%, 24.6%, and 23.11% lower than that of the IHDA method at MCS indices 6 (QPSK), 12 (16-QAM), and 17 (64-QAM), respectively. Overall, the proposed method requires 30–36% lower ANI for the LDPC decoder, compared to the PCE method, and 23–32% lower

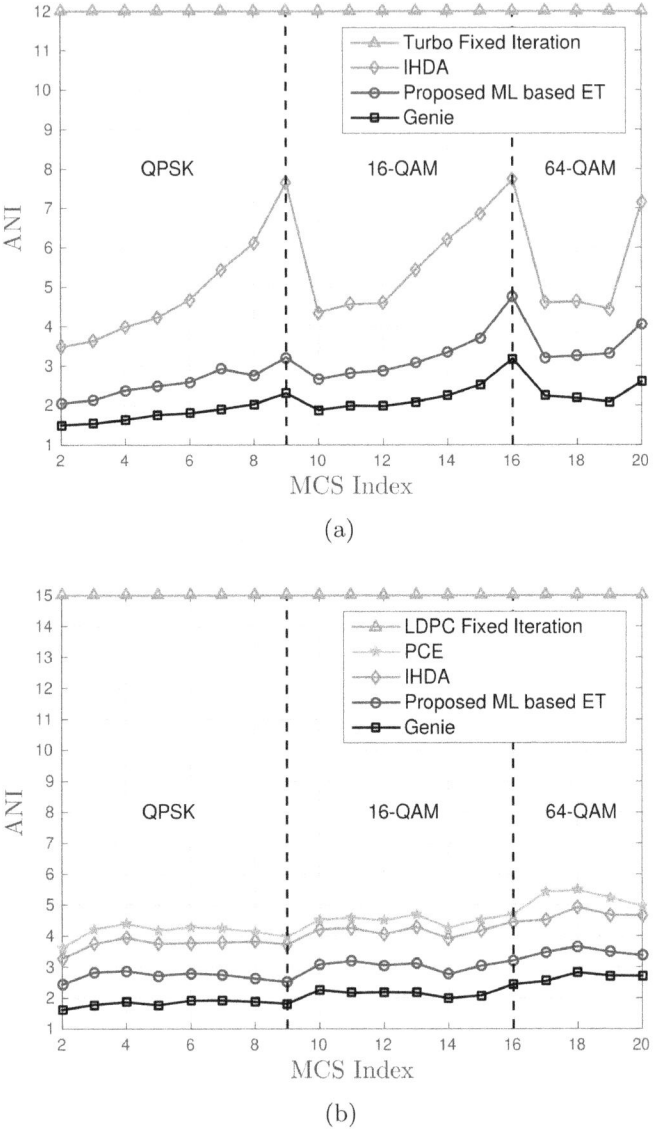

Figure 4.16 ANI as a function of the MCS index for turbo and LDPC decoders. (a) LTE turbo decoder, channel: EPA-5Hz [59], I_{MAX} = 12. (b) NR 5G LDPC decoder. Channel: TDL-A with DS = 43 ns, f_D = 5Hz, I_{MAX} = 15. Each MCS index is simulated at the SNR corresponding to a 10% BLER.

ANI, compared to the IHDA method, respectively, considered across all MCS indices as shown in Figure 4.16b. The reduction observed in ANI is significant for both turbo and LDPC decoders, and consistent in all three modulation schemes.

We have shown that the ML-based ET method consistently outperforms at all of the ranges of BLER, and across all of the modulation schemes: QPSK, 16-QAM, and 64-QAM. We have shown that the proposed algorithm outperforms the IHDA method by 25–57% for the turbo decoder, and the PCE method by 30–36% for the LDPC decoder, in terms of ANI reduction at a 10% BLER, considered across all of the modulation schemes.

4.5 POWER AMPLIFIER NONLINEARITY CORRECTION

In wireless communication systems, we use a PA to boost the signal power level before transmitting the signal over the air. This helps us compensate for the pathloss experienced by the wireless devices. With the increased data rate requirements in wireless systems, PA efficiency has become very critical. PAs exhibit nonlinearity when operated at higher power. This nonlinearity decreases the signal quality and also causes adjacent channel interference.

To overcome PA nonlinearities, DPDs have been explored over the past two decades. The DPD pre-distorts the baseband signal such that the modified signal when passed through the PA reduces nonlinearity. DPD achieves this by learning the inverse of the PA distortion and applying it to the input signal. Thus, the DPD technique has become indispensable for operating the PA at desired efficiency and also meeting the 3GPP requirements.

Initially, the DPDs were implemented using look-up table (LUT)-based methods. Later, mathematical model-based methods, such as Volterra series–based DPDs, were explored, resulting in memory polynomial (MP) [60] and generalized memory polynomial (GMP) [61] DPDs. In the past few years, with ML and DL gaining traction, various DL-based DPDs have been proposed.

In a real-valued focused time-delay neural network (RVFTDNN) [62], the current and past in-phase (I), quadrature-phase (Q) samples were used to obtain the DPD output. In an augmented real-valued time-delay neural network (ARVTDNN) [63], the authors made use of the magnitude and its powers on top of the I, Q samples of the current and past samples, showing an improvement over the RVFTDNN. Both of these approaches make use of densely connected NNs. Even though the performance of these architectures is much better than the conventional MP-based approaches, it comes at the expense of the computational complexity. An envelope time-delay neural network (ETDNN) [64] is proposed to address the computational complexity while maintaining the performance obtained by previously proposed NN-based approaches. This is achieved by initially training the densely connected NN and later pruning the connections with weights below a threshold. Apart from densely connected networks, other architectures were also explored, such as bi-long short-term memory (Bi-LSTM) [65, 66] and CNNs [67], for learning DPDs. The computational complexity of these architectures is quite high, making them highly difficult to implement in real-time systems. In literature, all of the samples (current and past) were given the same importance, with networks trying to figure out the importance by themselves.

In such networks, there is no straightforward extension for the case when a priori information about the extent of impact of previous samples is available.

The DL-based DPDs perform better, as they can capture the nonlinearity more effectively compared to Volterra series–based DPDs.

4.5.1 System model

The PA used at the transmitter end of the wireless communication system introduces undesired nonlinearity into the signal, which, if left uncorrected, corrupts the signal transmitted in the current and neighboring channels.

Let $y(n)$ represent the output samples of the PA. It is given by:

$$y(n) = f_{PA}(x(n)), \tag{4.19}$$

where $f_{PA}(\cdot)$ denotes the nonlinear PA's gain function, and $x(n)$ denotes the input signal. Now, we need to find the DPD function $f_{DPD}(\cdot)$, such that the cascade of DPD and PA results in a signal that is very close to the input signal with linear gain. We denote the output of the cascade of the DPD and PA by $y_c(n)$. It is given by:

$$y_c(n) = f_{PA}(f_{DPD}(x(n); \theta)), \tag{4.20}$$

where θ denotes the parameters of the DPD model.

Now, let $y_d(n)$ denote the desired output given by $Gx(n)$, where G is the linear gain of the PA; then the problem boils down to finding the right parameters θ for $f_{DPD}(\cdot)$, which minimizes the error between $y_c(n)$ and $y_d(n)$.

There are three major approaches to finding the DPD parameters: direct learning architecture (DLA) [68], indirect learning architecture (ILA) [69], and iterative learning control (ILC) [70]. In this section, we make use of the ILA principle to find the DPD parameters. In ILA, the principle is to find the inverse of the PA by modeling the PA input $x(n)$, using the normalized PA output $\frac{y(n)}{G}$, as shown in Figure 4.17. Here we fit the parameters θ by minimizing the error

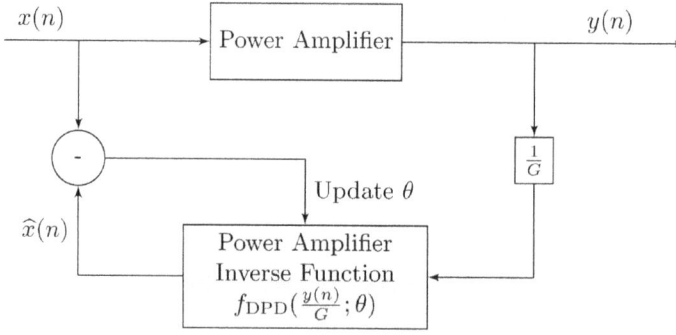

Figure 4.17 Indirect learning architecture principle for DPDs.

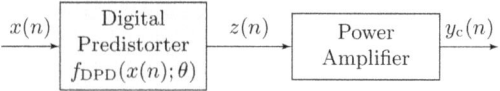

Figure 4.18 Inserting the learned inverse function as a DPD before the PA.

between the estimated PA input $\hat{x}(n)$ and the actual PA input $x(n)$. Here, we chose G to be the gain of the PA operating in the linear region.

Now, the learned inverse function is applied on the input signal $x(n)$ to digitally distort it, resulting in $z(n) = f_{\mathrm{DPD}}(x(n); \theta)$. The distorted signal $z(n)$ is then passed to PA, resulting in $y_c(n)$, as shown in Figure 4.18. The $y_c(n)$ thus obtained will be very close to the desired output $y_c(n) \approx Gx(n)$.

4.5.2 DL architecture for DPDs

In the case of memoryless nonlinear PA, the DPD output $z(n)$ depends only on baseband input $x(n)$ and its magnitude powers as:

$$z(n) = \sum_{k=0}^{K} \theta_k x(n) \left| x(n) \right|^k ,$$

(4.21)

where K represents the highest order of nonlinearity [71].

It can be seen from Equation (4.21) that $z(n)$ is a nonlinear function of $x(n)$ and can be modeled as a linear combination of $x(n)|x(n)|^k$. Even though we can learn the function that maps $x(n)$ to $z(n)$ using a NN, the complexity of such NNs will be quite high because we need more parameters to learn complex nonlinear functions. This results in more hidden units and layers, thereby increasing the computational complexity. Instead, if we try to learn the function that maps $[x(n), |x(n)|, ..., |x(n)|^k]$ to $z(n)$ using a NN, we can achieve this with a network whose complexity is much lower. So we can design the NN as shown in Figure 4.19. The complex valued $x(n)$ is separated into in-phase and quadrature-phase components, so that we can use the real valued NN.

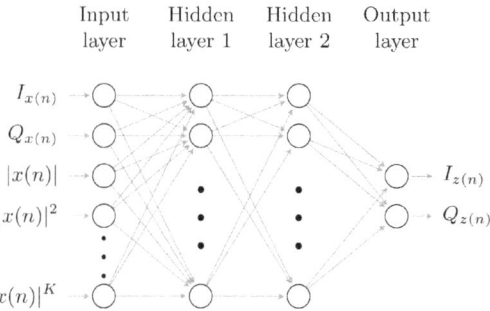

Figure 4.19 NN-based DPD for a memoryless nonlinear PA.

The PAs used for practical purposes contain some time delay circuits as well, such as bias line circuits with capacitors. This results in affecting the output of the PA based on the past samples $x(n-m)$. Hence, the DPD model used for practical purposes is also dependent on the past samples. One of the most widely used models to design the DPD for a nonlinear PA with memory is given by the MP model [60]. According to this, the DPD output $z(n)$ is given by:

$$z(n) = \sum_{k=0}^{K} \sum_{m=0}^{M} \theta_{km} x(n-m) \left| x(n-m) \right|^k, \tag{4.22}$$

where M denotes the memory length.

Now Equation (4.22) can be realized as a linear combination of Equation (4.21) over multiple memory taps. Inspired by the MP, we design the NN with separate densely connected layers for each of the memory taps $(x(n), x(n-1),..., x(n-m))$. So, for each of the memory taps, we can have a sub-network as shown in Figure 4.19 without the output layer. The outputs of hidden layer 2 from all of the memory taps are then concatenated and fed to the hidden layer 3, which is then followed by the output layer. The hidden layer 3 and output layer can then help in capturing the effect of nonlinear memory. The complete architecture of the proposed method is shown in Figure 4.20.

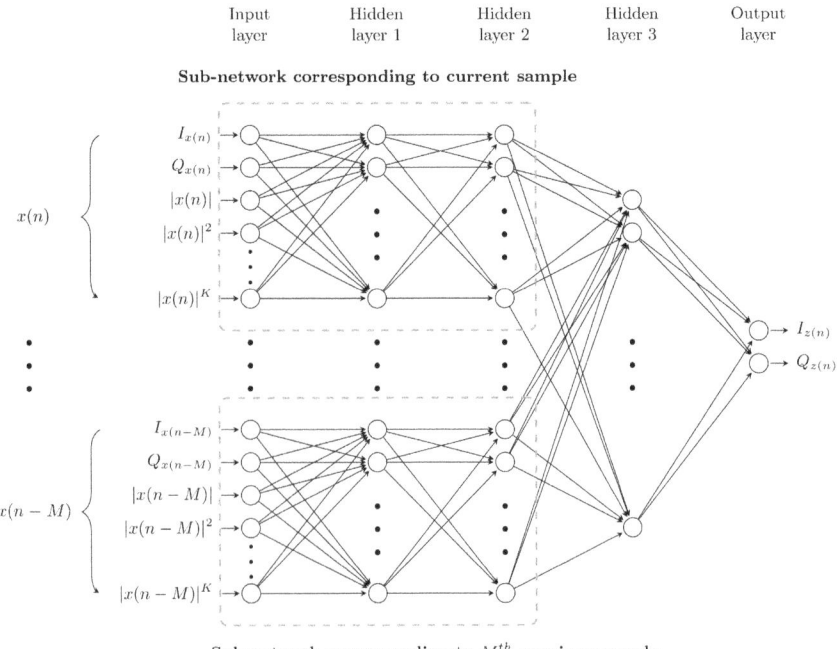

Figure 4.20 Proposed NN-based DPD to compensate for PA nonlinearities.

The number of nodes in hidden layers 1 and 2 is given by the sum of the number of nodes corresponding to each memory tap. The total number of nodes in hidden layers 1 and 2 is given by:

$$HL_C = HL_{C,0} + HL_{C,1} + \cdots + HL_{C,M}, \tag{4.23}$$

where HL_C corresponds to the total number of nodes in hidden layer C, and $HL_{C,m}$ corresponds to the number of nodes in hidden layer C, which are densely connected with nodes of the previous layer corresponding to the memory tap m. The activation function used for all of the hidden layers is the LReLU, which is given by:

$$LReLU(X) = \begin{cases} X & \text{if } X \geq 0, \\ \alpha X & \text{otherwise}, \end{cases} \tag{4.24}$$

where α is the scaling factor.

In order to provide more importance to the current sample $x(n)$, we suggest using more nodes for corresponding subnetworks ($HL_{1,0}$ and $HL_{2,0}$). This enables the network to learn more complex combinations of the current input sample compared to that of the previous samples. The number of nodes corresponding to previous samples ($x(n-1), \ldots, x(n-M)$) can be the same ($HL_{1,1} = HL_{1,2} = \ldots = HL_{1,M}$ and $HL_{2,1} = HL_{2,2} = \ldots = HL_{2,M}$), giving equal importance to all of the previous samples, or we can have chronological importance for previous samples ($HL_{1,1} > HL_{1,2} > \ldots > HL_{1,M}$ and $HL_{2,1} > HL_{2,2} > \ldots > HL_{2,M}$) as well. In this section, we have shown the experimental results with equal importance to all of the memory taps. Also, with the proposed architecture, we can have the flexibility to define the highest nonlinear order for each of the memory taps separately.

4.5.3 Simulation results

4.5.3.1 Evaluation setup

The Simulink system model is used for generated conventional DPD data. An OFDM baseband signal $x(t)$ is generated using the baseband generation block. This signal is scaled to the desired power level and extrapolated to get $x(n)$. Extrapolation is needed to capture higher-frequency nonlinearities in the output. $x(n)$ is modified using a coefficient matrix $\bar{a}$ from the DPD coefficient estimator in the DPD block to obtain $z(n)$. The baseband signal is upconverted to RF operation frequency F using a local oscillator and IQ modulator. After amplification from the PA, the signal is analyzed to measure the adjacent channel power ratio (ACPR) and error vector magnitude (EVM) metrics by a spectrum analyzer and constellation blocks. The PA output at RF is then downconverted to baseband frequency to get $y(n)$, which is passed to the coefficient estimator along with $z(n)$ to calculate the coefficient matrix. For a DL-based

DPD algorithm, the DPD and coefficient estimator blocks are replaced with a single block that pre-distorts the input signal $x(n)$ according to $y(n)$ to get $z(n)$.

4.5.3.2 Performance analysis

Our proposed DPD was compared with conventional (GMP [61]) and DL-based (ETDNN [64], Bi-LSTM [66], and real-valued time-delay convoluted neural network [RVTDCNN] [67]) DPDs using the EVM and ACPR reported for both the upper and lower channels.

For conventional DPD, the pre-distorter uses a generalized memory polynomial (GMP) to get a basis vector of $x(n)$. The vector is then multiplied by the previous iteration's coefficients to get $z(n)$. To update the coefficients, the cumulative error between $z(n)$ and a basis vector function of $y_c(n)$ is minimized in every iteration using a recursive LS algorithm, denoted by:

$$z(n) = \overline{a}(n-1) * f_b(x(n)), \tag{4.25}$$

$$e(n) = z(n) - \left[\overline{a}(n-1) * f_b\left(\frac{y_c(n)}{G} \right) \right], \tag{4.26}$$

$$J(n) = \sum_i e(i) * \beta^{n-i}, \tag{4.27}$$

where $e(i)$ corresponds to error, $\overline{a}$ corresponds to the coefficient vector, f_b corresponds to the basis vector generator function for the GMP, and $J(n)$ corresponds to cumulative error.

M is chosen to be 5 for all of the DL-based DPDs. The proposed method is implemented with $HL_{1,0} = 9, HL_{1,1},..., HL_{1,5} = 7, HL_{2,0} = 7, HL_{2,1},..., HL_{2,5} = 5$, and HL_3, consisting of 10 nodes. The α is chosen to be 0.5 for LReLu. The maximum degree K used at the input layer is 3. The ETDNN [64] architecture consists of a single hidden layer in which the number of hidden nodes experimented with were between 12 and 200. We found the optimal value of hidden nodes to be 80, beyond which there is no improvement in the performance. The ETDNN used here is the fully connected version. The Bi-LSTM-based DPD [66] consisted of a Bi-LSTM layer of size (310×2), followed by an LSTM layer of size (150×1). The activation function for both these layers was *tanh*. The LSTM layer was followed by three fully connected layers of sizes 150, 75, and 30, respectively, and the activation function was linear. A time-distributed layer was used at the output layer to obtain the sequence-to-sequence regression. An RVTDCNN [67] was implemented with three kernels of size $3 \times 3 \times 1$, followed by a fully connected layer of six neurons and an output layer with two neurons. The activation function used for the first two layers was *tanh*, and the last layer was linear.

The performance of the proposed method is compared with the conventional and DL-based DPDs in Simulink, as mentioned in Section 4.5.3.1 using the Simulink fit of the data generated from ADS for A2I25D012N. The

Table 4.2 EVM and ACPR benchmarking of proposed DPD

Method	EVM (dB)	ACPR (dBc)		
		Lower	Upper	Average
No DPD	−21.4	−27.19	−26.62	−26.905
GMP [61]	−30	−36.71	−33.79	−35.25
ETDNN [64]	−39.6	−37.36	−36.84	−37.1
Bi-LSTM [66]	−36	−40.43	−36.89	−38.66
RVTDCNN [67]	−32.9	−33.35	−33.21	−33.28
Proposed	−36.1	−39.45	−38.06	−38.755

experiments were carried out for 64-QAM data while maintaining the average output power to be 30.62 dBm, in accordance with the operating point (3 dB point) of the PA. The center frequency and bandwidth of the generated data are 2.58 GHz and 100 MHz, respectively. Table 4.2 provides the EVM and ACPR for various DPDs. It is observed that the ETDNN performs the best with respect to the EVM with a margin of 3.5 dB compared to the next-best method (the proposed method), whereas the proposed method performs the best for the ACPR. Most of the PAs are already meeting the EVM requirement to transmit 64-QAM or 256-QAM with conventional DPDs. The improvement in the ACPR, where the proposed method is the best, will help in reducing the interference at the network level.

4.6 BEAM PREDICTION

In this section, we cover a case of a millimeter-wave receiver with a receive beam selection problem. A typical UE performs beam measurements periodically in a round-robin fashion [72, 73]. Research is ongoing on the methods to find intelligent ways of scheduling beams for measurement by periodically prioritizing a few beams in the measurement set and reducing the measurement set size. Using the sensor data, a few beams are prioritized periodically for measurement based on the device orientation in Ref. [74]. ML-based methods have also been proposed for beam management such as using motion sensors and past mobility data, and future mobility has been predicted in order to track the best beam in Ref. [75]. In Refs. [76, 77], using environmental data such as GPS, traffic simulator, and LIDAR (light detection and ranging) data, DL methods have been proposed to shortlist the beam pairs while the training has been done using ray-tracing data.

Beam tracking at a BS has also been a topic of interest for research. Using UE's position estimate, ML methods have been developed for antenna alignment at a BS [78]. In Ref. [79], using an extended Kalman filter, beam tracking has been done at a BS with user's mobility, and a method has been proposed to update the beamforming weights for proper alignment of BS and UE beams [80].

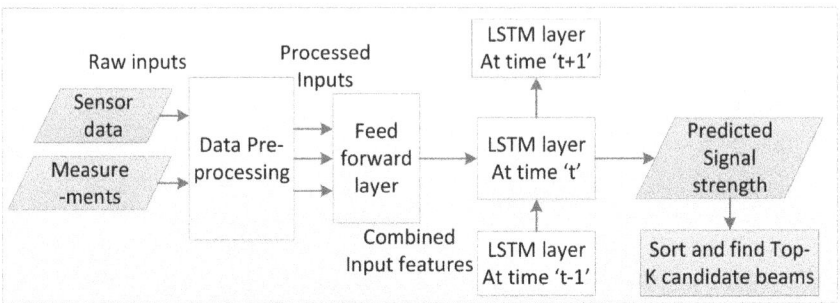

Figure 4.21 System model: Flowchart.

In this section, we describe a method for shortlisting the beam pairs periodically using a recurrent neural network (RNN) with sensor data and measurements as inputs [16]. These shortlisted beams are the candidates for best beam pair selection. The shortlisted beams are scheduled in upcoming measurement occasions instead of scheduling beams in a round-robin fashion.

As shown in Figure 4.21, UE sensor data and measurements are used as inputs for the prediction of top-K candidates. Inputs are pre-processed in order to extract the desirable input features. Full details of the pre-processing block are provided in the following part of this section. Input features are then combined for all of the UE beams, and the combined vector is fed to a long short-term memory (LSTM) network layer. The signal strength of all beams is predicted as the output of the LSTM layer, and then beams are sorted with decreasing predicted signal strength in order to find the top-K candidates.

4.6.1 Beam prediction algorithm

In this subsection, we explain the architecture of the ML model that is used for predicting the top candidates for the best UE beam [16]. We run the algorithm periodically with the period T_{RC}. Inputs such as the beam's reference signal received power (RSRP), its correlation, and sensor gain (SG) are extracted for every UE beam at the end of every reduced measurement cycle. These three input vectors are then combined using a feedforward neural network (FNN) for every beam, as shown in Figure 4.22. Combined features are then fed to an LSTM layer to incorporate the temporal features. The LSTM layers are connected throughout time and contain the information of the past inputs in terms of cell memory, while the feedforward layer combines the current inputs in order to make input features for the LSTM layer. The beam strength of the UE beams is predicted as the output of the LSTM layer. The predicted beam strength vector is then sorted to find top-K candidates for the best UE beam, which are then scheduled for measurements for the next K measurement occasions.

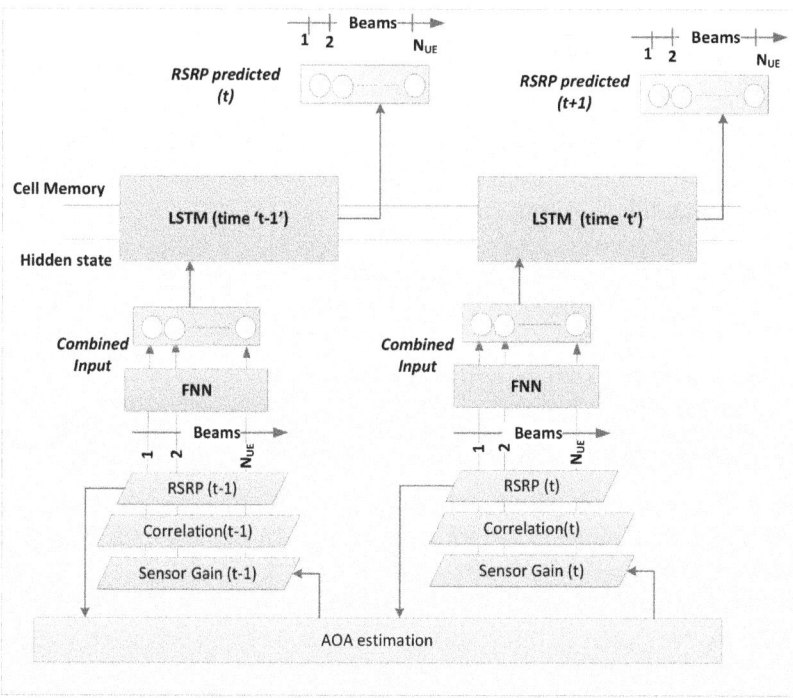

Figure 4.22 An ML model for beam candidates prediction.

Algorithm 4.1: Beam candidates prediction

1: If $mod(t, T_{\mathrm{RC}}) = 0$, where $T_{\mathrm{RC}} = KT_{\mathrm{MO}}$, do the following:

2: Obtain RSRP vector ($Input_1$), correlation vector ($Input_2$), and SG ($Input_3$) from the input database as explained in Section 4.6.1.

3: Combine the inputs using a dense layer to get input features for each beam as follows:

4: for $b \leftarrow 1, N_{UE}$ do

5: Obtain the combined input:

$$Input(b) = [Input_1(b),\ Input_2(b),\ Input_3(b)]$$

6: Feed the combined input to a dense layer of a feedforward neural network to get input features.

$$Inputfeature(b) = Dense(Input(b))$$

7: end for

8: Concatenate input features of all of the beams to obtain input feature vector.

$$Feature\,vector = [Input\,feature(1)....Input\,feature(N_{UE})]$$

9: Apply an LSTM layer with input feature vector as input that predicts beam strength vector as output.

$$Predicted\,Beam\,strength = LSTM(Feature\,vector)$$

10: Sort the predicted beam strength vector with decreasing values to get top-K candidate beams.

$$Top - K\,candidates = \left\{argsort(-Predicted\,beam\,strength)\right\}_{1:K}$$

4.6.2 Simulation setup and performance evaluation

4.6.3 Simulation setup

A system-level simulator (SLS) is developed in MATLAB for generating data based on a 3GPP channel model for an urban (UMi) scenario [38]. The 3GPP-based channel models the channel power for all of the gNB-UE beam pairs, using many system-level inputs such as the shadowing factor, the Rician factor for LoS and NLoS power, the number of clusters and rays for signal transmission and reception, and the coupling of receiver and transmitter rays with phase information. This 3GPP-based channel also takes specific inputs such as the location and orientation of the UE and gNB, and the beam field gain pattern of antennas of UE and gNB. Six antenna panels are considered for generating a total of 44 beams at UE [74]. The antenna panel at the front generates 16 beams, each occupying different angular space in both the azimuth and zenith. Similarly, the rear panel generates another 16 beams, and the four side panels generate three beams each.

Furthermore, in this section, we show the accuracy of the ML model with the percentage of times the best beam is in the top-five predicted candidate beams. In addition, we show the gain in SE for scheduling of the top-five predicted candidate beams using a proposed algorithm compared with the conventional scheduling of beams in a round-robin manner.

For training of the ML model, we have considered one data sample as one reduced measurement cycle in time. We have generated a total of 20,000 samples using SLS as described earlier in the section, out of which the first 18,000 samples are considered for training and the remaining 2,000 samples are considered for testing. For performance evaluation, an accuracy metric is calculated, which is the number of times the best beam is in the top-five predicted candidate beams. For top-five accuracy, data is generated considering different UE orientation change scenarios, such as a varying rotation rate from 15 degrees per second (dps) to 90 dps and different directions of rotation such as pitch and roll. The accuracy of these scenarios is summarized in Table 4.3. Table 4.3 shows that the best beam is in the top-five predicted candidate beams almost 99% in all of the scenarios.

Table 4.3 Accuracy: Number of times the best beam appeared among the top-five predicted beams

UE orientation change rate (dps)	% of times the best beam is in the top-five predicted beams	
	Rotation in roll (%)	Rotation in pitch (%)
15	99.6	99.9
30	99.6	99.9
60	98.7	99.8
90	98.0	98.6

Using the proposed algorithm, we predict the top-five candidate beams periodically with the period of a reduced measurement cycle (T_{RC}), and these top-five predicted beams are scheduled for measurement in the next reduced measurement cycle. We show SE gain between the conventional scheduling method and proposed model-based scheduling in Table 4.4, where the conventional method is scheduling beams in a round-robin fashion. The gain in SE is found to be 10–20% for the slower rotation rate and around 50% for the higher rotation rates, as shown in Figure 4.23. For the proposed method, as the device rotation rate increases, the gain in SE increases compared to the conventional scheduling method. This is because, at a higher rotation rate, there is a constant need to change the UE serving beam, and the proposed algorithm is able to predict the beams to be measured efficiently in order to update the serving beam. However, the conventional algorithm is unable to cope with the changes in orientation, which results in an inferior beam selected for data transmission for the conventional algorithm. With the proposed method, only the top-K predicted candidate beams are scheduled, which have almost 99% accuracy of having the best beam based on results shown in Table 4.3; the best beam can be found faster, thus ensuring that data transmission and reception occur on the best beam pair, which results in increasing the SE.

Table 4.4 Performance: Average SE (bits/Hz/sec) comparison: conventional versus proposed scheduling

Rotation direction	Rotation rate (dps)	Conventional (bits/Hz/sec)	Proposed (bits/Hz/sec)	% Gain
Roll	15	6.7688	6.9786	3
Roll	30	6.2614	6.9784	11
Roll	60	5.6292	6.7690	20
Roll	90	4.2611	6.6926	57
Pitch	15	7.2226	7.4543	3
Pitch	30	6.9635	7.3367	6
Pitch	60	5.7328	7.0636	23
Pitch	90	4.5592	7.0369	54

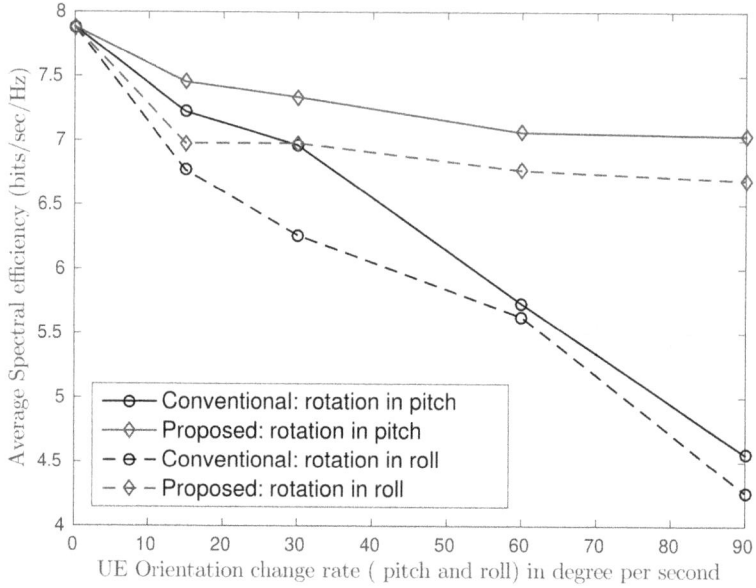

Figure 4.23 Average SE versus the user equipment (UE) rotation rate.

We showed that this algorithm achieves significant gains in SE of up to 50% at a 90 dps rotation rate. Furthermore, UE can search for the best beam pair faster, thus enhancing link quality. This algorithm is feasible to implement in terms of time and space complexity on a 5G UE and can be implemented in future 5G products.

REFERENCES

1. Elsayed, M. and Erol-Kantarci, M., "AI-enabled future wireless networks: Challenges, opportunities, and open issues," *IEEE Veh. Tech. Mag*, vol. 14, no. 3, pp. 70–77, 2019.
2. Gündüz, D., de Kerret, P., Sidiropoulos, N. D., Gesbert, D., Murthy, C. R. and van der Schaar, M., "Machine learning in the air," *IEEE J. Sel. Areas Commun.*, vol. 37, no. 10, pp. 2184–2199, 2019.
3. O'Shea, T. J. and Hoydis, J., "An introduction to deep learning for the physical layer," *IEEE Transactions on Cognitive Communications and Networking*, vol. 3, no. 4, pp. 563–575, December 2017.
4. Kibria, M. G., Nguyen, K., Villardi, G. P., Zhao, O., Ishizu, K. and Kojima, F., "Big data analytics, machine learning, and artificial intelligence in next-generation wireless networks," *IEEE Access*, vol. 6, pp. 32328–32338, 2018.
5. Dörner, S., Cammerer, S., Hoydis, J. and Brink, S. T., "Deep learning based communication over the air," *IEEE J. Sel. Top. Signal Process.*, vol. 12, no. 1, pp. 132–143, 2018.

6. Simeone, O., "A very brief introduction to machine learning with applications to communication systems," *IEEE Trans. Cogn. Commun. Netw*, vol. 4, no. 4, pp. 648–664, 2018.

7. Soltani, M., Pourahmadi, V., Mirzaei, A. and Sheikhzadeh, H., "Deep learning-based channel estimation," *IEEE Commun. Lett.*, vol. 23, no. 4, pp. 652–655, 2019.

8. RP-221348, "Study on Artificial Intelligence (AI)/Machine Learning (ML) for NR Air Interface," Source: Qualcomm. https://www.3gpp.org/ftp/tsg_ran/TSG_RAN/TSGR_96/Docs/RP-221348.zip

9. R1-2210955, "Discussions on AI-CSI," Source: Ericsson. https://www.3gpp.org/ftp/tsg_ran/WG1_RL1/TSGR1_111/Docs/R1-2210955.zip

10. R1-2210855, "AI/ML Based Positioning Enhancement," Source: Ericsson. https://www.3gpp.org/ftp/tsg_ran/WG1_RL1/TSGR1_111/Docs/R1-2210855.zip

11. R1-2210955, "Discussion on AI/ML for beam management," Source: Ericsson. https://www.3gpp.org/ftp/tsg_ran/WG1_RL1/TSGR1_111/Docs/R1-2210955.zip

12. O'Shea, T. J. and Hoydis, J., "An introduction to deep learning for the physical layer," *IEEE Trans. Cognitive Commun. Net.*, vol. 3, no. 4, pp. 563–575, December 2017.

13. Shental, O. and Hoydis, J., ""Machine LLRning": Learning to Softly Demodulate," *2019 IEEE Globecom Workshops (GC Wkshps)*, Waikoloa, HI, USA, 2019, pp. 1–7, doi: 10.1109/GCWkshps45667.2019.9024433.

14. Anusha, G., Avani, A, Chavva, A. K. R. and Saikrishna, P., "Machine Learning Based Early Termination for Turbo and LDPC Decoders," *IEEE Wireless Commun. and Netw. Conf. (WCNC)*, Nanjing, China, 2021, pp. 1–6.

15. Klautau, A., Gonz´alez-Prelcic, N. and Heath, R. W. Jr., "LIDAR data for deep learning-based mmWave beam-selection," *IEEE Wireless Commun. Lett.*, vol. 8, no. 3, June 2019.

16. Shubham, K. and Chavva, A. K. R., "Recurrent Neural Network Based Beam Prediction for Millimeter-Wave 5G Systems," *IEEE Wireless Commun. and Netw. Conf. (WCNC)*, Nanjing, China, 2021, pp. 1–6.

17. Sripada, K., Anirudh, R. G., Chavva, A. K. R., Mukul, B. and Vaishal, T., "Learning Based CSI Feedback Prediction for 5G NR," *IEEE Consumer Commun. and Netw. Conf. (CCNC)*, Vitrual, 2021, pp. 1–6.

18. Liao, Y., Yao, H., Hua, Y. and Li, C., "CSI feedback based on deep learning for massive MIMO systems," *IEEE Access*, vol. 7, pp. 86810–86820, 2019.

19. Kay, S. M., "Fundamentals of Statistical Signal Processing: Estimation Theory," Prentice Hall, 1997.

20. Ye, H., Li, G. Y. and Juang, B., "Power of deep learning for channel estimation and signal detection in OFDM systems," *IEEE Wireless Commun. Letters*, vol. 7, no. 1, pp. 114–117, 2018.

21. Han, S., Oh, Y. and Song, C., "A Deep Learning Based Channel Estimation Scheme for IEEE 802.11p Systems," *IEEE International Conference on Communications (ICC)*, Shanghai, China, 2019, pp. 1–6.

22. Balevi, E. and Andrews, J. G., "Deep learning-based channel estimation for high-dimensional signals," Apr. 2019, doi: https://arxiv.org/pdf/1904.09346.pdf

23. Dong, C., Loy, C. C., He, K. and Tang, X., "Image super-resolution using deep convolutional networks," *IEEE Trans. Pattern Anal. Mach. Intell*, vol. 38, no. 2, pp. 295–307, 2016.

24. Zhang, K., Zuo, W., Chen, Y., Meng, D. and Zhang, L., "Beyond a gaussian denoiser: Residual learning of deep CNN for image denoising," *IEEE Trans. Image Process*, vol. 26, no. 7, pp. 3142–3155, 2017.
25. Goldsmith, A., "Wireless Communications," Cambridge: Cambridge University Press, 2005.
26. Saikrishna, P., Chavva, A. K. R., Mukul, B. and Ankur, G., "Deep Learning Based Channel Estimation with Flexible Delay and Doppler Networks for 5G NR," *IEEE Wireless Commun. and Netw. Conf. (WCNC)*, Nanjing, China, 2021, pp. 1–6.
27. Truong, K. T. and Heath, R. W., "Effects of channel aging in massive MIMO systems," *J.Commn.Net.*, vol. 15, no. 4, pp. 338–351, 2013.
28. Kong, C., et al., "Sum-rate and power scaling of massive MIMO systems with channel aging," *IEEE Trans. Commun.*, vol. 63, no. 12, pp. 4879–4893, 2015.
29. Deng, R., et al., "Intermittent CSI update for massive MIMO systems with heterogeneous user mobility," *IEEE Trans. Commun.*, vol. 67, no. 7, pp. 4811–4824, 2019.
30. Kashyap, S., et al., "Performance Analysis of (TDD) Massive MIMO with Kalman Channel Prediction," *2017 IEEE International Conference on Acoustics, Speech and Signal Processing (ICASSP)*, IEEE, 2017.
31. 3GPP TS 38.214-ge0, "NR Physical layer procedures for data." https://www.3gpp.org/ftp/Specs/archive/38_series/38.214/38214-ge0.zip
32. Schwarz, S., Mehlführer, C. and Rupp, M., "Calculation of the Spatial Preprocessing and Link Adaption Feedback for 3GPP UMTS/LTE," *2010 Wireless Advanced 2010*, IEEE, 2010.
33. Hanzaz, Z. and Dieter Schotten, H., "Analysis of Effective SINR Mapping Models for MIMO OFDM in LTE System," 2013 9th International Wireless Communication and Mobile Computing Conference (IWCMC), IEEE, 2013.
34. Chu, E., Yoon, J. and Chul Jung, B., "A novel link-to-system mapping technique based on machine learning for 5G/IoT wireless networks," *Sensors*, vol. 19, no. 5, p. 1196, 2019.
35. Ahmed, R., Jayasinghe, K. and Wild, T., "Comparison of Explicit CSI Feedback Schemes for 5G New Radio," *2019 IEEE 89th Vehicular Technology Conference (VTC2019-Spring)*. IEEE, 2019.
36. Ameigeiras, Pablo, et al., "Traffic models impact on OFDMA scheduling design," *EURASIP J. Wireless Commun. Net.*, vol. 2012, no. 1, p. 61, 2012.
37. Pan, Sinno Jialin and Yang, Qiang, "A survey on transfer learning," *IEEE Transactions on Knowledge and Data Engineering*, vol. 22, no. 10, pp. 1345–1359, 2009.
38. 3GPP TS 38.901, Study on channel model for frequencies from 0.5 to 100 GHz. https://www.3gpp.org/ftp//Specs/archive/38_series/38.901/38901-f10.zip
39. Tse, D. and Viswanath, P., "Fundamentals of Wireless Communication," Cambridge University Press, 2005.
40. 3GPP TS 38.211, "NR; Physical channels and modulation." https://www.3gpp.org/ftp/Specs/archive/38_series/38.211/38211-ga0.zip.
41. Berrou, C., Glavieux, A. and Thitimajshima, P., "Near Shannon limit error-correcting coding and decoding: Turbo-codes. 1," *Proceedings of ICC '93 - IEEE International Conference on Communications*, Geneva, Switzerland, 1993, pp. 1064–1070 vol. 2.
42. Gallager, R., "Low-density parity-check codes," *IEEE Trans. Inf. Theory.*, vol. 8, no. 1, pp. 21–28, January 1962.

43. MacKay, D. J. C. and Neal, R. M., "Near Shannon limit performance of low density parity check codes," *Electron. Lett.*, vol. 33, no. 6, pp. 457–458, 13 March 1997.

44. Shao, S. et al., "Survey of Turbo, LDPC, and polar decoder ASIC implementations," *IEEE Commun. Surv. Tutor.*, vol. 21, no. 3, pp. 2309–2333, 2019, doi: 10.1109/COMST.2019.2893851.

45. Shao, R. Y., Lin, S. and Fossorier, M. P. C., "Two simple stopping criteria for turbo decoding," *IEEE Trans. Commun.*, vol. 47, pp. 1117–1120, 1999.

46. Wu, Y., Woerner, B. D. and Ebel, W. J., "A simple stopping criterion for turbo decoding," *IEEE Commun. Lett.*, vol. 4, no. 8, pp. 258–260, 2000.

47. Ngatched, T. and Takawira, F., "Simple stopping criterion for turbo decoding," *Electron. Lett.*, vol. 37, no. 22, pp. 1350–1351, Oct. 2001.

48. Amamra, I. and Derouiche, N., "A Stopping Criteria for Turbo Decoding Based on the LLR Histogram," *16th IEEE Mediterranean Electrotechnical Conference*, Yasmine Hammamet, 2012, pp. 699–702.

49. Li, J., You, X.-H. and Li, J., "Early stopping for LDPC decoding: Convergence of mean magnitude (CMM)," *IEEE Commun. Lett.*, vol. 10, no. 9, pp. 667–669, 2006.

50. Kienle, F. and Wehn, N., "Low Complexity Stopping Criterion for LDPC Code Decoders," *IEEE 61st Vehicular Technology Conference*, Stockholm, 2005, pp. 606–609, vol. 1.

51. Wang, F. et al., "Efficient early termination strategy for LDPC codes in GPS systems," *J. Harbin Institute Technol. (New Series)*, vol. 20, no. 6, pp. 118–122, Jun. 2013.

52. Nasir, M. Y. M., Mohamad, R., Kassim, M., Tahir, N. M. and Abdullah, E., "Performance Analysis of Cross-Entropy Stopping Criterion for Quadrature Amplitude Modulation," *IEEE 9th International Conference on System Engineering and Technology (ICSET)*, Shah Alam, Malaysia, 2019, pp. 273–276.

53. Wu, H., Wang, F. and Yuan, Y., "A Distributed CRC Early Termination Scheme for High Throughput QC-LDPC Codes," *10th International Conference on Wireless Communications and Signal Processing (WCSP)*, Hangzhou, 2018, pp. 1–5.

54. 3GPP TS 36.212-g70, "E-UTRA Multiplexing and channel coding." https://www.3gpp.org/ftp/Specs/archive/36_series/36.212/36212-g70.zip

55. 3GPP TS 38.212-gb0, "NR Multiplexing and channel coding." https://www.3gpp.org/ftp/Specs/archive/38_series/38.212/38212-gb0.zip

56. Bahl, L., Cocke, J., Jelinek, F. and Raviv, J., "Optimal decoding of linear codes for minimizing symbol error rate (Corresp.)," *IEEE Trans. Inf. Theory*, vol. 20, no. 2, pp. 284–287, 1974.

57. AlMahamdy, M. and Dill, J., "Half-Iteration Early Termination of Turbo Decoding," *IEEE 7th Annual Computing and Communication Workshop and Conference (CCWC)*, Las Vegas, NV, 2017, pp. 1–5.

58. Witten, I. H., Frank, E., Hall, M. A., and Pal, C. J. "Data Mining: Practical Machine Learning Tools and Techniques (4th Edition)". Morgan Kaufmann, 2017.

59. 3GPP TS 36.141-gh0, "E-UTRA Base Station conformance testing." https://www.3gpp.org/ftp/Specs/archive/36_series/36.141/36141-gh0.zip

60. Ding, Lei, Zhou, G. T., Morgan, D. R., Ma, Z., Kenney, J. S., Kim, J. and Giardina, C. R., "A robust digital baseband predistorter constructed using

memory polynomials," *IEEE Trans. Commun.*, vol. 52, no. 1, pp. 159–165, Jan. 2004, doi: 10.1109/TCOMM.2003.822188.

61. Morgan, D. R., Ma, Z., Kim, J., Zierdt, M. G. and Pastalan, J., "A generalized memory polynomial model for digital predistortion of RF power amplifiers," *IEEE Trans. Signal Process.*, vol. 54, no. 10, pp. 3852–3860, Oct. 2006, doi: 10.1109/TSP.2006.879264.

62. Rawat, M. and Ghannouchi, F. M., "A mutual distortion and impairment compensator for wideband direct-conversion transmitters using neural networks," *IEEE Trans. Broadcast.*, vol. 58, no. 2, pp. 168–177, June 2012, doi: 10.1109/TBC.2012.2189338.

63. Wang, D., Aziz, M., Helaoui, M. and Ghannouchi, F. M., "Augmented real-valued time-delay neural network for compensation of distortions and impairments in wireless transmitters," *IEEE Trans. Neural Netw. Learn. Syst.*, vol. 30, no. 1, pp. 242–254, Jan. 2019, doi: 10.1109/TNNLS.2018.2838039.

64. Tanio, M., Ishii, N. and Kamiya, N., "Efficient digital predistortion using sparse neural network," *IEEE Access*, vol. 8, pp. 117841–117852, 2020, doi: 10.1109/ACCESS.2020.3005146

65. Sun, J., Shi, W., Yang, Z., Yang, J. and Gui, G., "Behavioral modeling and linearization of wideband RF power amplifiers using BiLSTM networks for 5G wireless systems," *IEEE Trans. Veh. Technol.*, vol. 68, no. 11, pp. 10348–10356, Nov. 2019, doi: 10.1109/TVT.2019.2925562.

66. Sun, J., Wang, J., Guo, L., Yang, J. and Gui, G., "Adaptive deep learning aided digital predistorter considering dynamic envelope," *IEEE Trans. Veh. Technol.*, vol. 69, no. 4, pp. 4487–4491, April 2020, doi: 10.1109/TVT.2020.2974506.

67. Hu, X. et al., "Convolutional neural network for behavioral modeling and predistortion of wideband power amplifiers," *IEEE Trans. Neural Netw. Learn. Syst.*, doi: 10.1109/TNNLS.2021.3054867.

68. Zhou, D. and DeBrunner, V. E., "Novel adaptive nonlinear predistorters based on the direct learning algorithm," *IEEE Trans. Signal Process.*, vol. 55, no. 1, pp. 120–133, Jan. 2007, doi: 10.1109/TSP.2006.882058.

69. Eun, C. and Powers, E. J., "A new Volterra predistorter based on the indirect learning architecture," *IEEE Trans. Signal Process.*, vol. 45, no. 1, pp. 223–227, Jan. 1997, doi: 10.1109/78.552219.

70. Chani-Cahuana, J., Landin, P. N., Fager, C. and Eriksson, T., "Iterative learning control for RF power amplifier linearization," *IEEE Trans. Microw. Theory Tech.*, vol. 64, no. 9, pp. 2778–2789, Sept. 2016, doi: 10.1109/TMTT.2016.2588483.

71. Saikrishna, P., Goyal, A., Kumar, A., Kumar Reddy Chavva, A., Kim, S. and Lee, S., "Memory Polynomial-Inspired Neural Network to Compensate the Power Amplifier Non-linearities," *IEEE 33rd Annual International Symposium on Personal, Indoor and Mobile Radio Communications (PIMRC)*, 2022, pp. 1203–1208, doi: 10.1109/PIMRC54779.2022.9977802.

72. Giordani, M., Polese, M., Roy, A. and Castor, D., M. Zorzi, "A Tutorial on Beam Management for 3GPP NR at mmWave Frequencies," arXiv:1804.01908v2 [cs.NI] 4 Nov 2019.

73. Li, Y.R., Gao, B., Zhang, X. and Huang, K., "Beam Management in Millimeter-Wave Communications for 5G and Beyond," Special Section on Millimeter wave Communications, IEEE ACCESS, 2019, doi: 10.1109/ACCESS.2019.2963514.

74. Chavva, A. K. R. and Khunteta, S. et al., "Sensor Intelligence Based Beam Tracking for 5G mmWave Systems: A Practical Approach," *IEEE Global Communications Conference (GLOBECOM)*, 2019.

75. Jia, C., Gao, H., Chen, N. and He, Y., "Machine Learning Empowered Beam Management for Intelligent Reflecting Surface Assisted MmWave Networks," arXiv:2003.01306v1 [eess.SP] 3 Mar 2020.

76. Klautau, A., Batista, P., González-Prelcic, N., Wang, Y. and Heath, R.W. Jr., "5G MIMO Data for Machine Learning: Application to Beam-Selection using Deep Learning," *Information Theory and Applications Workshop (ITA)*, Feb. 2018. doi: 10.1109/ITA.2018.8503086.

77. Klautau, A., González-Prelcic, N. and Heath, R.W. Jr., "LIDAR data for deep learning-based mmWave beam-selection," *IEEE Wireless Commun. Lett.*, vol. 8, no. 3, pp. 909–912, 2019.

78. Aviles, J. and Kouki, A., "Position-aided mm-wave beam training under NLOS conditions," *IEEE Access*, vol. 4, pp. 8703–8714, 2016.

79. Jayaprakasam, S., Ma, X., Choi, J. and Kim, S., "Robust beam-tracking for mmWave mobile communications," *IEEE Commun. Lett.*, vol. 21, no. 12, pp. 2654–2657, 2017.

80. Zhu, D., Choi, J., Cheng, Q., Xiao, W. and Heath, R., "High-resolution angle tracking for mobile wideband millimeter-wave systems with antenna array calibration," *IEEE Trans. Wireless Commun.*, vol. 17, no. 11, pp. 7173–7189, 2018.

Chapter 5

AI at the beyond 5G edge

Jiasi Chen
University of California
Riverside, California

5.1 INTRODUCTION

Artificial intelligence (AI) and deep learning have recently been highly successful across a variety of application domains, including computer vision, natural language processing, and big data analysis, among others. For example, deep learning methods have consistently outperformed traditional methods for object recognition and detection in the ImageNet Large Scale Visual Recognition Challenge (ISLVRC) computer vision competition since 2012 [1]. However, deep learning's high accuracy comes at the expense of high computational and memory requirements for both the training and inference phases of deep learning. Training a deep learning model is space and computationally expensive due to millions of parameters that need to be iteratively refined over multiple time periods. Inference is computationally expensive due to the potentially high dimensionality of the input data (e.g., a high-resolution image) and the millions of computations that need to be performed on the input data. High accuracy and high resource consumption are defining characteristics of deep learning. Many emerging applications at the beyond 5G edge are envisioned to involve deep learning, such as augmented reality and virtual reality (AR/VR) [2], vehicular communications [3], and unmanned aerial vehicles [4].

To meet the computational requirements of deep learning, a common approach is to leverage cloud computing. To use cloud resources, data must be moved from the data source location on the network edge (e.g., from smartphones and internet of things [IoT] sensors) to a centralized location in the cloud. This potential solution of moving the data from the source to the cloud introduces several challenges: (1) *Latency*: Real-time inference is critical for many applications. For example, camera frames from an autonomous vehicle need to be quickly processed to detect and avoid obstacles, or a voice-based assistive application needs to quickly parse and understand the user's query and return a response. However, sending data to the cloud for inference or training may incur additional queuing and propagation delays from the network, and cannot satisfy strict end-to-end low-latency requirements needed for real-time, interactive applications; for example, real experiments have shown that offloading a camera frame to an Amazon Web Services (AWS)

DOI: 10.1201/9781003303527-6

server and executing a computer vision task take more than 200 ms end-to-end [5]. (2) *Scalability*: Sending data from the sources to the cloud introduces scalability issues, as network access to the cloud can become a bottleneck as the number of connected devices increases. Uploading all data to the cloud is also inefficient in terms of network resource utilization, particularly if not all data from all sources is needed by the deep learning. Bandwidth-intensive data sources such as video streams are particularly a concern. (3) *Privacy*: Sending data to the cloud risks privacy concerns from the users who own the data or whose behaviors are captured in the data. Users may be wary of uploading their sensitive information to the cloud (e.g., faces or speech) and of how the cloud or application will use this data. For example, recent deployment of cameras and other sensors in a smart city environment in New York City incurred serious concerns from privacy watchdogs [6].

Edge computing at the beyond 5G edge is a viable solution to meet the latency, scalability, and privacy challenges described above. In edge computing, a fine mesh of compute resources provides computational abilities close to the end devices [7]. For example, an edge compute node could be co-located with a cellular base station, with an IoT gateway, or on a campus network. Edge computing is already being deployed by industry; for example, a major cellular Internet Service Provider (ISP) in the United States and a national fast-food chain have both deployed edge compute services [8, 9]. To address latency challenges, edge computing's proximity to data sources on the end devices decreases end-to-end latency and thus enables real-time services. To address scalability challenges, edge computing enables a hierarchical architecture of end devices, edge compute nodes, and cloud data centers that can provide computing resources and scale with the number of clients, avoiding network bottlenecks at a central location. To address privacy challenges, edge computing enables data to be analyzed close to the source, perhaps by a local trusted edge server, thus avoiding traversal of the public internet and reducing exposure to privacy and security attacks.

While edge computing can provide the latency, scalability, and privacy benefits discussed above, several major challenges remain to realize deep learning at the beyond 5G edge. One major challenge is accommodating the high resource requirements of deep learning on less powerful edge compute resources. Deep learning needs to execute on a variety of edge devices, ranging from reasonably provisioned edge servers equipped with a graphics processing unit (GPU), to smartphones with mobile processors, to barebones Raspberry Pi devices. A second challenge is understanding how edge devices should coordinate with other edge devices and with the cloud, under heterogeneous processing capabilities and dynamic network conditions, to ensure good end-to-end application-level performance. Finally, privacy remains a challenge, even though edge computing naturally improves privacy by keeping data local to the network edge, as some data often still needs to be exchanged between edge devices, and possibly the cloud. Researchers have proposed various approaches from diverse angles to tackle these challenges, ranging from hardware design to system architecture to theoretical modeling and analysis. The purpose of this chapter is to survey works at the confluence of the two major trends of deep learning and edge computing, in particular focusing on the software aspects, and their unique challenges therein. While excellent surveys exist on deep learning [10] as well as edge computing [11, 12] individually, this chapter focuses on works at their intersection.

Deep learning on edge devices has similarities to, but also differences from, other well-studied areas in the literature. Compared to cloud computing, which can help run computationally expensive machine learning (e.g., machine learning as a service), edge computing has several advantages, such as lower latency and greater geospatial specificity, which have been leveraged by researchers [13]. Several works have combined edge computing with cloud computing, resulting in hybrid edge–cloud architectures [14]. Compared to traditional machine learning methods (outside of deep learning), deep learning's computational demands are particularly a challenge, but deep learning's specific internal structure can be exploited to address this challenge (e.g., Refs. [15–17]). Compared to the growing body of work on deep learning for resource-constrained devices, edge computing has additional challenges relating to shared communication and computation resources across multiple edge devices.

In the rest of this chapter, we define *edge devices* as including both end devices (e.g., smartphones and IoT sensors) as well as edge compute nodes or servers, as shown in Figure 5.1. The chapter is organized as follows. We first provide a brief background on deep learning, including frameworks and measurements (Section 5.2). We then discuss AI on the edge (Section 5.3), that is, how to carry out the entire process of building AI models, starting with application domains where deep learning on the network edge can be useful, different architectures and methods to speed up deep learning inference, and training deep learning models on edge devices. Following this, we discuss AI for the edge (Section 5.4), where key problems in edge computing are addressed with the help of popular and effective AI technologies, including for resource

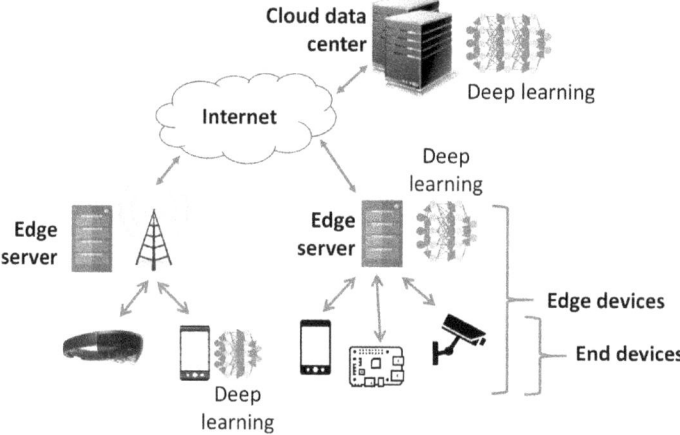

Figure 5.1 Deep learning can execute on edge devices (i.e., end devices and edge servers) and on cloud data centers.

management, network functions, and beyond 5G. Finally, we conclude with open research challenges (Section 5.5) and conclusions (Section 5.6).

5.2 BACKGROUND, MEASUREMENTS, AND FRAMEWORKS

5.2.1 Background on deep learning

Since some of the techniques discussed in this chapter rely on the specific internals of deep learning, we first provide a brief background on deep learning. Further details can be found in reference texts (e.g., Ref. [10]).

A deep learning prediction algorithm, also known as a model, consists of a number of layers, as shown in Figure 5.2. In deep learning inference, the input data passes through the layers in sequence, and each layer performs matrix multiplications on the data. The output of a layer is usually the input to the subsequent layer. After data is processed by the final layer, the output is either a feature or a classification output. When the model contains many layers in sequence, the neural network is known as a deep neural network (DNN). A special case of DNNs is when the matrix multiplications include convolutional filter operations, which are common in DNNs designed for image and video analysis. Such models are known as convolutional neural networks (CNNs). There are also DNNs designed especially for time series prediction; these are called recurrent neural networks, or RNNs [10], which have loops in their layer connections to maintain state and enable predictions on sequential inputs.

In deep learning training, the computation proceeds in reverse order. Given the ground truth training labels, multiple passes are made over the layers to optimize the parameters of each layer of matrix multiplications, starting from the final layer and ending with the first layer. The algorithm used is typically a stochastic gradient descent. In each pass, a randomly selected "mini-batch" of samples is selected and used to update the gradients in the direction that minimizes the training loss (where *training loss* is defined as the difference

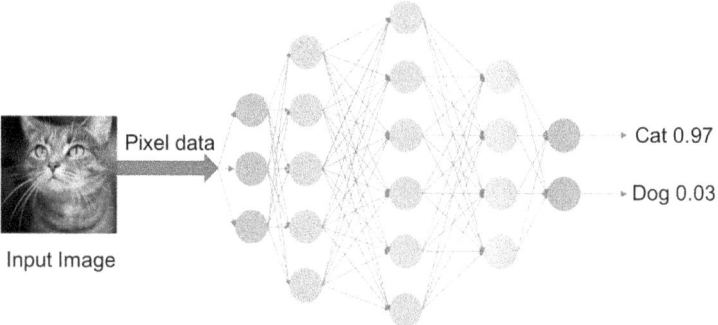

Figure 5.2 Deep neural network example of image classification.

between the predictions and the ground truth). One pass through the entire training dataset is called a training epoch [18].

A key takeaway for the purposes of this chapter is that there are a large number of parameters in the matrix multiplications, resulting in many computations being performed and thus the latency issues that we see on end devices. A second takeaway is that there are many choices (hyperparameters) on how to design the DNN models (e.g., the number of parameters per layer, and the number of layers), which makes model design more of an art than a science. Different DNN design decisions result in trade-offs between system metrics; for example, a DNN with higher accuracy likely requires more memory to store all the model parameters, and it will have higher latency because of all the matrix multiplications being performed. On the other hand, a DNN model with fewer parameters will likely execute more quickly and use less computational resources and energy, but it may not have sufficient accuracy to meet the application's requirements. Several works exploit these trade-offs, which will be discussed later in this chapter.

5.2.2 Measurements of deep learning performance

Deep learning can be used to perform both supervised and unsupervised learning. The metrics of success depend on the particular application domain where deep learning is being applied. For example, in object detection, the accuracy may be measured by the mean average precision (mAP) [1], which measures how well the predicted object location overlaps with the ground truth location, averaged across multiple categories of objects. In machine translation, accuracy can be measured by the BiLingual Evaluation Understudy (BLEU) score metric [19], which compares a candidate translation with several ground truth reference translations. Other general system performance metrics not specific to the application include throughput, latency, and energy. These metrics are summarized in Table 5.1.

Designing a good DNN model or selecting the right DNN model for a given application is challenging due to the large number of hyperparameter decisions. A good understanding of the trade-offs between the speed, accuracy, memory, energy, and other system resources can be helpful for the DNN model designer or the application developer. These comparative measurements are typically presented in research papers proposing new models, or in

Table 5.1 Common performance metrics

Performance metrics
Latency (s)
Energy (mW, J)
Concurrent requests served (no.)
Network bandwidth (Mbps)
Accuracy (application-specific)

standalone measurement papers [20]. An especially important consideration in the context of edge computing is the testbed that the measurements are conducted on. Machine learning research typically focuses on accuracy metrics, and their system performance results are often reported from powerful server testbeds equipped with GPUs. For example, Huang et al. [20] compare the speed and accuracy trade-offs when running on a high-end gaming GPU (Nvidia Titan X). The YOLO (you only look once) DNN model [21], which is designed for real-time performance, provides timing measurements on the same server GPU.

Specifically targeting mobile devices, Lu et al. [22] provide measurements for a number of popular DNN models on mobile central processing units (CPUs) and GPUs (Nvidia TK1 and TX1). Ran et al. [23] further explore accuracy–latency trade-offs on mobile devices by measuring how reducing the dimensionality of the input size reduces the overall accuracy and latency. DNN models designed specifically for mobile devices, such as MobileNets [24], report system performance in terms of the number of multiply–add operations, which could be used to estimate latency characteristics and other metrics on different mobile hardware, based on the processing capabilities of the hardware.

Once the system performance is understood, the application developer can choose the right model. There has also been much recent interest in automated machine learning, which uses AI to choose which DNN model to use for running and tuning the hyperparameters. For example, Tan et al. [25] and Taylor et al. [26] propose using reinforcement learning and traditional machine learning, respectively, to choose the right hyperparameters for mobile devices, which is useful in edge scenarios.

5.2.3 Frameworks available for DNN inference and training

To experiment with deep learning models, researchers commonly turn to open-source software libraries and hardware development kits. Several open-source software libraries are publicly available for deep learning inference and training on end devices and edge servers. Google's TensorFlow [27], released in 2015, is an interface for expressing machine learning algorithms, and an implementation for executing such algorithms on heterogeneous distributed systems. TensorFlow's computation workflow is modeled as a directed graph, and it utilizes a placement algorithm to distribute computation tasks based on estimated or measured execution time and communication time [28]. The placement algorithm uses a greedy approach that places a computation task on the node that is expected to complete the computation the soonest. TensorFlow can run on edge devices such as Raspberry Pi and smartphones. TensorFlow Lite was proposed in late 2017 [29]; it is an optimized version of TensorFlow for mobile and embedded devices, with mobile GPU support added in early 2019. TensorFlow Lite only provides on-device inference abilities, not training, and achieves low latency by compressing a pre-trained DNN model.

Caffe [30–32] is another deep learning framework, originally developed by Yangqing Jia, with the current version, Caffe2, maintained by Facebook. It seeks to provide an easy and straightforward way for deep learning with a focus on mobile devices, including smartphones and Raspberry Pis. PyTorch [33] is another deep learning platform developed by Facebook, with its main goal differing from Caffe2 in that it focuses on integration of research prototypes to production development. Facebook has recently announced that Caffe2 and PyTorch will be merging.

GPUs are an important factor in efficient DNN inference and training. Nvidia provides GPU software libraries to make use of Nvidia GPUs, such as CUDA [34] for general GPU processing, and the CUDA Deep Neural Network (cuDNN) [35], which is targeted toward deep learning. While such libraries are useful for training DNN models on a desktop server, cuDNN and CUDA are not widely available on current mobile devices such as smartphones. To utilize smartphone GPUs, Android developers can currently make use of TensorFlow Lite, which provides experimental GPU capabilities. To experiment with edge devices other than smartphones, researchers can turn to edge-specific development kits, such as the Nvidia Jetson TX2 development kit for experimenting with edge computing (e.g., as used in Ref. [36]), with Nvidia-provided software development kits (SDKs) used to program the devices. The Intel Edison kit is another popular platform for experimentation, which is designed for IoT experiments (e.g., as used in Ref. [37]).

5.3 AI ON THE EDGE

5.3.1 Applications

We now describe several examples of applications where deep learning on edge devices is useful, and what *real time* means for each of these applications. Other applications of deep learning exist alongside the ones described throughout this section; here, for brevity, we highlight several that are relevant in the edge computing context. The common theme across these applications is that they are complex machine learning tasks in which deep learning has been shown to provide good performance, and they need to run in real time and/or have privacy concerns, hence necessitating inference and/or training on the edge.

5.3.1.1 Virtual and augmented reality

In 360° virtual reality, deep learning has been proposed to predict the user's field of view [38–40]. These predictions are used to determine which spatial regions of the 360° video to fetch from the content provider, and must be computed in real time to minimize stalls and maximize the quality of experience of the user. In augmented reality (AR), deep learning can be used to detect objects of interest in the user's field of view and apply virtual overlays

[36, 41], or for hand gesture recognition, depth estimation, localization, or other functions. Moreover, the deep learning models can form a dependency graph, for example to first detect if a hand is present and, if so, run hand-tracking models thereafter [2].

Latency in AR/VR is often measured in terms of the *motion-to-photons delay*. This is defined as the end-to-end delay starting from when the user moves her headset to when the display is updated in response to her movement. Motion-to-photons latency is typically required to be on the order of tens to hundreds of milliseconds [42]. Since deep learning is only one possible part of the AR/VR pipeline (retrieving virtual objects from memory and rendering them can also consume significant latency), the motion-to-photons latency requirement is an upper bound on the latency requirement of deep learning. The motion-to-photons latency requirement also depends on the specific application and the type of user interaction in that application; Chen et al. provide latency requirements for different cognitive assistance AR applications [43]. Since offloading AR computation to the cloud can incur latencies on the order of hundreds of milliseconds, edge computing is needed to provide satisfactory performance, as is done for cognitive assistance using Google Glass [44] and for localization for AR devices [45].

5.3.1.2 Internet of things

Automatic understanding of IoT sensor data is desired in several verticals, such as wearables for healthcare, smart cities, and smart grids. The type of analysis that is performed on this data depends on the specific IoT domain, but deep learning has been shown to be successful in several of them. Examples include human activity recognition from wearable sensors [46], pedestrian traffic in a smart city [47], and electrical load prediction in a smart grid [48]. One difference in the IoT context is that there may be multiple streams of data that need to be fused and processed together, and these data streams typically have space and time correlations that should be leveraged by machine learning. DeepSense [46] is one framework geared toward IoT data fusion leveraging spatiotemporal relationships. It proposes a general deep learning framework that incorporates a hierarchy of CNNs (to capture multiple sensor modalities) and RNNs (to capture temporal correlations), and demonstrates how this general framework can be applied to different tasks with multiple sensor inputs: car tracking, human activity recognition, and biometric identification using inertial sensors (gyroscope, accelerometer, and magnetometer).

Another line of work in the context of IoT deep learning focuses on compressing the deep learning models to fit onto computationally weak end devices, such as Arduino and Raspberry Pi, which typically have only kilobytes of memory and low-power processors. Bonsai [49] does experiments with Arduino Uno, DeepThings [50] experiments with Raspberry Pi 3, and DeepIoT [37] works with Intel's IoT platform, the Edison Board. More details on how they shrink the deep learning model to fit in memory and run on these lightweight devices are discussed later. Other examples of applying deep learning to IoT scenarios, including agriculture, industry, and smart homes, can be found in the excellent survey by Mohammadi et al. [51].

Another motivation for edge computing with IoT devices is the significant privacy concerns that arise when IoT sensors are placed in public locations; for example, the Hudson Yards smart city development in New York City seeks to use air quality, noise, and temperature sensors, along with cameras, to provide advertisers with estimates of how many and how long people looked at advertisements, as well as their sentiment based on facial expressions. However, this has raised significant warnings from privacy watchdogs [6]. Thus, while analyzing IoT sensor data in real time is not always a requirement, and communication bandwidth requirements from sensors are typically small (unless cameras are involved), privacy is a major concern that motivates IoT processing on the edge.

5.3.1.3 Computer vision

Since the successes of deep learning in ISLVRC computer vision competitions from 2012 onward [1], deep learning has been recognized as the state of the art for image classification and object detection. Image classification and object detection are fundamental computer vision tasks that are needed in a number of specific domains, such as video surveillance, object counting, vehicle detection, etc. Such data naturally originates from cameras located at the network edge, and there have even been commercial cameras released with built-in deep learning capabilities [52]. Real-time inference in computer vision is typically measured in terms of frame rate [53], which could be as much as the frame rate of the camera, typically 30–60 frames per second. Uploading camera data to the cloud also leads to privacy concerns, especially if the camera frames contain sensitive information, such as people's faces or private documents, further motivating computation at the edge. Scalability is a third reason why edge computing is useful for computer vision tasks, as the uplink bandwidth to a cloud server may become a bottleneck if there are a large number of cameras uploading large video streams.

Vigil [54] is one example of an edge-based computer vision system. Vigil consists of a network of wireless cameras that perform processing at edge compute nodes to intelligently select frames for analysis (object detection or counting), for example to search for missing people in surveillance cameras or analyze customer queues in retail environments. The motivation for edge computing in Vigil is twofold: to reduce the bandwidth consumption compared to a naïve approach of uploading all frames to the cloud for analysis, and for scalability as the number of cameras increases.

VideoEdge [55] similarly motivates edge-based video analysis from a scalability standpoint. It uses a hierarchical architecture of edge and cloud compute nodes to help with load balancing while maintaining high prediction accuracy (further details are provided later on). Commercial devices such as Amazon DeepLens [52] also follow an edge-based approach, where image detection is performed locally in order to reduce latency, and scenes of interest are uploaded to the cloud for remote viewing only if an interesting object is detected, in order to save bandwidth.

5.3.1.4 Natural language processing

Deep learning has also become popular for natural language processing tasks [56], including for speech synthesis [57], named entity recognition [58] (understanding different parts of a sentence), and machine translation [59] (translating from one language to another). For conversational AI, latency on the order of hundreds of milliseconds has been achieved in recent systems [60]. At the intersection of natural language processing and computer vision, there are also visual question-and-answer systems [61], where the goal is to pose questions about an image (e.g., "How many zebras are in this image?") and receive natural language answers. Latency requirements differ based on how information is presented; for example, conversational replies are preferably returned within 10 ms, while a response to a written web query can tolerate around 200 ms [62].

An example of natural language processing on the edge is voice assistants such as Amazon Alexa or Apple Siri. While voice assistants perform some of their processing in the cloud, they typically use on-device processing to detect wake words (e.g., "Alexa" or "Hey Siri"). Only if the wake word is detected is the voice recording sent to the cloud for further parsing, interpretation, and query response. In the case of Apple Siri, the wake word processing uses two on-device DNNs to classify speech into one of 20 classes (including general speech, silence, and the wake word) [63]. The first DNN is smaller (five layers with 32 units) and runs on a low-power always-on processor. If the first DNN's output is above a threshold, it triggers a second, more powerful DNN (five layers with 192 units) on the main processor.

Wake word detection methods need to be further modified to run on even more computationally constrained devices, such as a smartwatch or an Arduino. On the Apple Watch, a single DNN is used, with a hybrid structure borrowing from the aforementioned two-pass approach. For speech processing on an Arduino, researchers from Microsoft optimized a RNN-based wake word ("Hey Cortana") detection module to fit in 1 KB of memory [64]. Overall, while edge computing is currently used for wake word detection on edge devices, latency remains a significant issue for more complex natural language tasks (e.g., a professional translator can translate 5× faster than Google Translate with the Pixel Buds earbuds [65]), as well as the need for constant cloud connectivity.

5.3.2 Inference

To enable the above applications to meet their latency requirements, different architectures for quickly performing DNN inference have been proposed. In this section, we discuss research centered around three major architectures:

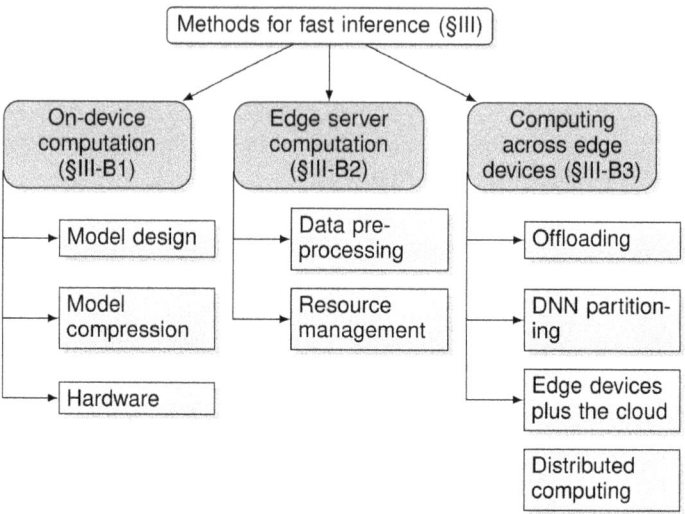

Figure 5.3 Taxonomy of DNN inference speedup methods on the edge.

(1) on-device computation, where DNNs are executed on the end device; (2) edge server–based architectures, where data from the end devices is sent to one or more edge servers for computation; and (3) joint computation between end devices, edge servers, and the cloud. Figure 5.3 shows the taxonomy of these methods, and Figure 5.5 depicts examples of different scenarios, which will be discussed in further detail below. Table 5.2 provides a summary of the discussed works.

5.3.2.1 On-device computation

Many research efforts have focused on ways to reduce the latency of deep learning when it is executed on a resource-constrained device (Figure 5.5a). Such efforts can have benefits throughout the edge ecosystem, by reducing the

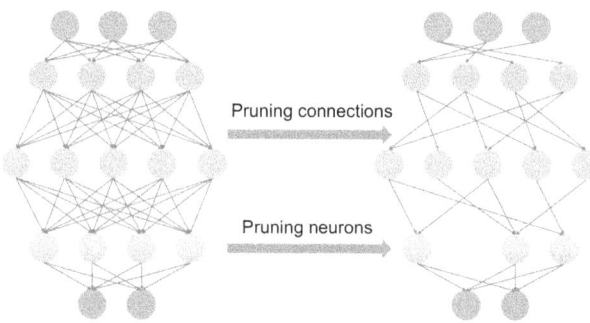

Figure 5.4 Pruning a neural network.

Table 5.2 Summary of selected works on fast deep learning inference with edge computing

Architecture	Work	DNN model	Application	End devices	Speedup method	Key metrics
On-device computation (Section 3.2.1)	Taylor et al. [26]	MobileNet [24], others	Image classification	Nvidia Jetson TX2	Model selection	Latency, accuracy
On-device computation (Section 3.2.1)	DeploT [37]	LeNet5 [93], VGGNet, BiLSTM [94], others	Text, image, speech recognition	Intel Edison computing platform	Model pruning	Latency, energy, memory
On-device computation (Section 3.2.1)	Lai et al. [69]	7-layer CNN	Image classification	Arm Cortex-M	Model quantization	Memory, number of operations
On-device computation (Section 3.2.1)	ESE [70]	LSTM [95]	Speech recognition	XCKU060 FPGA	Model pruning, quantization	Number of operations, memory
On-device computation (Section 3.2.1)	Bhattacharya et al. [71]	AlexNet [96], VGGNet [97]	Speech, image recognition	Qualcomm Snapdragon 400, Nvidia Tegra K1, ARM Cortex M0 and M3	Model sparsification	Memory
On-device computation (Section 3.2.1)	Adadeep [74]	LeNet, AlexNet, and VGGNet	Image, audio, activity classification	Smartphones, wearable devices, development boards, smart home devices	Model selection	Latency, memory, energy
On-device computation (Section 3.2.1)	DeepMon [75]	Yolo YOLO [21], MatConvNet [98]	Object detection	Samsung Galaxy S7	GPU	Latency, caching hit rates
On-device computation (Section 3.2.1)	RSTensorFlow [84]	24-layer CNN, LSTM	Image and hand gestures classification	Nexus 6 and Nexus 5X	GPU	Latency

(Continued)

Table 5.2 Summary of selected works on fast deep learning inference with edge computing (Continued)

Architecture	Work	DNN model	Application	End devices	Speedup method	Key metrics
On-device computation (Section 3.2.1)	DeepX [85]	AlexNet, others	Speech, image recognition	Qualcomm Snapdragon 800, Nvidia Tegra K1	Heterogeneous processors	Energy, memory
On-device computation (Section 3.2.1)	Precog [12]	General image classifiers	Image classification	Nexus 7	Cached specialized models	Latency, accuracy, energy
Edge server computation (Section 3.2.2)	Glimpse [88]	GoogleNet [99]	Feature extraction	Samsung Galaxy Nexus, Google Glass	Pre-processing, offloading	Accuracy, latency
Edge server computation (Section 3.2.2)	Liu et al. [89]	AlexNet with one more NN layer	Image classification	Xiaomi Note	Pre-processing, offloading	Accuracy, latency, energy
Edge server computation (Section 3.2.2)	VideoStorm [90]	Caffe models	Image classification	N/A (video dataset)	Parameter tuning	Quality of queries, latency
Edge server computation (Section 3.2.2)	Chameleon [91]	Faster RCNN [53], YOLO	Object detection	N/A (video dataset)	Parameter tuning	Accuracy, GPU resource usage
Edge server computation (Section 3.2.2)	VideoEdge [55]	AlexNet, others	Image classification	Nvidia Tegra K1	Offloading, parameter tuning	Accuracy, latency
Edge server computation (Section 3.2.2)	Mainstream [92]	MobileNets, others	Image classification and event detection	N/A (video dataset)	Transfer learning, offloading	Number of concurrent apps, accuracy
Edge server computation (Section 3.2.2)	Liu et al. [36]	Faster RCNN, ResNet-50 [100]	Object detection	Nvidia Jetson TX2	Selective offloading	Accuracy, latency

(Continued)

Table 5.2 Summary of selected works on fast deep learning inference with edge computing (Continued)

Architecture	Work	DNN model	Application	End devices	Speedup method	Key metrics
Computing across edge devices (Section 3.2.3)	DeepDecision [23]	YOLO	Object detection	Samsung Galaxy S7	Offloading, parameter tuning	Accuracy, latency, energy, network bandwidth
Computing across edge devices (Section 3.2.3)	MCDNN [101]	AlexNet, VGGNet, DeepFace [102]	Image classification	NVIDIA Jetson board TK1	Offloading, application scheduling	Memory, energy, latency
Computing across edge devices (Section 3.2.3)	Li et al. [14]	AlexNet	Image classification	IoT device and gateways	DNN partitioning	Number of deployed tasks
Computing across edge devices (Section 3.2.3)	DeepThings [50]	YOLO	Object detection	Raspberry Pi 3	DNN partitioning, distributed computing	Memory, latency
Computing across edge devices (Section 3.2.3)	MoDNN [103]	MXNet [104]	Image classification	LG Nexus 5	DNN partitioning, distributed computing	Latency
Computing across edge devices (Section 3.2.3)	DDNN [105]	GoogleNet, BranchyNet [106]	Image classification	N/A (simulation)	DNN partitioning	Accuracy, communication cost, number of end devices

DDNN, distributed deep neural network; LSTM, long short-term memory; MCDNN, mobile–cloud deep neural network; MoDNN, memory optimal deep neural network; RCNN, region-based convolutional neural network.

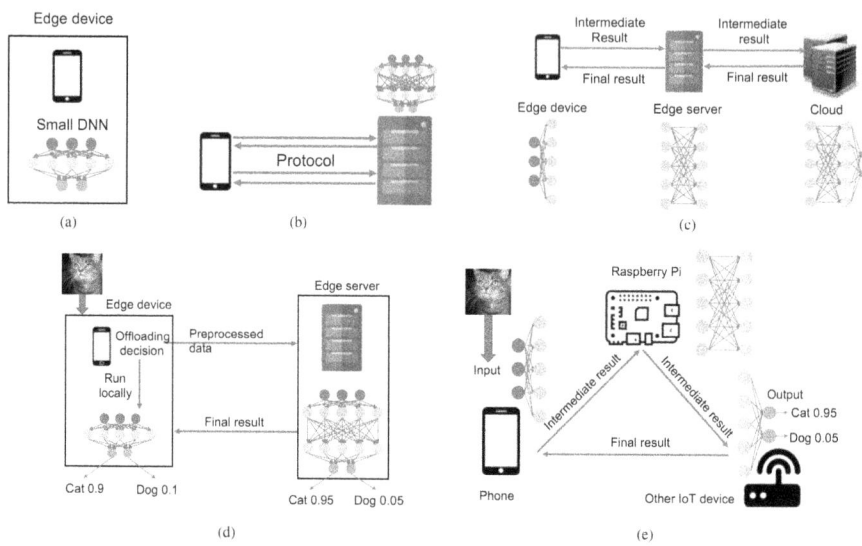

Figure 5.5 Architectures for deep learning inference with edge computing. (a) On-device computation. (b) Secure two-part communication. (c) Computing against edge devices with DNN model partitioning. (d) Offloading with model selection. (e) Distributed computing with DNN model partitioning.

latency of the DNN while running on the end devices or edge servers. Here we describe major efforts in efficient hardware and DNN model design.

5.3.2.1.1 Model design

When designing DNN models for resource-constrained devices, machine learning researchers often focus on designing models with a reduced number of parameters in the DNN model, thus reducing memory and execution latency, while aiming to preserve high accuracy. There are many techniques for doing so, and we briefly mention several popular deep learning models for resource-constrained devices drawn from computer vision. These models include MobileNets [24], Single Shot MultiBox Detector (SSD) [66], YOLO [21], and SqueezeNet [67], and the state of the art is evolving rapidly. MobileNets decompose the convolution filters into two simpler operations, reducing the number of computations needed. SqueezeNet downsamples the data using special 1×1 convolution filters. YOLO and SSD are both single-shot detectors that jointly predict the location and class of the object at the same time, which is much faster than performing these steps sequentially. Many of these models, with pre-trained weights, are available for download on open-source machine learning platforms such as TensorFlow [27] and Caffe [31] for fast bootstrapping.

5.3.2.1.2 Model compression

Compressing the DNN model is another way to enable DNNs on edge devices. Such methods usually seek to compress existing DNN models with minimal accuracy loss compared to the original model. There are several popular model compression methods: parameter quantization, parameter pruning, and knowledge distillation. We briefly outline these approaches here.

Parameter quantization takes an existing DNN and compresses its parameters by changing from floating-point numbers to low-bit width numbers, thus avoiding costly floating-point multiplications. Pruning involves removing the least important parameters (e.g., those that are close to 0), as shown in Figure 5.4 (on page 90). Quantization and pruning approaches have been considered individually as well as jointly [68]. Specifically for edge and mobile devices, DeepIoT [37] presents a pruning method for commonly used deep learning structures in IoT devices, and the pruned DNN can be immediately deployed on edge devices without modification. Lai et al. [69] provide CMSIS-NN, a library for ARM Cortex-M processors that maximizes DNN performance through quantization. It also optimizes data reuse in matrix multiplication to speed up DNN execution. Han et al. [70] propose pruning and quantization for a RNN model, with $10\times$ speedup resulting from pruning and $2\times$ from quantization. Bhattacharya et al. [71] compress the neural network by sparsifying the fully connected layers and decomposing the convolutional filters on wearable devices.

Knowledge distillation involves creating a smaller DNN that imitates the behavior of a larger, more powerful DNN [72]. This is done by training the smaller DNN using the output predictions produced from the larger DNN. Essentially, the smaller DNN approximates the function learned by the larger DNN. Fast exiting [73] is another technique where not all layers are computed; only the result from computing the initial layers is used to provide approximate classification results.

Several works have explored combinations of these model compression techniques. Adadeep [74] automatically chooses between different compression techniques, including pruning and the special filter structures borrowed from MobileNet and SqueezeNet, to meet application requirements and satisfy mobile resource constraints. DeepMon [75] combines quantization with caching of results from intermediate layers on GPUs. The caching leverages the insight that an input video does not change much between subsequent frames, so some computation results from a previous frame can be reused in the current frame, reducing redundant computations and speeding up execution.

5.3.2.1.3 Hardware

To speed up inference of deep learning, hardware manufacturers are leveraging existing hardware such as CPUs and GPUs, as well as producing custom application-specific integrated circuits (ASICs) for deep learning, such as Google's Tensor Processing Unit (TPU [76]). ShiDianNao [77] is another recently proposed custom ASIC, which focuses on efficient memory access in order to reduce latency and energy consumption. It is part of the DianNao [78] family of DNN accelerators, but is geared toward embedded devices, which is useful in the edge computing context. Field-programmable gate array (FPGA)-based DNN accelerators are another promising approach, as FPGAs can provide fast computation while maintaining re-configurability [79]. These custom ASICs and FPGA designs are generally more energy-efficient than traditional CPUs and GPUs, which are designed for flexible support of various workloads at the expense of higher energy consumption.

Vendors also provide software tools for application developers to leverage the accelerations provided by the hardware. Chip manufacturers have developed software tools to optimize deep learning on existing chips, such as Intel's OpenVINO Toolkit to leverage Intel chips, including Intel's CPUs, GPUs, FPGAs, and vision processing units (VPUs) [80, 81]. Nvidia's EGX platform [82] is another recent entrant into this space, with support for Nvidia hardware ranging from lightweight Jetson Nanos to powerful T4 servers. Qualcomm's Neural Processing SDK is designed to utilize its Snapdragon chips [83]. There are also general libraries developed for mobile devices not tied to specific hardware, such as RSTensorFlow [84], which uses the GPU to speed up matrix multiplication in deep learning. Software approaches have also been developed to efficiently utilize hardware; for example, Lane et al. [85] decomposes DNNs and assigns them to heterogeneous local processors (e.g., CPU or GPU) to accelerate execution. More details on hardware-accelerated deep learning can be found in the excellent survey by Sze et al. [86]. Since Sze's survey has covered hardware-based DNN accelerations in great depth, the remainder of this chapter mainly focuses on software-based approaches.

5.3.2.2 Edge server computation

While the above hardware speedup and compression techniques can help DNNs run on end devices, deploying large, powerful DNNs with real-time execution requirements on edge devices is still challenging because of resource limitations (e.g., power, computation, and memory). Thus, it is natural to consider offloading DNN computations from end devices to more powerful entities, such as edge servers or the cloud. However, the cloud is not suitable for edge applications that require short response times [11]. Since the edge server is close to users and can respond quickly to users' requests, it becomes the first-choice helper.

The most straightforward method to utilize the edge server is to offload all the computation from end devices to the edge server. In such scenarios, the end devices will send their data to a nearby edge server, and receive the corresponding results after server processing. Wang et al. [87], for example, always offload DNNs to the edge server (an IoT gateway) to analyze wireless signals.

5.3.2.2.1 Data pre-processing

When sending data to an edge server, data pre-processing is useful to reduce data redundancy and thus decrease communication time. Glimpse [88] offloads all DNN computation to a nearby edge server, but uses change detection to filter which camera frames are offloaded. If no changes are detected, Glimpse will perform frame tracking locally on the end device. This pre-processing improves system processing ability and makes real-time object recognition on mobile devices possible. Along similar lines, Liu et al. [89] build a food recognition system with two pre-processing steps: First, they discard blurry images, and second, they crop the image so that it only contains objects of interest. Both pre-processing steps are lightweight and can reduce the amount of offloaded data. We note that while feature extraction is a common pre-processing step in computer vision, it does not apply in the context of deep learning, because the DNNs themselves serve as the feature extractors.

5.3.2.2.2 Edge resource management

When DNN computations run on edge servers, DNN tasks from multiple end devices need to run and be efficiently managed on shared compute resources. Several works have explored this problem space, focusing on the trade-offs between accuracy, latency, and other performance metrics, such as the number of requests served. VideoStorm [90] was one of the first works in this space, and profiles these trade-offs to choose the right DNN configuration for each request, to meet accuracy and latency goals. The configuration can also be updated online during the streaming video input, as is done in Chameleon [91]. VideoEdge [55] additionally considers computation that is distributed across a hierarchy of edge and cloud servers, and how to jointly tune all the DNN hyperparameters. Mainstream [92] considers a similar problem setup of accuracy versus latency trade-offs on edge servers, but their solution uses transfer learning to reduce the computational resources consumed by each request. Transfer learning enables multiple applications to share the common lower layers of the DNN model, and computes higher layers unique to the specific application, thus reducing the overall amount of computation.

5.3.2.3 Computing across edge devices

Although the edge server can accelerate DNN processing, it is not always necessary to have the edge devices execute DNNs on the edge servers—intelligent offloading can be used instead. We next discuss four offloading scenarios: (1) binary offloading of DNN computation, where the decision is whether to offload the entire DNN or not; (2) partial offloading of partitioned DNNs, where the decision is what fraction of the DNN computations should be offloaded; (3) hierarchical architectures, where offloading is performed across a combination of edge devices, edge servers, and the cloud;

and (4) distributed computing approaches, where the DNN computation is distributed across multiple peer devices.

5.3.2.3.1 Offloading

Recent approaches such as DeepDecision [23, 107] and mobile-cloud deep neural network (MCDNN) [101] take an optimization-based offloading approach with constraints such as network latency and bandwidth, device energy, and monetary cost. These decisions are based on empirical measurements of the trade-offs between these parameters, such as energy, accuracy, latency, and input size for the different DNN models. The catalogue of different DNN models can be chosen from existing popular models, or new model variants can be constructed through knowledge distillation or by "mix-and-matching" DNN layers from multiple models [101]. An example of offloading, combined with model selection where a powerful DNN is available on the edge server and a weaker DNN is available on the end device, is shown in Figure 5.5d.

We note that while offloading has long been studied in the networking literature [108], even in the context of edge computing [109], DNN offloading can consider the additional degree of freedom of not only where to run, but which DNN model or which portion of the model to run. The decision of whether to offload or not thus depends on the size of the data, the hardware capabilities, the DNN model to be executed, and the network quality, among other factors.

5.3.2.3.2 DNN model partitioning

A fractional offloading approach can also be considered that leverages the unique structure of DNNs, specifically their layers. In such model-partitioning approaches, some layers are computed on the device, and some layers are computed by the edge server or the cloud, as shown in Figure 5.5c. This is known as DNN model partitioning. These approaches can potentially offer latency reductions by leveraging the compute cycles of other edge devices; however, care must also be taken that the latency of communicating the intermediate results at the DNN partition point still leads to overall net benefits. The intuition behind model partitioning is that, after the first few layers of the DNN model have been computed, the size of the intermediate results is relatively small, making them faster to send over the network to an edge server than the original raw data [50]. This motivates approaches that partition after the initial layers. Neurosurgeon [16] is one work that intelligently decides where to partition the DNN, layer-wise, while accounting for network conditions.

In addition to partitioning the DNN by layers, the DNN can also be partitioned along the input dimension (e.g., select rows of the input image). Such input-wise partitioning allows finer-grained partitioning, because the input and output data size and the memory footprint of each partition can be arbitrarily chosen, instead of the minimum partition size being defined by the discrete DNN layer sizes. This is especially important for extremely lightweight devices, such as IoT sensors, which may not have the necessary memory to hold an entire DNN layer. However, input-wise partitioning can result in increased data dependency, as computing subsequent DNN layers requires data results from adjacent partitions. Two examples of input-wise partitioning are memory optimal deep neural networks (MoDNNs) [103] and DeepThings [50].

Overall, these partial offloading approaches through DNN partitioning are similar in spirit to past, non-DNN offloading approaches such as MAUI [108] and Odessa [110], which divide an application into its constituent subtasks, and decide which subtasks to execute where based on energy and/or latency considerations. However, a new decision in the deep learning scenario is how to decide the constituent subtasks, as the DNN can be divided layer-wise, input-wise, or possibly in other ways yet to be explored.

5.3.2.3.3 Edge devices plus the cloud

Deep learning computation can not only be performed on edge devices but also utilize the cloud, as shown in Figure 5.5c. While solely offloading to the cloud can violate the real-time requirements of the deep learning applications under consideration, judicious use of the powerful compute resources in the cloud can potentially decrease the total processing time. Different from a binary decision of whether to perform computation on the edge server or cloud, approaches in this space often consider DNN partitioning, where some layers can execute in the cloud, edge server, and/or end device.

Li et al. [14] divide the DNN model into two parts—the edge server computes the initial layers of the DNN model, and the cloud computes the higher layers of the DNN. The edge server receives input data, performs lower-layer DNN processing, then sends the intermediate results to the cloud. The cloud, after computing the higher layers, sends back the final results to the end devices. Such designs utilize both the edge server and the cloud, where the cloud can help with computationally heavy requests and increase the edge server's request-processing rate, while at the same time reducing the network traffic between the edge server and the cloud. A distributed deep neural network (DDNN) [105] also distributes computation across a hierarchy of cloud, edge servers, and end devices, and additionally combines this with the fast exiting idea, so that the computation requests do not always reach the cloud.

A unique characteristic of edge computing is that the edge server typically serves users within a limited geographical area, suggesting that their input data and thus their DNN outputs may be similar. Precog [13] leverages this insight in the case of image recognition, and places smaller, specialized image classification models on the end devices, based on what has recently been observed by other devices served by the same edge server. If on-device classification fails, the query is sent to the edge server, which stores all the classification models. Although their evaluation does not use DNNs, they discuss how their classification model placement decisions would apply to DNNs. This approach has similarities to knowledge distillation for compressed models, in that it uses a combination of weaker and stronger classification models, but provides a more careful look at what specialized models are needed on the end devices in edge scenarios.

5.3.2.3.4 Distributed computation

The above approaches mainly consider offloading computation from end devices to other more powerful devices (e.g., edge servers or the cloud). Another line of work considers the problem from a distributed computing perspective, where the DNN computations can be distributed across multiple helper edge devices, as shown in Figure 5.5e. For example, MoDNN [103] and DeepThings [50] distribute DNN executions using fine-grained partitioning on lightweight end devices such as Raspberry Pis and Android smartphones. The DNN partition decision is made based on the computation capabilities and/or memory of the end devices. At runtime, the input data is distributed to helpers according to load-balancing principles, with MoDNN using a MapReduce-like model, and DeepThings designing a load-balancing heuristic. The assignment of data to the helper devices can be adjusted online to account for dynamic changes in compute resource availability or network conditions. More formal mechanisms from distributed systems could also be applied in these scenarios to provide provable performance guarantees.

5.3.3 Training

Thus far, edge computing and deep learning have mostly been discussed for inference, with goals including low latency, privacy, and bandwidth savings. These methods assume that a deep learning model has already been trained offline on a centralized, existing dataset. In this section, we discuss methods of training deep learning models with edge computing, primarily with a focus on communication efficiency and privacy (Figure 5.6).

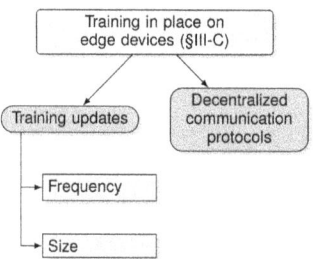

Figure 5.6 Taxonomy of DNN training in place on edge devices.

Traditionally, training data produced by end devices would be sent to the cloud, which would then perform the training with its large computational resources, and finally distribute the trained model back to the edge devices as needed. However, sending the data to the cloud can consume large amounts of bandwidth, and also causes privacy concerns. Leaving data *in situ* on the end devices is useful when privacy is desired, and also helps reduce the network bandwidth requirements. For example, a deep learning–based typing prediction model for smartphones may benefit from training data from multiple users, but individual users may not wish to upload their raw keystroke data to the cloud; similarly, in an image classification service, uploading all camera frames from end devices to the cloud would consume large amounts of bandwidth and risk uploading sensitive information.

Edge-based training borrows from DDNN training in data centers. In data centers, training is performed across multiple workers, with each worker holding either a partition of the dataset (known as data parallelism) or a partition of the model (known as model parallelism). While both system designs have been explored, data parallelism is widely used in practical systems [111], and is the focus of the remainder of this section. In data parallelism, each worker computes the gradients of its local partition of the dataset, which are then collected by a central parameter server, some aggregate computation is performed, and the updates are sent back to the workers (Figure 5.7a).

Training on edge devices borrows from the data center setup, where the workers are end devices instead of powerful servers in a data center, and the central parameter server is an edge compute node or server. For example, DeepCham [112] consists of a master edge server that trains domain-aware object recognition on end devices, leveraging the insight that users connected to the same edge server may have similar domains (e.g., time of day, physical environment). In an edge scenario, communication latency, network bandwidth, and the compute capabilities of the end device are key considerations of training performance.

Training deep learning on edge devices typically involves distributed deep learning training techniques. This section discusses techniques to perform

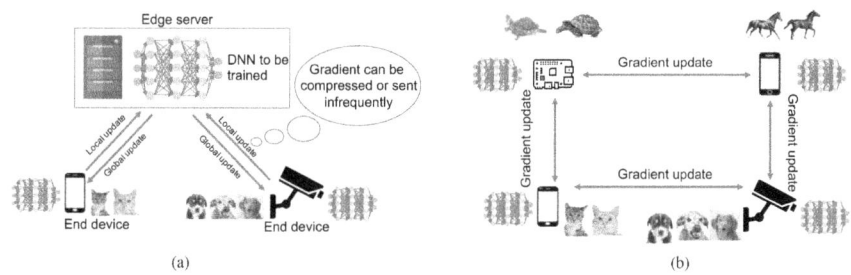

Figure 5.7 Architectures for deep learning training on the edge. (a) Centralized training. (b) Decentralized training.

distributed training on edge devices from the following perspectives: the frequency and size of training updates, which both contribute to communication costs and decentralized information sharing. A taxonomy of these techniques is shown in Figure 5.6, and a summary of the works discussed below is shown in Table 5.3.

Table 5.3 Summary of selected works on distributed training

Category	Work	DNN model	Main ideas	Key metrics
Communication frequency	EASGD [114]	7-layer CNN	Allow local parameters to deviate from central parameters	Training loss, test loss
Communication frequency	Federated learning [115]	CNN and LSTM	Trade off local computation for communication rounds	Training loss, test loss, number of communication rounds
Communication frequency	Gaia [117]	Caffe model	Hierarchical communication of geodistributed nodes	Training time
Communication frequency	Co-distillation [118]	LSTM	Teacher–student models	Accuracy
Communication frequency	Dean et al. [111]	Fully connected DNN with 42 million parameters	Partition DNN across different machines	Number of training nodes, training time
Communication size	Lin et al. [119]	AlexNet, ResNet-5, 2- or 5-layer LSTM	Send sparsified gradient	Gradient size
Communication size	Hardy et al. [120]	CNN with 2 convolution layers and 2 fully connected layers	Send sparsified and nonstale gradients	Accuracy
Communication size	Blot et al. [121]	7-layer CNN	Gossip with random neighbors	Training loss
Gossip-based communication	Jin et al. [122]	ResNet	Scalability of synchronous and asynchronous SGD	Test error, training time/epochs
Gossip-based communication	INCEPTIONN [123]	ResNet-50, AlexNet, VGG-16	Lossy gradient compression and hierarchical gossip	Gradient size, number of training nodes, gradient exchange time

EASGD, elastic averaging stochastic gradient descent.

5.3.3.1 Frequency of training updates

Communication costs are a major concern for edge devices. Reducing the frequency of communications and the size of each communication are key methods to reduce communication costs. In this subsection, we discuss distributed training methods that focus on communication timing and frequency, while in the next subsection, we discuss the size of the communicated data. There are two general methods for synchronizing updates to a central edge server: synchronous and asynchronous stochastic gradient descent (SGD) [113]. In synchronous SGD, individual devices update their parameters in lockstep, when all the devices have finished computing the gradients on their current batch of training data. In asynchronous SGD, the devices update their parameters independently to the central server. Both synchronous SGD and asynchronous SGD have their own pros and cons. Although synchronous SGD typically converges to better solutions, it is often slower in practice because of the need to wait for straggler devices in each iteration. Asynchronous SGD, on the other hand, tends to converge faster than synchronous SGD, but may update parameters using stale information from devices, and can suffer from convergence to poor solutions.

Distributed training algorithms usually focus on how to make synchronous SGD faster, or how to make asynchronous SGD converge to better solutions. In a distributed setting, communication frequency and data volume are also important. Elastic averaging [114] reduces the communication costs of synchronous and asynchronous SGD training methods, by allowing each device to perform more local training computations, and deviate/explore further from the globally shared solution, before synchronizing its updates. This reduces the amount of communication between local devices and the edge server. Federated learning [115] is similar in spirit, but considers non-ideal scenarios, such as non-iid (independent and identically distributed) data distributions (e.g., one device has more data samples of a given class than another device). Computing more local gradient updates without uploading the raw training data to the server trades off accuracy for communication costs: Doing more computation locally lowers the prediction accuracy (due to overfitting to local datasets) but can also save on communication costs, and vice versa. Wang et al. [116] further explored this issue by considering some practical concerns with implementation on a real testbed. They proposed a control policy for deciding how much computation should be performed locally in between global gradient updates, and performed experiments with Raspberry Pis and laptops.

Tiered architectures and their communication costs have also been considered. Gaia [117] studies synchronous SGD in the scenario where devices are geographically distributed across a large area. In their test setup, the clients are servers inside a data center and across data centers. Because bandwidth constraints are tighter across geodistributed data centers than within a single data center, gradient updates need to be carefully coordinated between workers. Gaia proposes a policy where updates are synchronized across different data centers only when the aggregated updates are higher than a given threshold.

Along with synchronous and asynchronous updates, distillation is another method that has been applied to reduce communication frequency. Distillation uses the prediction outputs of one model to help train another model. Anil et al. [118] proposed incorporating distillation into distributed training of DNNs. In their method, each device trains on a subset of the data and updates its gradients based on its computed training loss as usual, but also uses the prediction outputs from other devices (that are also simultaneously training) to improve training efficacy. Since they find that the training is robust to stale prediction results from other devices, information needs to be exchanged with other devices less frequently (compared to the gradient sharing methods described above). In this way, frequent communication of gradients is avoided or reduced. Furthermore, distillation can be combined with distributed SGD, and can improve training efficacy even when distributed SGD is not possible due to network constraints.

Finally, if some devices have poor connectivity and are subject to atypically long latencies, they can hold up distributed training. Chen et al. [113] proposed improvements to synchronous SGD to mitigate such straggler effects. Their main idea is to have backup devices, which are "on call" to compute the gradient updates of any straggling regular devices. Once the server receives the gradient updates from a sufficient number of devices, the training process will update the global parameters and move on to the next iteration without waiting for the straggler devices, thereby reducing training latency.

5.3.3.2 Size of training updates

Along with the frequency of training updates, the size of training updates also contributed to bandwidth usage. With model sizes on the order of hundreds of megabytes, and multiple rounds of communication needed, the bandwidth demands can be considerable. Bandwidth concerns are crucial in the edge scenario, where last-mile bandwidth (e.g., wireless, access networks) can be quite constrained. In this subsection, we review gradient compression techniques, which can reduce the size of the updates communicated to a central server.

There are two general approaches to gradient compression: gradient quantization and gradient sparsification [119]. Gradient quantization approximates floating-point gradients using low-bit width numbers. For example, a 32-bit floating-point number can be approximated by an 8-bit number, reducing the size by a factor of 4. Note that gradient quantization is similar to parameter quantization, with the difference being whether the quantization is applied to the model gradients or the model parameters. Gradient sparsification discards unimportant gradient updates and only communicates updates that exceed a certain threshold. Gradient quantization and sparsification can work together. For example, Lin et al. [119] do gradient sparsification combined with other training tricks such as momentum correction [124] and warm-up training [125] techniques to speed up training convergence. Hardy et al. [126] perform gradient sparsification and also choose which gradients to communicate based on their staleness.

5.3.3.3 Decentralized communication protocols

Thus far, we have considered centralized training architectures where multiple end devices communicate with an edge server. Having a central edge compute or server node helps ensure that all devices converge to the same model parameters. However, communication throughput of a centralized architecture is limited by bandwidth of the central node. To overcome this, a gossip-type algorithm has been proposed as a method to exchange training information in a decentralized fashion. In gossip-type algorithms, each device computes its own gradient updates based on its training data, then communicates its updates to some of the other devices (see Figure 5.7b). The overall goal is to design a gossiping algorithm that allows the devices to reach a consensus on a good DNN model. Gossiping can be considered as a decentralized version of elastic averaging, where clients are allowed to deviate more significantly from each other.

Blot et al. [121] proposed an asynchronous algorithm for gossip-based training of deep learning. Their experiments show faster convergence than the elastic averaging. Jin et al. [122] also proposed gossiping SGD based on their study of convergence rates for synchronous and asynchronous SGD. Their primary concern was scalability (i.e., which SGD methods would be appropriate for different numbers of clients). They found that asynchronous methods such as gossiping and elastic averaging converged more quickly with a small number of workers (32 workers in their simulations), whereas synchronous SGD scaled up better and had higher accuracy when there were more workers (100 workers in their simulations). Li et al. [123] developed a distributed system called INCEPTIONN, which combines gradient compression and gossiping. Their gossiping method involves dividing devices into different groups, and within each group, each device shares some of its gradients with the next device. The algorithm guarantees that all parts of the DNN across all devices will be updated after several iterations. Within each group, the parameters can be shared either in the traditional centralized way or through gossiping.

5.4 AI FOR THE EDGE

5.4.1 Resource management

5.4.1.1 Management and scheduling

Deep learning is often treated as a black box by application developers and network administrators. However, deep learning models have many trade-offs between latency, accuracy, battery life, etc. While several of the works described earlier have discussed how to tune such control knobs to achieve overall good system performance [23, 90], exposing these control knobs in a consistent and unified manner to the application developer and/or server administrator through a standard specification could be valuable. This would enable developers and server administrators without in-depth machine learning knowledge to understand the available knobs and tune them to achieve good system performance, especially on edge compute nodes with limited resources. Specifying the application's needs and the trade-offs of the DNN model being run can allow the edge server to effectively schedule the end device requests. Not doing this carefully (e.g., incurring long latency on a video frame analysis request from an AR headset) would negate the latency benefits of edge computing.

A natural question, then, is how to schedule such requests, given knowledge of the trade-offs and control knobs. The question is complicated by time dependency between sequential inputs from an end device (e.g., multiple frames from a camera), which could introduce priority into the scheduling policy and thus influence the decisions made by the edge server of which requests to serve when. For example, should a new camera frame inference request from device A receive higher priority than the hundredth frame from device B? Incorporating freshness metrics, such as the Age of Information [127], could allow for more intelligent scheduling decisions by the edge server. While this problem has some overlap with task scheduling in cloud data centers, edge computing brings new challenges in that the number and variety of requests are likely fewer on an edge server serving geolocated end devices, so statistical multiplexing cannot necessarily be relied on. New analysis of load-balancing and request-scheduling mechanisms is needed. Furthermore, the compute resource allocations may be coupled with the traffic steering from the end devices to the edge server. Existing work mainly considers proximity as the primary factor behind traffic-steering decisions [128].

5.4.1.2 Migration

Migrating edge computing applications between different edge servers can be useful for load balancing or to accommodate user movement, with the goal of minimizing the end-to-end latency of the user. While edge migration has been studied in general cases, for example using virtual machine (VM) migration techniques [129] or Docker containers [130], or using Multipath Transmission Control Protocol (MPTCP) to speed up the migration [131], understanding how deep learning applications should be migrated is still an area of consideration. DNN models can be fairly large; for example, a pre-trained YOLO model [21] is approximately 200 MB, and recent vision transformer models [132] contain up to 632 million parameters. Loading such models can take upward of several seconds. What parts of the DNN model should be migrated and what parts should be included in the standalone virtual image? Can the program state be migrated in the midst of a DNN execution, similar to the DNN partitioning approaches for offloading? Addressing these challenges requires system measurements and experiments to gain an empirical understanding of the migration challenges.

5.4.2 Network functions

5.4.2.1 Usage

Using deep learning for network functions (NFs), such as for intrusion detection [133, 134] and wireless scheduling [135], has been proposed. Such systems by definition live on the network edge and need to operate with stringent latency requirements. For example, an intrusion detection system that actively responds to a detected attack by blocking malicious packets needs to perform detection at line rate to avoid creating a bottleneck (e.g., 40 μs) [136]. If the intrusion detection system operates in passive mode, however, its latency requirements are less strict. A wireless scheduler also needs to operate at line rate in order to make real-time decisions on which packets should be delivered where.

In-network caching is another example of a NF that can use deep learning at the network edge. In an edge computing scenario, different end devices in the same geographical region may request the same content many times from a remote server. Caching such contents at an edge server can significantly reduce the perceived response time and network traffic. There are generally two approaches to apply deep learning in a caching system: Use deep learning for content popularity prediction, or use deep reinforcement learning to decide a caching policy [137]. Saputra et al. [138], for example, use deep learning to predict content popularity. To train the deep learning model, the cloud collects content popularity information from all of the edge caches. Deep reinforcement learning for caching, on the other hand, avoids popularity prediction, and is solely based on reward signals from its actions. Chen et al. [139], for example, train deep reinforcement learning for caching using the cache hit rate as the reward.

5.4.2.2 Future work

Recently, network abstractions such as software-defined networking (SDN, to abstract the data plane from the control plane) and network function virtualization (NFV, to abstract the NFs from the hardware) are gaining importance and being adopted by the telecommunications industry. If deep learning grows in popularity and these flows containing deep learning data appear on the edge network, this leads to questions of how SDN and NFV should manage these types of flows, and what types of quality of service (QoS) guarantee the flows require. How can deep learning flows be identified, even under encryption? Given a set of NFs that need to operate on deep learning flows, how can a SDN controller be designed to best manage these flows (e.g., by carving out network slices for deep learning traffic)? How should network resources be shared between competing deep learning flows or with other non–deep learning traffic, such as web or video?

Another direction is using deep learning itself as a NF, such as the network intrusion detection and caching applications described earlier.

If deep learning is adopted for various network tasks, NFV platforms need to account for the resource requirements of deep learning in order for the NFs to run in real time. While fast instantiation and performance of NFVs have been investigated [140], deep learning inference can be greatly accelerated with GPU access on the edge server, necessitating GPU support in NFV platforms.

5.4.3 Beyond 5G

3GPP's Network Data Analytics Function (NWDAF) is a specific NF that offers data collection abilities in the 5G core network. Data such as user mobility, load, QoS, communication patterns, and radio analytics can be collected and used to drive machine learning to optimize performance. Any other NF can also request data analytics. This opens up opportunities for data-driven approaches to optimizing network configurations and deployments in beyond 5G networks [141, 142]. Some recent examples of machine learning for cellular networks include traffic analysis to provision slice resources [143] and suggestions to proactively fix network failures noticed by devices [144] or customers [145]. Extreme mobility is a key concern of beyond 5G networks, with high mobility in many use cases such as satellites, high-speed rails, vehicular networks, and drones [146]. Thus, AI has been applied to user mobility analysis by inferring road mobility patterns from sequences of cell tower signals [147], or for handover prediction [148]. Ultra-low latency is another key concern for emerging edge applications such as AR/VR, and application-layer approaches to encourage low-latency connections have been studied [149]. On the wireless side, with increasing reliance on higher-frequency spectrums, there has been much work on millimeter-wave beam alignment and blockage prediction [150–152], as well as some work on subcarrier configuration using collaborative filtering [153]. Finally, the federated learning paradigm can aid cellular networks, for example through distributed spectrum sharing, or to avoid aggregating all data and models at the centralized NWDAF and instead perform machine learning at different locations in the core network [142]. A key challenge for researchers exploring AI for beyond 5G networks is the lack of public operational data that is needed to train and evaluate machine learning models, which typically require large amounts of data to avoid overfitting. While software implementations of 3GPP standards exist, such as OpenAirInterface, it is still hard for researchers to drive such software without realistic input data.

5.5 OPEN CHALLENGES

Many challenges remain in deploying deep learning on the edge, not only on end devices but also on edge servers and on a combination of end devices, edge servers, and the cloud. In this section, we discuss some of the open challenges.

5.5.1 Systems challenges

5.5.1.1 Latency

While several of the works described earlier in this chapter have focused on reducing inference latency, the current state of the art still results in quite high latency, particularly when operating on high-dimensional input data such as images and on mobile devices. For example, even DNN models designed for mobile devices execute at 1–2 frames per second on modern smartphones [23, 75]. Much work is still needed for DNN model compression to enable deep learning to run on edge devices, particularly on IoT devices that tend to have the most severe resource constraints. Furthermore, while the offloading approaches described earlier propose innovative approaches to minimize latency, machine learning experts are also constantly innovating, leading to new DNN models with ever more parameters and new layer designs. For example, the DNN partitioning approach may work well for standard sequential DNNs, but not as well for other deep learning methods such as RNNs, which have loops in their layer structure. Keeping up with new deep learning designs will continue to be a major systems challenge.

5.5.1.2 Energy

Minimizing the energy consumption of deep learning is very important for battery-powered edge devices, such as smartphones. While reducing the amount of computation implicitly reduces energy consumption, understanding the interactions of the deep learning computations with other battery management mechanisms, such as CPU throttling or sensor hardware optimizations [154], is an important avenue for investigation. Performing change detection on the input data, in either software or hardware [155], can help reduce the frequency of deep learning executions and the overall energy consumption. Reducing energy consumption of the specific hardware chips (e.g., GPUs and TPUs) is already a key priority for hardware designers, but understanding their interaction with the rest of the system (e.g., battery management mechanisms, and trade-offs with edge server compute resources) is needed to reduce overall energy consumption.

5.5.2 Deep learning benchmarks on edge devices

The state of the art of deep learning is evolving rapidly. For researchers and developers wishing to deploy deep learning on edge devices, choosing the right DNN model is difficult due to a lack of apples-to-apples comparisons on the target hardware. Even though new machine learning papers contain comparative evaluations with prior existing models, the subsets of models compared are chosen at the discretion of the researchers and may not include the desired comparisons or hardware platforms. Furthermore, standalone measurement papers can quickly become outdated as new DNN models emerge. A public repository containing apples-to-apples benchmark comparisons between models on different hardware could be of great benefit to the community. This task is made slightly easier by the existence of standard datasets in certain application domains, such as image classification and natural language processing, as well as standard machine learning platforms such as TensorFlow, Caffe, and PyTorch. Especially important to edge computing is comparison on a variety of edge device hardware, including the simple devices (e.g., Raspberry Pi), smartphones, home gateways, and edge servers. Much of the current work has focused either on powerful servers or on smartphones, but as deep learning and edge computing become prevalent, a comparative understanding of deep learning performance on heterogeneous hardware is needed.

5.5.3 Privacy

While privacy has been studied generally in the context of distributed deep learning, there are several implications for edge computing that merit further investigation. One possible concern is membership attacks. A membership attack seeks to determine whether a particular item was part of the training set used to generate the deep learning model [156]. This attack gains significance in edge computing, as a successful attack on an edge server's DNN training process means that the data item can be more easily pinpointed as belonging to a small subset of users who accessed that edge server. Another concern is data obfuscation. While data obfuscation techniques have been studied in cases where there are a large number of users, such as in the cloud, whether such obfuscation can still be successful in an edge computing scenario, where more specialized deep learning models are being used [13, 112] or smaller training sets are available due to fewer end devices connected to each edge server, is unclear. Finally, the definition of *differential privacy* [157] means that as there are fewer devices, more noise must be added. This is exactly the scenario of edge computing, where a smaller set of geolocated end devices communicates with an edge server. How much noise must be added to compensate for fewer end devices? Overall, the privacy problems described above have been studied mainly in the context of general distributed machine learning, but their study with regard to edge computing, which has a smaller set of users and more specialized deep learning models, could be valuable.

5.6 CONCLUSION

This chapter reviewed the current state of the art for deep learning operating at the beyond 5G network edge. Computer vision, natural language processing, network functions, and virtual and augmented reality were discussed as example application drivers, with the commonality being the need for real-time processing of data produced by end devices. Methods for accelerating deep learning inference across end devices, edge servers, and the cloud were described, which leverage the unique structure of DNN models as well as the geospatial locality of user requests in edge computing. The trade-offs between accuracy, latency, and other performance metrics were found to be important factors in several of the works discussed. Training of deep learning models, where multiple end devices collaboratively train a DNN model (possibly with the help of an edge server and/or the cloud), was also discussed, including techniques for further enhancing privacy.

Many open challenges remain, in terms of further performance improvements as well as privacy, resource management, benchmarking, and integration with other networking technologies such as SDN and NFV. These challenges can be addressed through technological innovations in algorithms, system design, and hardware accelerations. As the pace of deep learning innovation remains high in the near term, new technical challenges in edge computing may emerge in the future, alongside existing opportunities for innovation.

REFERENCES

1. Olga Russakovsky, Jia Deng, Hao Su, Jonathan Krause, Sanjeev Satheesh, Sean Ma, Zhiheng Huang, Andrej Karpathy, Aditya Khosla, Michael Bernstein, Alexander C. Berg and Li Fei-Fei. ImageNet large scale visual recognition challenge. *International Journal of Computer Vision (IJCV)*, 115(3):211–252, 2015.
2. Hyoukjun Kwon, Krishnakumar Nair, Jamin Seo, Jason Yik, Debabrata Mohapatra, Dongyuan Zhan, Jinook Song, Peter Capak, Peizhao Zhang and Peter Vajda, et al. Xrbench: An extended reality (XR) machine learning benchmark suite for the metaverse. *MLSys*, 2023.
3. Hang Qiu, Fawad Ahmad, Fan Bai, Marco Gruteser and Ramesh Govindan. Avr: Augmented vehicular reality. In *Proceedings of the 16th Annual International Conference on Mobile Systems, Applications, and Services*, pages 81–95, 2018.
4. Moustafa Abdelbaky, Jiasi Chen, Alexander Fedin, Kenneth Freeman, Mohana Gurram, Abraham K Ishihara, Carlee Joe-Wong, Christopher Knight, Kalmanje Krishnakumar and Isaias Reyes, et al. DRF: A software architecture for a data marketplace to support advanced air mobility. *AIAA AVIATION 2021 FORUM*, page 2387, 2021.
5. Mahadev Satyanarayanan. The emergence of edge computing. *Computer*, 50(1): 30–39, 2017.
6. David Jeans. Related's Hudson Yards: Smart city or surveillance city? https://therealdeal.com/2019/03/15/hudson-yards-smart-city-or-surveillance-city/, March 2019.
7. Mahadev Satyanarayanan, Victor Bahl, Ramón Caceres and Nigel Davies. The case for VM-based cloudlets in mobile computing. *IEEE Pervasive Computing*, 2009.
8. At&t multi-access edge computing. https://www.business.att.com/products/multi-access-edge-computing.html.
9. Chick-Fil-A Tech Blog. Edge computing at chick-fil-a. https://linkprotect.cudasvc.com/url?a=https%3a%2f%2fmedium.com%2fchick-fil-atech%2fedge-computing-at-chick-fil-a-2621f4b5a969&c=E,1,N1Di1nqD9wfyIPCfjyJagbCWSBRM uvJxzcWefU5iBOREr056Q_yK3PBblYekAaln8lN6r0ipj2ssjAOHlo0vYcYc5k-D4qrcBtYbKbR550hJK0Y7P__tsil4ngQ,,&typo=1.

10. Ian Goodfellow, Yoshua Bengio, Aaron Courville and Yoshua Bengio. *Deep learning*, volume 1. MIT press Cambridge, 2016.
11. Weisong Shi, Jie Cao, Quan Zhang, Youhuizi Li and Lanyu Xu. Edge computing: Vision and challenges. *IEEE Internet of Things Journal*, 3(5):637–646, 2016.
12. Yuyi Mao, Changsheng You, Jun Zhang, Kaibin Huang and Khaled B Letaief. A survey on mobile edge computing: The communication perspective. *IEEE Communications Surveys & Tutorials*, 19(4):2322–2358, 2017.
13. Utsav Drolia, Katherine Guo and Priya Narasimhan. Precog: prefetching for image recognition applications at the edge. In *ACM/IEEE Symposium on Edge Computing*, 2017.
14. He Li, Kaoru Ota and Mianxiong Dong. Learning IoT in edge: Deep learning for the internet of things with edge computing. *IEEE Network*, 32(1):96–101, 2018.
15. Loc N Huynh, Youngki Lee and Rajesh Krishna Balan. Deepmon: Mobile GPU-based deep learning framework for continuous vision applications. In *Proceedings of the 15th Annual International Conference on Mobile Systems, Applications, and Services*, pages 82–95. ACM, 2017.
16. Yiping Kang, Johann Hauswald, Cao Gao, Austin Rovinski, Trevor Mudge, Jason Mars and Lingjia Tang. Neurosurgeon: Collaborative intelligence between the cloud and mobile edge. *ACM SIGPLAN Notices*, 52(4):615–629, 2017.
17. Reza Shokri and Vitaly Shmatikov. Privacy-preserving deep learning. In *Proceedings of the 22nd ACM SIGSAC Conference on Computer and Communications Security*, pages 1310–1321. ACM, 2015.
18. Sebastian Ruder. An overview of gradient descent optimization algorithms. *CoRR*, abs/1609.04747, 2016.
19. Kishore Papineni, Salim Roukos, Todd Ward and Wei-Jing Zhu. Bleu: A method for automatic evaluation of machine translation. In *Proceedings of the 40th Annual Meeting on Association for Computational Linguistics*, pages 311–318. Association for Computational Linguistics, 2002.
20. Jonathan Huang, Vivek Rathod, Chen Sun, Menglong Zhu, Anoop Korattikara, Alireza Fathi, Ian Fischer, Zbigniew Wojna, Yang Song and Sergio Guadarrama, et al. Speed/accuracy trade-offs for modern convolutional object detectors. *IEEE CVPR*, 4, 2017.
21. Joseph Redmon and Ali Farhadi. Yolo9000: Better, faster, stronger. IEEE CVPR, 2017.
22. Zongqing Lu, Swati Rallapalli, Kevin Chan and Thomas La Porta. Modeling the resource requirements of convolutional neural networks on mobile devices. *ACM Multimedia*, 2017.
23. Xukan Ran, Haoliang Chen, Xiaodan Zhu, Zhenming Liu and Jiasi Chen. Deepdecision: A mobile deep learning framework for edge video analytics. *IEEE INFOCOM*, 2018.
24. Andrew G Howard, Menglong Zhu, Bo Chen, Dmitry Kalenichenko, Weijun Wang, Tobias Weyand, Marco Andreetto and Hartwig Adam. MobileNets: Efficient convolutional neural networks for mobile vision applications. *arXiv preprint arXiv:1704.04861*, 2017.
25. Mingxing Tan, Bo Chen, Ruoming Pang, Vijay Vasudevan and Quoc V Le. MnasNet: Platform-aware neural architecture search for mobile. *arXiv preprint arXiv:1807.11626*, 2018.

26. Ben Taylor, Vicent Sanz Marco, Willy Wolff, Yehia Elkhatib and Zheng Wang. Adaptive deep learning model selection on embedded systems. LCTES. ACM, 2018.

27. TensorFlow. https://www.tensorflow.org/.

28. Martn Abadi, Ashish Agarwal, Paul Barham, Eugene Brevdo, Zhifeng Chen, Craig Citro, Gregory S. Corrado, Andy Davis, Jeffrey Dean, Matthieu Devin, Sanjay Ghemawat, Ian J. Goodfellow, Andrew Harp, Geoffrey Irving, Michael Isard, Yangqing Jia, Rafal Józefowicz, Lukasz Kaiser, Manjunath Kudlur, Josh Levenberg, Mané Dan, Rajat Monga, Sherry Moore, Derek Gordon Murray, Chris Olah, Mike Schuster, Jonathon Shlens, Benoit Steiner, Ilya Sutskever, Kunal Talwar, Paul A. Tucker, Vincent Vanhoucke, Vijay Vasudevan, Fernanda B. Viégas, Oriol Vinyals, Pete Warden, Martin Wattenberg, Martin Wicke, Yuan Yu and Xiaoqiang Zheng. TensorFlow: Large-scale machine learning on heterogeneous distributed systems. *CoRR*, abs/1603.04467, 2016.

29. TensorFlow lite. https://www.tensorflow.org/lite.

30. Yangqing Jia, Evan Shelhamer, Jeff Donahue, Sergey Karayev, Jonathan Long, Ross Girshick, Sergio Guadarrama and Trevor Darrell. Caffe: Convolutional architecture for fast feature embedding. In *Proceedings of the 22nd ACM international conference on Multimedia*, pages 675–678. ACM, 2014.

31. Caffe2. https://caffe2.ai/.

32. Caffe. https://caffe.berkeleyvision.org/.

33. Pytorch. https://pytorch.org.

34. NVIDIA. CUDA. https://developer.nvidia.com/cuda-zone.

35. NVIDIA. cuDNN. https://developer.nvidia.com/cudnn.

36. Luyang Liu, Hongyu Li and Macro Gruteser. Edge assisted real-time object detection for mobile augmented reality. *ACM MobiCom*, 2019.

37. Sicong Liu, Yingyan Lin, Zimu Zhou, Kaiming Nan, Hui Liu and Junzhao Du. DeepIoT: Compressing deep neural network structures for sensing systems with a compressor-critic framework. In *Proceedings of SenSys*. ACM, 2017.

38. Xueshi Hou, Sujit Dey, Jianzhong Zhang and Madhukar Budagavi. Predictive view generation to enable mobile 360-degree and VR experiences. In *Proceedings of the 2018 Morning Workshop on Virtual Reality and Augmented Reality Network*, pages 20–26. ACM, 2018.

39. Yanyu Xu, Yanbing Dong, Junru Wu, Zhengzhong Sun, Zhiru Shi, Jingyi Yu and Shenghua Gao. Gaze prediction in dynamic 360 immersive videos. In *Proceedings of the IEEE Conference on Computer Vision and Pattern Recognition*, pages 5333–5342, 2018.

40. Shahryar Afzal, Jiasi Chen and KK Ramakrishnan. Characterization of 360-degree videos. *ACM SIGCOMM Workshop on Virtual Reality and Augmented Reality Network*, 2017.

41. Amit Jindal, Andrew Tulloch, Ben Sharma, Bram Wasti, Fei Yang, Georgia Gkioxari, Jaeyoun Kim, Jason Harrison, Jerry Zhang, Kaiming He, Orion Reblitz-Richardson, Peizhao Zhang, Peter Vajda, Piotr Dollar, Pradheep Elango, Priyam Chatterjee, Rahul Nallamothu, Ross Girshick, Sam Tsai, Su Xue, Vincent Cheung, Yanghan Wang, Yangqing Jia and Zijian He. Enabling full body AR with mask R-CNN2Go. https://research.fb.com/enabling-full-body-ar-with-mask-r-cnn2go/, January 2018.

42. Steven LaValle. *Virtual reality*. Cambridge University Press, 2016.

43. Zhuo Chen, Wenlu Hu, Junjue Wang, Siyan Zhao, Brandon Amos, Guanhang Wu, Kiryong Ha, Khalid Elgazzar, Padmanabhan Pillai and Roberta Klatzky, et al. An empirical study of latency in an emerging class of edge computing applications for wearable cognitive assistance. In *Proceedings of the Second ACM/IEEE Symposium on Edge Computing*, page 14. ACM, 2017.
44. Kiryong Ha, Zhuo Chen, Wenlu Hu, Wolfgang Richter, Padmanabhan Pillai and Mahadev Satyanarayanan. Towards wearable cognitive assistance. *ACM MobiSys*, 2014.
45. Aditya Dhakal, Xukan Ran, Yunshu Wang, Jiasi Chen and K. K. Ramakrishnan. SLAM-share: Visual simultaneous localization and mapping for real-time multi-user augmented reality. In *Proc. ACM CoNEXT*, 2022.
46. Shuochao Yao, Shaohan Hu, Yiran Zhao, Aston Zhang and Tarek Abdelzaher. Deepsense: A unified deep learning framework for time-series mobile sensing data processing. In *Proceedings of the 26th International Conference on World Wide Web*, pages 351–360. International World Wide Web Conferences Steering Committee, 2017.
47. Wanli Ouyang and Xiaogang Wang. Joint deep learning for pedestrian detection. In *Proceedings of the IEEE International Conference on Computer Vision*, pages 2056–2063, 2013.
48. Liangzhi Li, Kaoru Ota and Mianxiong Dong. When weather matters: IoT-based electrical load forecasting for smart grid. *IEEE Communications Magazine*, 55(10):46–51, 2017.
49. Ashish Kumar, Saurabh Goyal and Manik Varma. Resource-efficient machine learning in 2 kb RAM for the internet of things. In *Proceedings of the 34th International Conference on Machine Learning-Volume 70*, pages 1935–1944. JMLR.org, 2017.
50. Zhuoran Zhao, Kamyar Mirzazad Barijough and Andreas Gerstlauer. Deepthings: Distributed adaptive deep learning inference on resource-constrained IoT edge clusters. *IEEE Transactions on Computer-Aided Design of Integrated Circuits and Systems*, 37(11):2348–2359, 2018.
51. Mehdi Mohammadi, Ala Al-Fuqaha, Sameh Sorour and Mohsen Guizani. Deep learning for IoT big data and streaming analytics: A survey. *IEEE Communications Surveys & Tutorials*, 20(4):2923–2960, 2018.
52. Amazon. Aws deeplens. https://aws.amazon.com/deeplens/.
53. Shaoqing Ren, Kaiming He, Ross Girshick and Jian Sun. Faster r-CNN: Towards real-time object detection with region proposal networks. *Advances in Neural Information Processing Systems*, 91–99, 2015.
54. Tan Zhang, Aakanksha Chowdhery, Paramvir Victor Bahl, Kyle Jamieson and Suman Banerjee. The design and implementation of a wireless video surveillance system. In *Proceedings of the 21st Annual International Conference on Mobile Computing and Networking*, pages 426–438. ACM, 2015.
55. Chien-Chun Hung, Ganesh Ananthanarayanan, Peter Bodik, Leana Golubchik, Minlan Yu, Paramvir Bahl and Matthai Philipose. Videoedge: Processing camera streams using hierarchical clusters. *2018 IEEE/ACM Symposium on Edge Computing (SEC)*, pages 115–131. IEEE, 2018.
56. Tom Young, Devamanyu Hazarika, Soujanya Poria and Erik Cambria. Recent trends in deep learning based natural language processing. *IEEE Computational Intelligence Magazine*, 13(3):55–75, 2018.

57. Apple. Deep learning for Siri's voice: On-device deep mixture density networks for hybrid unit selection synthesis. https://machinelearning.apple.com/2017/08/06/siri-voices.html.

58. Guillaume Lample, Miguel Ballesteros, Sandeep Subramanian, Kazuya Kawakami and Chris Dyer. Neural architectures for named entity recognition. *arXiv preprint arXiv:1603.01360*, 2016.

59. Yonghui Wu, Mike Schuster, Zhifeng Chen, Quoc V Le, Mohammad Norouzi, Wolfgang Macherey, Maxim Krikun, Yuan Cao, Qin Gao and Klaus Macherey, et al. Google's neural machine translation system: Bridging the gap between human and machine translation. *arXiv preprint arXiv:1609.08144*, 2016.

60. Google AI Blog. Google duplex: An ai system for accomplishing real-world tasks over the phone. https://ai.googleblog.com/2018/05/duplex-ai-system-for-natural-conversation.html.

61. Stanislaw Antol, Aishwarya Agrawal, Jiasen Lu, Margaret Mitchell, Dhruv Batra, C Lawrence Zitnick and Devi Parikh. VQA: Visual question answering. In *Proceedings of the IEEE International Conference on Computer Vision*, pages 2425–2433, 2015.

62. Google. Pagespeed insights: Improve server response time.

63. Apple. Hey Siri: An on-device DNN-powered voice trigger for Apple's personal assistant. https://machinelearning.apple.com/2017/10/01/hey-siri.html, 2017.

64. Aditya Kusupati, Manish Singh, Kush Bhatia, Ashish Kumar, Prateek Jain and Manik Varma. FastGRNN: A fast, accurate, stable and tiny kilobyte sized gated recurrent neural network. *Advances in Neural Information Processing Systems*, 9017–9028, 2018.

65. Raymond Wong. Google's pixel buds are no match for professional interpreters. https://mashable.com/2017/12/05/google-pixel-buds-real-time-translations-vs-un-interpreter/?europe=true.

66. Wei Liu, Dragomir Anguelov, Dumitru Erhan, Christian Szegedy, Scott Reed, Cheng-Yang Fu and Alexander C Berg. SSD: Single shot multibox detector. In *European conference on computer vision*, pages 21–37. Springer, 2016.

67. Forrest N Iandola, Song Han, Matthew W Moskewicz, Khalid Ashraf, William J Dally and Kurt Keutzer. SqueezeNet: AlexNet-level accuracy with 50x fewer parameters and < 0.5 mb model size. *arXiv preprint arXiv:1602.07360*, 2016.

68. Song Han, Huizi Mao and William J Dally. Deep compression: Compressing deep neural networks with pruning, trained quantization and Huffman coding. *arXiv preprint arXiv:1510.00149*, 2015.

69. Liangzhen Lai and Naveen Suda. Enabling deep learning at the IoT edge. In *Proceedings of the International Conference on Computer-Aided Design*, ICCAD '18. ACM, 2018.

70. Song Han, Junlong Kang, Huizi Mao, Yiming Hu, Xin Li, Yubin Li, Dongliang Xie, Hong Luo, Song Yao, Yu Wang, Huazhong Yang and William (Bill) J. Dally. ESE: Efficient speech recognition engine with sparse LSTM on FPGA. In *Proceedings of the 2017 ACM/SIGDA International Symposium on Field-Programmable Gate Arrays*, FPGA '17. ACM.

71. Sourav Bhattacharya and Nicholas D. Lane. Sparsification and separation of deep learning layers for constrained resource inference on wearables. In *Proceedings of the 14th ACM Conference on Embedded Network Sensor Systems CD-ROM*, SenSys '16. ACM, 2016.

72. Geoffrey Hinton, Oriol Vinyals and Jeff Dean. Distilling the knowledge in a neural network. *arXiv preprint arXiv:1503.02531*, 2015.

73. Surat Teerapittayanon, Bradley McDanel and HT Kung. BranchyNet: Fast inference via early exiting from deep neural networks. *International Conference on Pattern Recognition*, 2016.

74. Shuochao Yao, Yiran Zhao, Zhang Aston, Lu Su and Tarek Abdelzaher. On-demand deep model compression for mobile devices: A usage-driven model selection framework. In *Proceedings of MobiSys*. ACM, 2018.

75. Loc N. Huynh, Youngki Lee and Rajesh Krishna Balan. Deepmon: Mobile gpu-based deep learning framework for continuous vision applications. *ACM MobiSys*, 2017.

76. Edge TPU. https://cloud.google.com/edge-tpu/.

77. Zidong Du, Robert Fasthuber, Tianshi Chen, Paolo Ienne, Ling Li, Tao Luo, Xiaobing Feng, Yunji Chen and Olivier Temam. Shidiannao: Shifting vision processing closer to the sensor. In *ACM SIGARCH computer architecture news*, volume 43, pages 92–104. ACM, 2015.

78. Yunji Chen, Tianshi Chen, Zhiwei Xu, Ninghui Sun and Olivier Temam. Diannao family: Energy-efficient hardware accelerators for machine learning. *Communications of the ACM*, 59(11):105–112, 2016.

79. Kalin Ovtcharov, Olatunji Ruwase, Joo-Young Kim, Jeremy Fowers, Karin Strauss and S. Eric Chung. Accelerating deep convolutional neural networks using specialized hardware. https://www.microsoft.com/en-us/research/wp-content/uploads/2016/02/CNN20Whitepaper.pdf.

80. VPU. https://www.movidius.com/solutions/vision-processing-unit.

81. S. Rivas-Gomez, A. J. Pena, D. Moloney, E. Laure and S. Markidis. Exploring the vision processing unit as co-processor for inference. *2018 IEEE International Parallel and Distributed Processing Symposium Workshops (IPDPSW)*, pages 589–598, May 2018.

82. Nvidia. Nvidia EGX edge computing platform. https://www.nvidia.com/en-us/data-center/products/egx-edge-computing/.

83. Qualcomm. Qualcomm neural processing SDK for AI. https://developer.qualcomm.com/software/qualcomm-neural-processing-sdk.

84. Moustafa Alzantot, Yingnan Wang, Zhengshuang Ren and Mani B. Srivastava. RSTensorFlow. In *Proceedings of the 1st International Workshop on Deep Learning for Mobile Systems and Applications - EMDL 17*, 2017.

85. Nicholas D. Lane, Sourav Bhattacharya, Petko Georgiev, Claudio Forlivesi, Lei Jiao, Lorena Qendro and Fahim Kawsar. DeepX: A software accelerator for low-power deep learning inference on mobile devices. *2016 15th ACM/IEEE International Conference on Information Processing in Sensor Networks (IPSN)*, 2016.

86. Vivienne Sze, Yu-Hsin Chen, Tien-Ju Yang and Joel S Emer. Efficient processing of deep neural networks: A tutorial and survey. *Proceedings of the IEEE*, 105(12):2295–2329, 2017.

87. Xuyu Wang, Xiangyu Wang and Shiwen Mao. RF sensing in the internet of things: A general deep learning framework. *IEEE Communications Magazine*, 56(9):62–67, 2018.

88. Tiffany Yu-Han Chen, Lenin Ravindranath, Shuo Deng, Paramvir Bahl and Hari Balakrishnan. Glimpse: Continuous, real-time object recognition on mobile devices. *ACM SenSys*, 2015.

89. Chang Liu, Yu Cao, Yan Luo, Guanling Chen, Vinod Vokkarane, Ma Yunsheng, Songqing Chen and Peng Hou. A new deep learning-based food recognition system for dietary assessment on an edge computing service infrastructure. *IEEE Transactions on Services Computing*, 11(2):249–261, 2018.

90. Haoyu Zhang, Ganesh Ananthanarayanan, Peter Bodik, Matthai Philipose, Paramvir Bahl and Michael J Freedman. Live video analytics at scale with approximation and delay-tolerance. USENIX NSDI, 2017.

91. Junchen Jiang, Ganesh Ananthanarayanan, Peter Bodik, Siddhartha Sen and Ion Stoica. Chameleon: scalable adaptation of video analytics. In *Proceedings of the 2018 Conference of the ACM Special Interest Group on Data Communication*, pages 253–266. ACM, 2018.

92. Angela H Jiang, Daniel L-K Wong, Christopher Canel, Lilia Tang, Ishan Misra, Michael Kaminsky, Michael A Kozuch, Padmanabhan Pillai, David G Andersen and Gregory R Ganger. Mainstream: Dynamic stem-sharing for multi-tenant video processing. *2018 USENIX Annual Technical Conference (USENIX ATC 18)*, pages 29–42, 2018.

93. Y. Lecun, L. Bottou, Y. Bengio and P. Haffner. Gradient-based learning applied to document recognition. *Proceedings of the IEEE*, 86(11):2278–2324, 1998.

94. Zhiheng Huang, Wei Xu and Kai Yu. Bidirectional LSTM-CRF models for sequence tagging. *CoRR*, 2015.

95. S. Hochreiter and J. Schmidhuber. Long short-term memory. *Neural Computation*, 1997.

96. Alex Krizhevsky, Ilya Sutskever and Geoffrey E Hinton. ImageNet classification with deep convolutional neural networks. *Advances in Neural Information Processing Systems*, 1097–1105, 2012.

97. Karen Simonyan and Andrew Zisserman. Very deep convolutional networks for large-scale image recognition. *CoRR 1409.1556*, 2014.

98. Andrea Vedaldi and Karel Lenc. MatConvNet. In *Proceedings of the 23rd ACM international conference on Multimedia - MM 15*, 2015.

99. Christian Szegedy, Wei Liu, Yangqing Jia, Pierre Sermanet, Scott E. Reed, Dragomir Anguelov, Dumitru Erhan, Vincent Vanhoucke and Andrew Rabinovich. Going deeper with convolutions. *CoRR*, abs/1409.4842, 2014.

100. Kaiming He, Xiangyu Zhang, Shaoqing Ren and Jian Sun. Deep residual learning for image recognition. *CoRR*, abs/1512.03385, 2015.

101. Seungyeop Han, Haichen Shen, Matthai Philipose, Sharad Agarwal, Alec Wolman and Arvind Krishnamurthy. MCDNN: An approximation-based execution framework for deep stream processing under resource constraints. *ACM Mobisys*, 2016.

102. Yaniv Taigman, Ming Yang, Marcaurelio Ranzato and Lior Wolf. Deepface: Closing the gap to human-level performance in face verification. *2014 IEEE Conference on Computer Vision and Pattern Recognition*, 2014.

103. Jiachen Mao, Xiang Chen, Kent W Nixon, Christopher Krieger and Yiran Chen. MoDNN: Local distributed mobile computing system for deep neural network. *2017 Design, Automation & Test in Europe Conference & Exhibition (DATE)*, pages 1396–1401. IEEE, 2017.

104. ARCore overview. https://mxnet.apache.org/.

105. Surat Teerapittayanon, Bradley McDanel and HT Kung. Distributed deep neural networks over the cloud, the edge and end devices. In *Distributed Computing Systems (ICDCS), 2017 IEEE 37th International Conference on*, pages 328–339. IEEE, 2017.

106. Surat Teerapittayanon, Bradley McDanel and H. T. Kung. BranchyNet: Fast inference via early exiting from deep neural networks. *CoRR*, 2017.

107. Xukan Ran, Haoliang Chen, Zhenming Liu and Jiasi Chen. Delivering deep learning to mobile devices via offloading. *ACM SIGCOMM Workshop on Virtual Reality and Augmented Reality Network*, 2017.

108. Eduardo Cuervo, Aruna Balasubramanian, Dae-ki Cho, Alec Wolman, Stefan Saroiu, Ranveer Chandra and Paramvir Bahl. MAUI: Making smartphones last longer with code offload. *ACM MobiSys*, 2010.

109. Shanhe Yi, Zijiang Hao, Qingyang Zhang, Quan Zhang, Weisong Shi and Qun Li. LAVEA: Latency-aware video analytics on edge computing platform. In *ACM/IEEE Symposium on Edge Computing*, 2017.

110. Moo-Ryong Ra, Anmol Sheth, Lily Mummert, Padmanabhan Pillai, David Wetherall and Ramesh Govindan. Odessa: enabling interactive perception applications on mobile devices. *ACM MobiSys*, 2011.

111. Jeffrey Dean, Greg Corrado, Rajat Monga, Kai Chen, Matthieu Devin, Mark Mao, Andrew Senior, Paul Tucker, Ke Yang and Quoc V Le, et al. Large scale distributed deep networks. *Advances in Neural Information Processing Systems*, 1223–1231, 2012.

112. Dawei Li, Theodoros Salonidis, Nirmit V Desai and Mooi Choo Chuah. DeepCham: Collaborative edge-mediated adaptive deep learning for mobile object recognition. In *Edge Computing (SEC), IEEE/ACM Symposium on*, pages 64–76. IEEE, 2016.

113. Jianmin Chen, Rajat Monga, Samy Bengio and Rafal Józefowicz. Revisiting distributed synchronous SGD. *CoRR*, abs/1604.00981, 2016.

114. Sixin Zhang, Anna E Choromanska and Yann LeCun. Deep learning with elastic averaging sgd. In C. Cortes, N. D. Lawrence, D. D. Lee, M. Sugiyama, and R. Garnett, editors, *Advances in Neural Information Processing Systems 28*, pages 685–693. Curran Associates, Inc., 2015.

115. H Brendan McMahan, Eider Moore, Daniel Ramage and Seth Hampson, et al. Communication-efficient learning of deep networks from decentralized data. *arXiv preprint arXiv:1602.05629*, 2016.

116. Shiqiang Wang, Tiffany Tuor, Theodoros Salonidis, Kin K. Leung, Christian Makaya, Ting He and Kevin Chan. When edge meets learning: Adaptive control for resource-constrained distributed machine learning. *CoRR*, 2018.

117. Kevin Hsieh, Aaron Harlap, Nandita Vijaykumar, Dimitris Konomis, Gregory R. Ganger, Phillip B. Gibbons and Onur Mutlu. Gaia: Geo-distributed machine learning approaching LAN speeds. In *14th USENIX Symposium on Networked Systems Design and Implementation (NSDI 17)*, pages 629–647, Boston, MA. USENIX Association, 2017.

118. Rohan Anil, Gabriel Pereyra, Alexandre Passos, Róbert Ormándi, George E. Dahl and Geoffrey E. Hinton. Large scale distributed neural network training through online distillation. *CoRR*, abs/1804.03235, 2018.

119. Yujun Lin, Song Han, Huizi Mao, Yu Wang and William J. Dally. Deep gradient compression: Reducing the communication bandwidth for distributed training. *CoRR*, abs/1712.01887, 2017.

120. Corentin Hardy and Erwan Le Merrer, and Bruno Sericola. Distributed deep learning on edge-devices: feasibility via adaptive compression. IEEE International Symposium on Network Computing and Applications (NCA), 2017.

121. Michael Blot, David Picard, Matthieu Cord and Nicolas Thome. Gossip training for deep learning. *CoRR*, abs/1611.09726, 2016.

122. Peter H. Jin, Qiaochu Yuan, Forrest N. Iandola and Kurt Keutzer. How to scale distributed deep learning? *CoRR*, abs/1611.04581, 2016.

123. Youjie Li, Jongse Park, Mohammad Alian, Yifan Yuan, Zheng Qu, Peitian Pan, Ren Wang, Alexander Schwing, Hadi Esmaeilzadeh and Nam Kim. A network-centric hardware/algorithm co-design to accelerate distributed training of deep neural networks: IEEE/ACM MICRO. 10:175–188, 2018.

124. Ning Qian. On the momentum term in gradient descent learning algorithms. *Neural Network*, 12(1):145–151, January 1999.

125. Priya Goyal, Piotr Dollár, Ross B. Girshick, Pieter Noordhuis, Lukasz Wesolowski, Aapo Kyrola, Andrew Tulloch, Yangqing Jia and Kaiming He. Accurate, large minibatch SGD: Training ImageNet in 1 hour. *CoRR*, abs/1706.02677, 2017.

126. Corentin Hardy, Erwan Le Merrer and Bruno Sericola. Distributed deep learning on edge-devices: Feasibility via adaptive compression. *Network Computing and Applications (NCA), 2017 IEEE 16th International Symposium on*, pages 1–8. IEEE, 2017.

127. Sanjit Kaul, Roy Yates and Marco Gruteser. Real-time status: How often should one update? In *INFOCOM, 2012 Proceedings IEEE*, pages 2731–2735. IEEE, 2012.

128. Junguk Cho, Karthikeyan Sundaresan, Rajesh Mahindra, Jacobus Van der Merwe and Sampath Rangarajan. Acacia: context-aware edge computing for continuous interactive applications over mobile networks. In *Proceedings of the 12th International on Conference on emerging Networking Experiments and Technologies*, pages 375–389. ACM, 2016.

129. Kiryong Ha, Yoshihisa Abe, Thomas Eiszler, Zhuo Chen, Wenlu Hu, Brandon Amos, Rohit Upadhyaya, Padmanabhan Pillai and Mahadev Satyanarayanan. You can teach elephants to dance: Agile VM handoff for edge computing. In *Proceedings of the Second ACM/IEEE Symposium on Edge Computing*, page 12. ACM, 2017.

130. Lele Ma, Shanhe Yi and Qun Li. Efficient service handoff across edge servers via docker container migration. In *Proceedings of the Second ACM/IEEE Symposium on Edge Computing*, page 11. ACM, 2017.

131. Lucas Chaufournier, Prateek Sharma, Franck Le, Erich Nahum, Prashant Shenoy and Don Towsley. Fast transparent virtual machine migration in distributed edge clouds. In *Proceedings of the Second ACM/IEEE Symposium on Edge Computing*, page 10. ACM, 2017.

132. Alexey Dosovitskiy, Lucas Beyer, Alexander Kolesnikov, Dirk Weissenborn, Xiaohua Zhai, Thomas Unterthiner, Mostafa Dehghani, Matthias Minderer, Georg Heigold and Sylvain Gelly, et al. An image is worth 16x16 words: Transformers for image recognition at scale. *ICLR*, 2021.

133. Jake Ryan, Meng-Jang Lin and Risto Miikkulainen. Intrusion detection with neural networks. *Advances in Neural Information Processing Systems*, 943–949, 1998.

134. Yisroel Mirsky, Tomer Doitshman, Yuval Elovici and Asaf Shabtai. Kitsune: an ensemble of autoencoders for online network intrusion detection. *arXiv preprint arXiv:1802.09089*, 2018.

135. Sandeep Chinchali, Pan Hu, Tianshu Chu, Manu Sharma, Manu Bansal, Rakesh Misra, Marco Pavone and Sachin Katti. Cellular network traffic scheduling with deep reinforcement learning. *Thirty-Second AAAI Conference on Artificial Intelligence*, 2018.

136. Nikos Tsikoudis, Antonis Papadogiannakis and Evangelos P Markatos. Leonids: A low-latency and energy-efficient network-level intrusion detection system. *IEEE Transactions on Emerging Topics in Computing*, 4(1):142–155, 2016.

137. Hao Zhu, Yang Cao, Wei Wang, Tao Jiang and Shi Jin. Deep reinforcement learning for mobile edge caching: Review, new features, and open issues. *IEEE Network*, 32(6):50–57, 2018.

138. Yuris Mulya Saputra, Dinh Thai Hoang, Diep N. Nguyen, Eryk Dutkiewicz, Dusit Niyato and Dong In Kim. Distributed deep learning at the edge: A novel proactive and cooperative caching framework for mobile edge networks. *CoRR*, 2018.

139. Zhong Chen, Cenk Gursoy Mustafa and Velipasalar Senem. A deep reinforcement learning-based framework for content caching. *CoRR*, 2017.

140. Wei Zhang, Jinho Hwang, Shriram Rajagopalan, KK Ramakrishnan and Timothy Wood. Flurries: Countless fine-grained NFS for flexible per-flow customization. In *Proceedings of the 12th International on Conference on emerging Networking Experiments and Technologies*, pages 3–17. ACM, 2016.

141. Konstantinos Samdanis and Tarik Taleb. The road beyond 5g: A vision and insight of the key technologies. *IEEE Network*, 34(2):135–141, 2020.

142. Solmaz Niknam, Harpreet S Dhillon and Jeffrey H Reed. Federated learning for wireless communications: Motivation, opportunities, and challenges. *IEEE Communications Magazine*, 58(6):46–51, 2020.

143. Chaoyun Zhang, Marco Fiore, Cezary Ziemlicki and Paul Patras. Microscope: Mobile service traffic decomposition for network slicing as a service. In *Proceedings of the 26th Annual International Conference on Mobile Computing and Networking*, pages 1–14, 2020.

144. Jinghao Zhao, Zhaowei Tan, Yifei Xu, Zhehui Zhang and Songwu Lu. Seed: A sim-based solution to 5g failures. In *Proceedings of the ACM SIGCOMM 2022 Conference*, pages 129–142, 2022.

145. Amit Sheoran, Sonia Fahmy, Matthew Osinski, Chunyi Peng, Bruno Ribeiro and Jia Wang. Experience: Towards automated customer issue resolution in cellular networks. In *Proceedings of the 26th Annual International Conference on Mobile Computing and Networking*, pages 1–13, 2020.

146. Yuanjie Li, Qianru Li, Zhehui Zhang, Ghufran Baig, Lili Qiu and Songwu Lu. Beyond 5g: Reliable extreme mobility management. In *Proceedings of the Annual conference of the ACM Special Interest Group on Data Communication on the applications, technologies, architectures, and protocols for computer communication*, pages 344–358, 2020.

147. Zhihao Shen, Wan Du, Xi Zhao and Jianhua Zou. DMM: Fast map matching for cellular data. In *Proceedings of the 26th Annual International Conference on Mobile Computing and Networking*, pages 1–14, 2020.

148. Jun Du, Chunxiao Jiang, Jian Wang, Yong Ren and Merouane Debbah. Machine learning for 6g wireless networks: Carrying forward enhanced bandwidth, massive access, and ultrareliable/low-latency service. *IEEE Vehicular Technology Magazine*, 15(4):122–134, 2020.

149. Zhaowei Tan, Yifei Xu and Songwu Lu. Device-based lte latency reduction at the application layer. In *NSDI*, pages 471–486, 2021.

150. Yuqiang Heng and Jeffrey G Andrews. Machine learning-assisted beam alignment for mmwave systems. *IEEE Transactions on Cognitive Communications and Networking*, 7(4):1142–1155, 2021.

151. Ke Ma, Zhaocheng Wang, Wenqiang Tian, Sheng Chen and Lajos Hanzo. Deep learning for mmwave beam-management: State-of-the-art, opportunities and challenges. *IEEE Wireless Communications*, 2022.

152. Muhammad Alrabeiah and Ahmed Alkhateeb. Deep learning for mmwave beam and blockage prediction using sub-6 GHZ channels. *IEEE Transactions on Communications*, 68(9):5504–5518, 2020.

153. Ajay Mahimkar, Ashiwan Sivakumar, Zihui Ge, Shomik Pathak and Karunasish Biswas. Auric: Using data-driven recommendation to automatically generate cellular configuration. In *Proceedings of the 2021 ACM SIGCOMM 2021 Conference*, pages 807–820, 2021.

154. Robert LiKamWa, Bodhi Priyantha, Matthai Philipose, Lin Zhong and Paramvir Bahl. Energy characterization and optimization of image sensing toward continuous mobile vision. In *Proceeding of the 11th Annual International Conference on Mobile Systems, Applications, and Services*, pages 69–82. ACM, 2013.

155. Saman Naderiparizi, Pengyu Zhang, Matthai Philipose, Bodhi Priyantha, Jie Liu and Deepak Ganesan. Glimpse: A programmable early-discard camera architecture for continuous mobile vision. In *Proceedings of the 15th Annual International Conference on Mobile Systems, Applications, and Services*, pages 292–305. ACM, 2017.

156. Reza Shokri, Marco Stronati, Congzheng Song and Vitaly Shmatikov. Membership inference attacks against machine learning models. In *Security and Privacy (SP), 2017 IEEE Symposium on*, pages 3–18. IEEE, 2017.

157. Cynthia Dwork, Frank McSherry, Kobbi Nissim and Adam Smith. Calibrating noise to sensitivity in private data analysis. In *Theory of cryptography conference*, pages 265–284. Springer, 2006.

Chapter 6

Intelligent edge computing for B5G networks

Prabhu Kaliyammal Thiruvasagam
and Manikantan Srinivasan
NEC Corporation India
Chennai, India
Indian Institute of Technology Madras
Chennai, India

6.1 INTRODUCTION

Network operators (NOs) have rolled out 5G networks and services all over the world, based on the 3rd Generation Partnership Project (3GPP) Releases 15 and 16, in phases [1, 2]. 5G networks are envisioned to support new use cases and business models and to satisfy future end-user needs (e.g., quality of experience [QoE]) [3]. The initial focus of 5G was to support enhanced mobile broadband (eMBB), massive machine-type communications (mMTC), and some ultra-reliable and low-latency communications (URLLC) use cases [4–6]. 3GPP Releases 17 and 18 are focusing on enhancements for 5G system (5GS) architecture to further expand use cases with the help of emerging technologies [7, 8]. To support real-time services and new use cases for multiple industry verticals while ensuring energy efficiency and sustainability, researchers from industries, academia, governments, and standards bodies across the globe have already started to work on the innovations of beyond-5G (B5G) networks [9–14]. The B5G network is expected to become the key infrastructure for providing real-time services to multiple industry verticals and societies in the 2030s [11]. It is also expected that B5G networks will act as drivers for achieving the United Nations' Sustainable Development Goals [13, 15].

B5G networks are envisioned to provide both human-centric and machine-centric services through billions of heterogeneous internet of things (IoT) devices [13, 16]. Hence, B5G is expected to support multiple industry verticals such as transportation, food and agriculture, healthcare, energy, manufacturing, entertainment and gaming, and smart cities. Industry vertical applications (e.g., self-driving vehicles and remote surgery) require highly reliable, low-latency, and secure communications [6]. To support services that require low latency to communicate securely in real time, a new networking paradigm called edge computing (EC) was introduced by a leading telecom operators and vendors [17].

EC is considered as one of the key pillars for 5G and beyond networks to meet the key performance indicators (KPIs) of multiple industry verticals [6, 18]. EC provides cloud computing capabilities and an IT service environment at

DOI: 10.1201/9781003303527-7

the edge of the network to process and store data close to the end users, which enables new business models to support multiple use cases and applications [17, 19]. EC was first initiated in the European Telecommunications Standards Institute (ETSI) in 2014 by a group of leading network operators and vendors as an Industry Specification Group (ISG) for multi-access edge computing (MEC) [17]. The purpose is to create a standardized and open environment to allow an efficient and seamless integration of applications from multiple parties such as network operators, service providers, vendors, and application developers. MEC was initially referred to as mobile edge computing [17]. The ETSI MEC ISG specifies the elements that are required to enable applications to be hosted in a multi-vendor and multi-access edge computing environment [20].

EC has evolved from cloud computing, and it moves computing and networking facilities from the centralized core cloud to the network edge in order to reduce latency and enhance security [17]. EC enables the hosting of services at the network edge that is close to the customer's location where the data is being generated [18]. The locations for EC clouds can be chosen carefully to cover an entire region with a minimum number of edge clouds while satisfying the service requirements of the users [21]. Integrating EC with B5G is essential for enabling versatile service platforms for various industry verticals and other segments. EC is particularly suitable for applications and services that are concerned about low latency, security, and bandwidth efficiency. EC plays a transformative role for the telecommunications business to support industry verticals and other customer-specific segments of society [18]. Since EC can be an enabler for various B5G edge use cases (e.g., autonomous vehicles and remote surgery), and it is suitable for multiple access technologies (e.g., 3GPP access and non-3GPP access), EC plays a vital role in B5G networks [6].

Furthermore, B5G networks are expected to be smart enough to make intelligent decisions automatically and to dynamically support the on-demand provisioning of services that require fast responses to meet the service requirements of customers [13]. It is also expected that B5G networks provide support to detect and recover network functions from failures quickly in order to maintain service continuity and enhance the QoE of users. But, these operations are so complex and beyond the capacity of human operators that it necessitates full automation to perform these operations instantly [22]. Hence, B5G networks rely on artificial intelligence (AI) and machine learning (ML) techniques to make such smart and right decisions automatically and to enable fully automated operations.

Integrating EC and AI/ML techniques into B5G networks is essential to enable innovative real-time and critical use cases and applications for multiple industry verticals such as smart manufacturing, intelligent transportation systems, gaming and entertainment, and e-healthcare [22, 23]. The data-driven AI/ML techniques train models using EC resources at the edge of the network, and use the trained models to make smart and right decisions autonomously in a short time. AI/ML-based distributed edge networks are expected to play a crucial role in B5G and 6G networks to realize the vision of 2030 [22].

In this chapter, we discuss the roles of EC and AI/ML techniques in B5G networks to enable ultra-low-latency services and self-learning, respectively, to ensure service continuity and to enhance the quality of service and experience of users. The rest of the chapter is structured as follows. Section 6.2 presents EC architecture and how EC can be integrated with a B5G system from a standardization point of view. Section 6.3 presents some of the key technology enablers for EC in B5G networks. Section 6.4 presents the role of AI/ML in B5G edge networks. Section 6.5 presents some future research directions in the area of AI/ML at B5G edge networks. Section 6.6 concludes the chapter.

6.2 EDGE COMPUTING ARCHITECTURE AND A STANDARDIZATION POINT OF VIEW

In this section, we discuss EC architecture and how EC can be considered as a part of B5G networks from a standardization point of view. Different standards development organizations (SDOs) and their market representation partners work to define and develop standards for EC to have a common platform for supporting new applications and interoperability in B5G networks [18].

6.2.1 EC at the ETSI MEC ISG

Figure 6.1 shows the ETSI MEC ISG's defined framework for MEC. The MEC framework is grouped into system-level, host-level, and network-level entities [24]. The management layer at host- and system-level administrative entities provides the foundation to operate in a distributed environment for instantiating and scaling mobile applications and services in a highly granular and dynamic manner. MEC framework–supported architecture enables the implementation of MEC applications as software modules that run on top of a virtualization infrastructure in the MEC host, and these applications are managed by the MEC platform [24].

The ETSI MEC ISG also defined the generic multi-access edge system reference architecture, which is shown in Figure 6.2; it consists of the MEC hosts and the MEC management system to run applications in an operator network [24]. In this reference architecture, three groups of reference points are defined between different system entities: (1) MEC platform-related reference points (Mp), (2) MEC management-related reference points (Mm), and (3) reference points connecting to external entities (Mx) [24].

A MEC system-level entity includes user devices, third-party entities (e.g., commercial enterprises), and MEC system-level management functions. MEC system-level management functions (the MEC orchestrator and operations support system) maintain an overall view of the MEC system based on the deployed MEC hosts, available resources, available MEC services, and network topology. A MEC host includes virtualization infrastructure, MEC applications, and the MEC platform. A virtualization infrastructure provides compute, network,

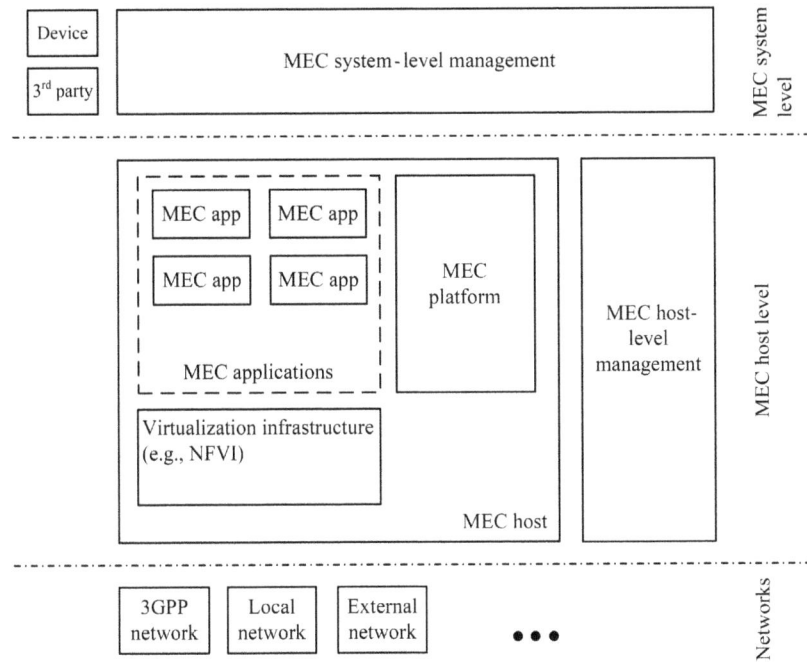

Figure 6.1 MEC framework.

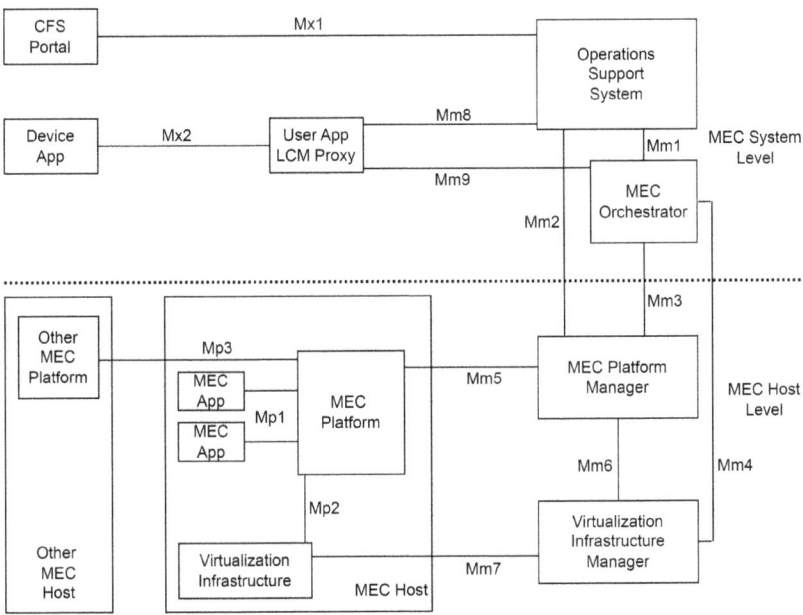

Figure 6.2 Multi-access edge system reference architecture.

and storage resources to run MEC applications as software modules. A MEC platform consists of essential functionalities (a MEC service, a service registry, traffic rules control, and DNS handling) to run MEC applications on top of a virtualization infrastructure. The services produced by MEC applications are registered in the service registry of the MEC platform. Service registration is part of the application enablement functionality [25]. MEC host-level management functions (a virtualization infrastructure manager and MEC platform manager) coordinate with the MEC host for lifecycle management of MEC applications and MEC platforms. MEC hosts can be connected with other MEC hosts. A MEC network-level entity can consist of different networks, which could be a subset of an operator network or some external network that is allowed to provide services on behalf of the network operator. An entire MEC system can be connected with other MEC systems through a MEC federation. MEC also allows direct access to real-time radio network information (e.g., subscriber location and cell load), which can be used by MEC applications to offer context- and location-related services [17].

6.2.2 EC at 3GPP

6.2.2.1 Networking-layer perspective

3GPP defines the 5G system (5GS) architecture as a service-based architecture (SBA) to cater to a wide range of use cases [26]. An enhanced 5GS SBA supporting EC is shown in Figure 6.3 [27]. The 5GS consists of user equipment (UE), a 5G access network (5G AN), and a 5G core network (5G CN). The 5G

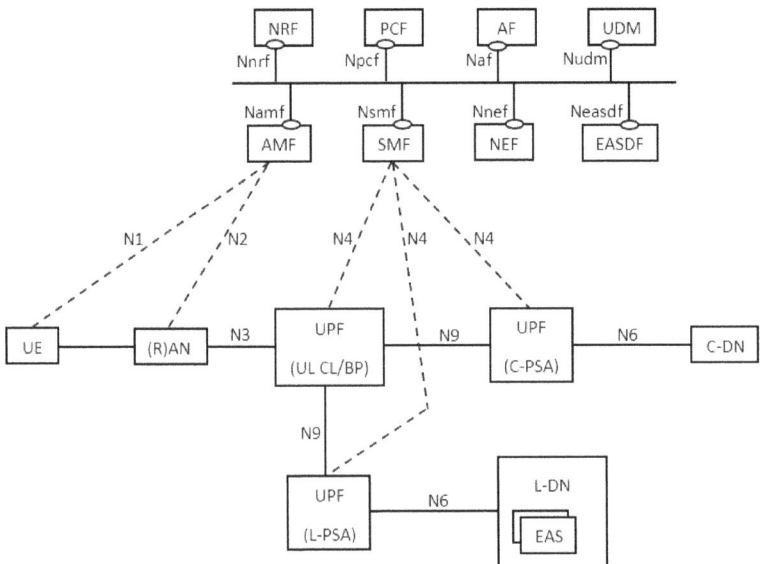

Figure 6.3 The enhanced 5G system architecture supporting edge computing.

AN supports both 3GPP access and non-3GPP access types, and it connects with a common 5G CN. The 5GS architecture separates user plane functions (UPFs) from control plane functions (CPFs) to allow scalability and flexible deployments. Since the 5GS architecture is designed as SBA, both service-based representation (e.g., Nnamf) and point-to-point representation (e.g., N4) are used for interactions between any two network functions. Multiple control plane (CP) network functions in the 5G core (5GC) are used to set up a connection between a UE and UPF to access services from a data network (DN) by establishing a protocol data unit (PDU) session. The UPF is acting as a PDU session anchor (PSA). The access and mobility management function (AMF) is responsible for providing access and handling the mobility of UE, and the session management function (SMF) is responsible for assigning Internet Protocol (IP) addresses to UEs and selecting UPFs for establishing PDU sessions.

The 5GS SBA supports communications between the core network CP functions via the service-based interfaces (SBIs). The core network CP functions can act as service providers and service consumers, and they provide and consume services using SBIs. The 5GS SBA application programming interface (API) framework supports a flexible way to efficiently expose and consume services from different core network functions through a network exposure function (NEF), and a common API framework for 3GPP northbound APIs is defined to securely expose and access services from network functions [28]. The core network functions and the services they offer are registered in the common network function called the network repository function (NRF). Hence, information about the list of available services provided by different CP network functions can be obtained from the NRF. The policy control function (PCF) is responsible for creating policy and charging control (PCC) rules and enforcing PCC rules on PDU sessions through the SMF and UPF. User subscription data and policy control data are managed by the unified data management (UDM) function. The application function (AF) is responsible for managing application servers and routing/steering service traffic through the SMF and UPF to a particular DN based on the demand and resource availability by altering PCC rules via the NEF and PCF.

The enhanced 5GS architecture supports an edge hosting environment (EHE). The EHE can be deployed in the local part of DN close to the UE's access point of attachment to achieve an efficient service delivery through the reduced end-to-end latency and load on the transport network [27]. The EHE provides support for executing edge application servers (EASs). The edge application server discovery function (EASDF) is introduced in the enhanced 5GS architecture supporting EC as shown in Figure 6.3 [27]. The EASDF supports UEs to discover a suitable EAS that is close to the UE's location to access edge application services. In the enhanced 5GS architecture, the UPF uplink classifier (UL CL) or uplink branching point (UL BP) is used for diverting certain user plane traffic to the local part of the DN, according to the classification rule given by the PCF, and the remaining traffic is routed to a central DN (C-DN) through a central PSA (C-PSA) UPF. The UE traffic that is allowed to access services from an EAS deployed in the local DN (L-DN) is routed to an EAS with the help of a UPF UL CL/BP and a local PSA (L-PSA) UPF. The EASDF is used to discover or rediscover a suitable EAS for UEs to access services and to relocate the EAS to a different DN in the case of UE mobility and/or application mobility due to maintenance or overloading.

6.2.2.2 Application-layer perspective

3GPP defined the application-layer architecture for enabling edge applications over 3GPP networks, which is shown in Figure 6.4. The architecture for enabling edge applications includes UE with an application client (AC) and edge enabler client (EEC), a 3GPP core network, an edge data network (EDN) with EASs and edge enabler servers (EESs), and an edge configuration server (ECS) [29]. In this architecture, interactions between any two entities (e.g., EEC and EES) are represented by point-to-point reference points (e.g., EDGE-1).

The EEC provides supporting functions (e.g., getting EES and EDN details from the ECS, registering with the EES, and getting suitable EAS details) needed for ACs to access services from the EAS. The ECS provides supporting functions (e.g., providing the unique identity of the EES with EDN details, registering different EES details, and providing a target location of the EES) needed for the EEC to connect with the EES. The EES provides supporting functions (e.g. registering EAS details and performing application context relocation) needed for the EAS and ECS, such that the AC can access services from a suitable EAS. The EAS is performing the application server functions, and it resides in the EDN. The EAS, the EES, and the ECS can interact with the 3GPP core network to expose EAS capabilities and consume 5GC services. The 3GPP core network provides connectivity for UEs and ACs to access services from EDNs.

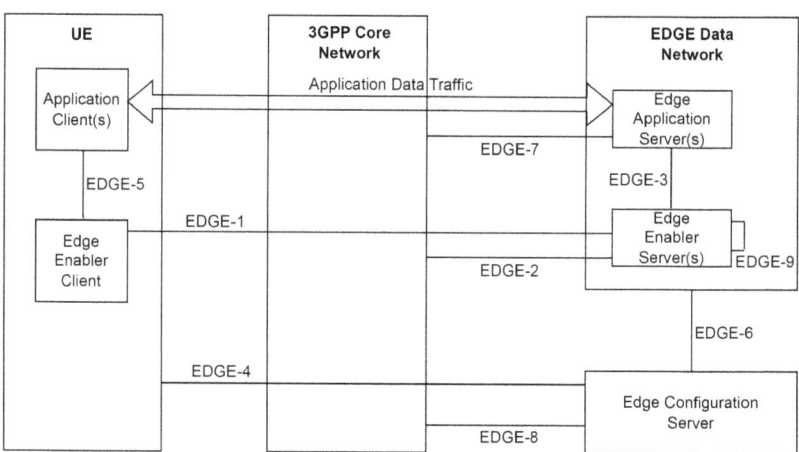

Figure 6.4 Architecture for enabling edge applications over 3GPP networks.

6.2.2.3 Other variants

MEC can be integrated with the 5G and B5G networks in multiple ways (e.g., MEC as an external or third-party AF in the 5GS), as discussed in Ref. [18]. However, an option that supports EC deployment close to the end users is preferred in order to minimize latency and enhance security. EC can also be integrated with multiconnectivity-enabled 5GS to improve the reliability of edge nodes, communication links, and services [30].

6.2.3 Relationship between ETSI MEC and 3GPP EC architectures

ETSI MEC ISG architecture and 3GPP EC application-layer architecture for enabling edge applications over 3GPP networks can complement each other. Both EASs in 3GPP architecture for enabling edge applications and the MEC application in ETSI MEC ISG reference architecture are application servers, and they can provide similar application-specific functionalities. Both EESs and MEC platforms provide application support capabilities for application servers (EASs and MEC applications). An EAS utilizes the services of EESs, and a MEC application utilizes the services of a MEC platform via EDGE-3 and Mp1 reference points. The EAS and MEC application can be collocated in an implementation to utilize the services offered by both the EES and MEC platform [24]. Similarly, the EES and MEC platform can be collocated in an implementation [29]. The EDGE-3 and Mp1 reference points and EDGE-9 and Mp3 reference points can be grouped. The alignment of these reference points is implementation specific [29]. The EES provides supporting functions not only to EASs but also to EECs residing in UEs, whereas the MEC platform provides support to MEC applications via a Mp1 reference point, and it is involved in MEC application management with the MEC platform manager via a Mp5 reference point. UEs can interact directly with the EES via an EDGE-1 reference point in 3GPP architecture for enabling edge applications, whereas UEs do not interact directly with the MEC platform and make requests via a Mx2 reference point [24]. As there are direct relations and differences between the functionalities of the entities involved in both the 3GPP EC and ETSI MEC architectures, collocation of entities and alignment of reference points are implementation specific.

6.3 KEY TECHNOLOGY ENABLERS FOR EDGE COMPUTING IN B5G NETWORKS

B5G edge networks that leverage the features of network functions virtualization (NFV), software-defined networking (SDN), service function chaining (SFC), and network slicing provide both human-centric and machine-centric services dynamically to utilize available resources efficiently, and to meet the diverse service requirements of users and industry verticals. An enhanced

5GS SBA supporting EC can leverage these technologies to make the network more flexible and scalable in order to construct slices and provision services dynamically as per demand.

6.3.1 Network functions virtualization

The NFV concept was introduced in 2012, and the specifications for NFV have been managed by the ETSI NFV ISG [31]. To date, the ETSI NFV ISG has created a number of technical specifications and reports, including an NFV reference architectural framework [32].

NFV decouples network functions from specialized hardware appliances by using a virtualization technique without affecting functionality [31]. NFV enables the transfer of network functions from dedicated hardware appliances to software-based applications. NFV gives network operators the ability to run and consolidate many physical network functions as software modules on top of virtual machines or containers using commercial off-the-shelf hardware (e.g., general purpose servers and storage devices), which brings flexibility, scalability, cost efficiency, and agility to network design and operations management [32]. The transferred network functions obtained through a software virtualization technique are referred to as virtualized network functions (VNFs).

Figure 6.5 shows the reference architectural framework of ETSI NFV. The framework consists of the NFV infrastructure (NFVI) layer, VNF layer, operations support system (OSS) or business support system (BSS) layer, and management and orchestration (MANO) layer [32]. Both physical and virtual resources reside at the NFVI layer, forming a cloud network infrastructure

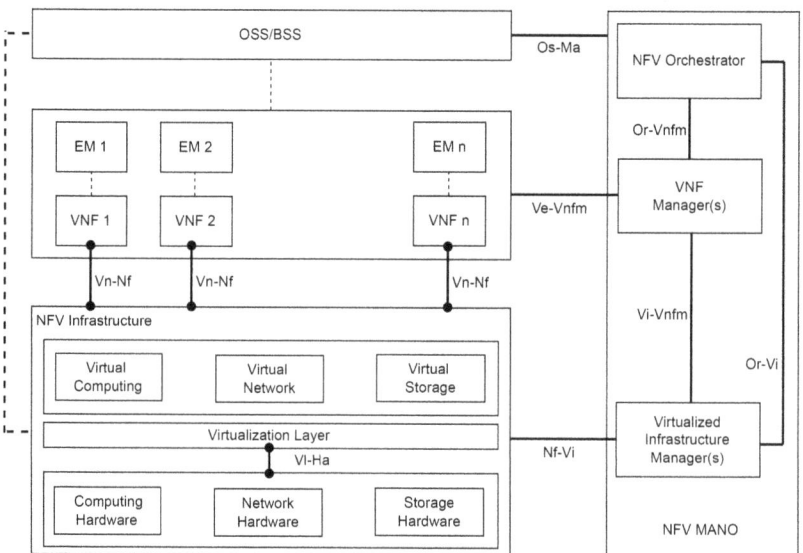

Figure 6.5 ETSI NFV reference architectural framework.

to provide services through the virtual network. The virtualization layer in NFVI is a virtual machine manager, container manager, or cloud operating system, which is used to virtualize the underlying physical network resources. VNFs can be deployed using either virtual machines or containers on top of NFVI. The MANO layer consists of three functional blocks, which are (1) the virtual infrastructure manager (VIM), (2) VNF managers (VNFMs), and (3) the NFV orchestrator (NFVO). The NFVO is responsible for lifecycle management of network services, management of global resources, management of network service deployment templates, and VNF packages management. In addition, the NFVO performs infrastructure resource requests validation and authorization, network service instances performance, and policy management. The VNFM controls and manages the lifecycle management of VNF instances and element managers. The VIM controls and manages the infrastructure resources, lifecycle management of software images, and collection of performance and fault information of hardware and software resources. Lifecycle management supported by different entities (e.g., the NFVO and VNFM) includes many operations such as preparation, instantiation, scaling, migration, performance monitoring, and termination.

NFV is considered as one of the key technology enablers for 5G and beyond future networks [33, 34]. ETSI MEC can be deployed in an NFV environment to leverage the features of NFV [24]. The NFV components can be used in MEC reference architecture (as shown in Figure 6.2) in the following manner [24]:

- The MEC platform and MEC applications can be deployed as VNFs on top of virtualization infrastructure.
- The virtualization infrastructure can be deployed as NFVI.
- NFVI virtualized infrastructure can be managed by the VIM of NFV reference architecture [32].
- The MEC platform manager can be replaced by one or more VNFMs to handle lifecycle management of VNFs.
- The MEC orchestrator can be replaced by the MEC application orchestrator and NFVO for resource and service orchestration.

Network functions that support services in B5G edge networks can be deployed as VNFs (e.g., using virtual machines or containers) on top of an NFV platform. NFV MANO can be used to manage resources and services at B5G edge networks. The NFV MANO and application enablement functions can be used to enable service environments in edge data centers, and the service APIs can be used to enable the exposure of underlying network information and capabilities to applications [19, 26].

6.3.2 Software-defined networking

Traditional networking devices (e.g., routers and switches) have an in-built control plane and data plane for identifying routing paths in the network and forwarding data packets via those paths, respectively. Networking devices run distributed control plane software to manage complex networks. Since vendor-developed control plane software is proprietary and closed, running new routing algorithms and changing flow table entries according to the user's need are not easy, and this hinders innovation in network traffic management [35].

The SDN concept was developed from an academic project [36], and it is presently managed and accelerated by the Open Networking Foundation. SDN enables more flexibility and easy network management by allowing the physical separation of the network control plane from the user data-forwarding plane in discrete networking devices [37]. The separated CPF is centralized logically to control multiple networking devices with the help of one or more SDN controllers.

Figure 6.6 shows an aerial view of an SDN architectural framework. The simplified SDN architecture has three layers [38]: (1) the application layer hosts applications, and the northbound interface enables relaying information between the controller and the applications; (2) the controller layer acts as a network operating system that enables network management and control, automation, and policy enforcement across physical and virtual environments; and (3) the infrastructure layer consists of physical networking elements or devices (e.g., routers, switches, and a firewall), and the southbound interface enables relaying information between the controller and the individual networking device.

An inside view of an OpenFlow-enabled SDN switch is shown in Figure 6.7. Secure communication between the controller and networking device is facilitated by the OpenFlow protocol [36, 39]. An SDN controller can directly modify

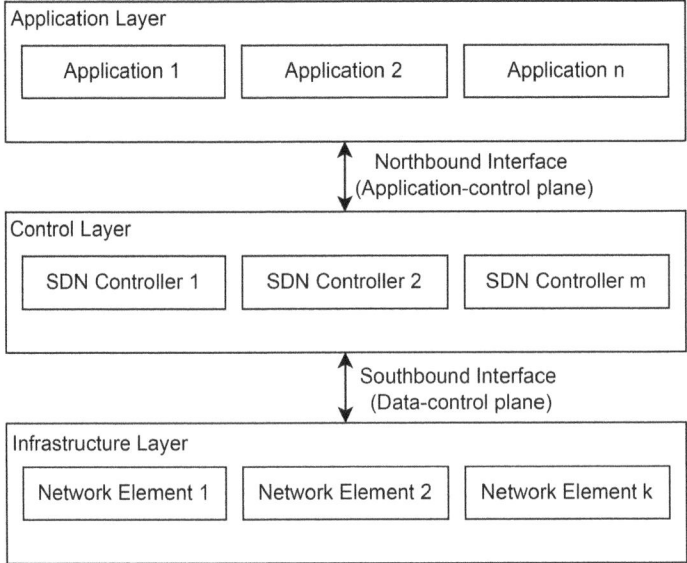

Figure 6.6 Aerial view of an SDN architectural framework.

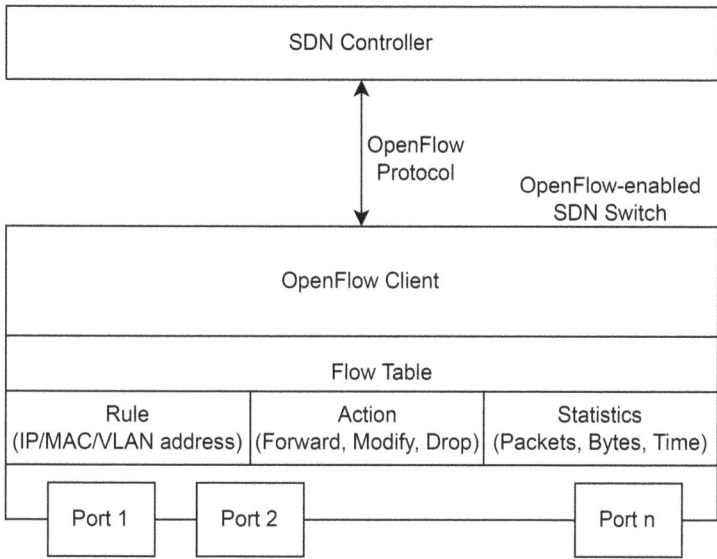

Figure 6.7 Inside view of an OpenFlow-enabled SDN switch.

the rule and actions in the flow table entry, and the statistics column in the flow table collects traffic information that can be used for further analysis.

MEC can use SDN-enabled networking devices to dynamically route the traffics to different VNFs (deployed on top of NFVI) by altering the flow table using SDN controllers. The 3GPP 5GS SBA leverages the concept of SDN (it separates the UPFs from CPFs) to allow independent scalability and flexible deployments [26].

6.3.3 Service function chaining

Network operators deploy multiple network functions (a network function also known as a service function or middlebox) to deliver end-to-end services by steering the service traffic through a series of network functions. In general, a service chain is created to deliver a service by deploying the required network functions and connecting them in a sequential order to steer the traffic through them as per the service policy [40]. The set of network functions required to provide service to a user will vary depending on the service or application type. In traditional networks, network functions are tightly coupled with network topology and physical resources; hence, the deployment model is rigid and static [40].

SFC is a mechanism that allows various network functions to be connected in an ordered form to create a service in a dynamic manner by leveraging the features of NFV and SDN. In NFV- and SDN-enabled 5G networks, SFC can be constructed to provide a specific service by instantiating a set of VNFs

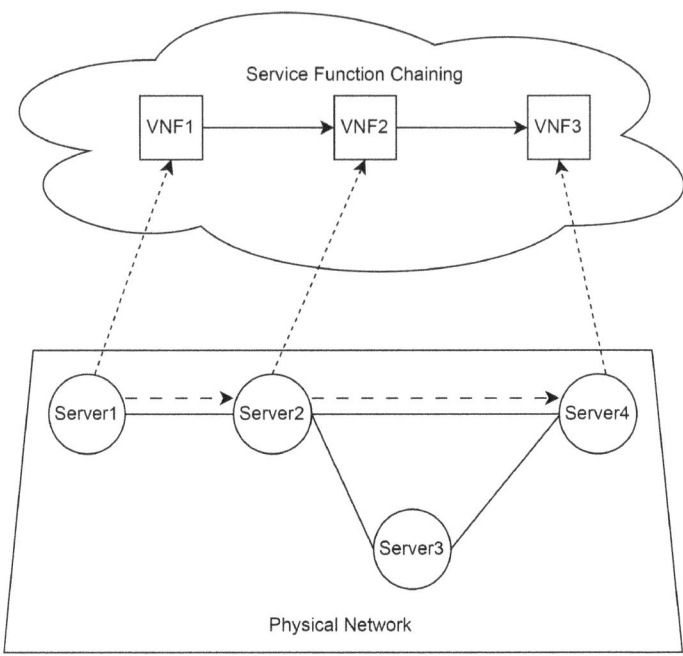

Figure 6.8 An example of VNF mapping and SFC construction.

(e.g., a firewall, a network address translator, a load balancer, and mobile gateway functions) and steering the traffic flows through them in an ordered manner as per policy [41]. The policy may be specific to the network, service, or customer.

SDN can be used to dynamically direct traffic to the appropriate VNFs of SFC in the required sequential order by altering the routing policy. Figure 6.8 shows an example of a constructed SFC with VNF mapping and a physical path in the substrate network, in which three VNFs {VNF1, VNF2, VNF3} are instantiated on top of the physical substrate nodes {Server1, Server2, Server4} and VNFs are chained using physical and virtual links to form the SFC [42].

In enhanced 5GS architecture, SFC policies can be defined to detect and classify user plane traffic and steer the traffic to a chain of ordered network or service functions for SFC processing [26, 43]. A UPF with SFC capabilities can support a flexible SFC configuration and traffic-steering policies for different applications' upstream and downstream traffic in EDNs. 5GC can support an AF to request predefined SFC policies and traffic-steering policies for certain traffic associated with the applications and target UEs [43].

6.3.4 Network slicing

Network slicing allows network operators to create multiple dedicated virtual or logical networks (or slices) with the required functionality over a common network infrastructure. Each network slice is an isolated end-to-end virtual network that is tailored to meet the service requirements of a user or industry vertical. NFV and SDN enable the implementation of flexible and scalable network slices on top of a shared physical infrastructure.

Network slicing plays a major role in 5G and B5G networks in order to support a multitude of use cases and new services (e.g., eMBB, URLLC, and mMTC). The available network resources will be sliced into multiple dedicated virtual networks that can support different service types [3]. Figure 6.9 shows an example of multiple slices concurrently operating on a common physical infrastructure. Slice 1 is created to provide services to smartphones, whereas slice 2 is created to provide services to autonomous driving. Similarly, slice 3 is created to provide services to massive IoT devices. In each category, the service requirements are different. For instance, the latency requirement

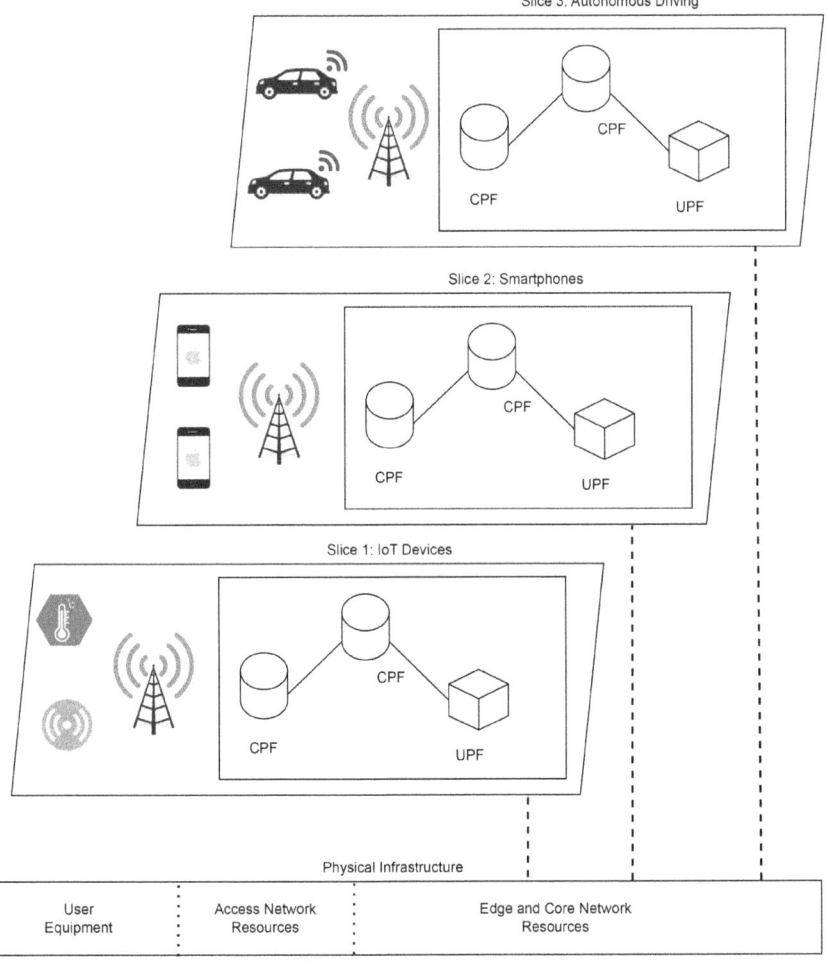

Figure 6.9 Network slices implemented on a common physical infrastructure.

for autonomous driving is much lesser than the other two use cases. Each slice is specifically designed with the required functionalities to provide a particular service and to meet the service requirements (e.g., data rate, latency, and availability). With the help of NFV, SFC, and SDN, network operators can create, scale, and modify network functions of a network slice dynamically to meet the demands and balance network traffic loads. Network slicing is primarily used to logically partition resources across mobile networks to support the diverse service requirements of multiple industry verticals. 3GPP defines the standards for 5G and beyond networks that are primarily based on the network slicing concept [26].

6.4 ROLE OF AI AT B5G EDGE NETWORKS

6.4.1 Introduction

In recent years, AI/ML-based techniques have been applied in diverse fields of science and technology to harness the features of learning techniques. Thus, AI/ML-based products and services are increasingly integrated into our daily lives and becoming more popular (e.g., intelligent personal assistants, recommender systems, and better route maps to destinations with less traffic). Furthermore, multiple industries are planning to use AI/ML techniques to automate their processes as part of the Industry 4.0 digital transformation [22]. It is expected that AI/ML techniques will play an important role in B5G networks for handling system dynamics and daunting tasks that are beyond the limit of human-only operations. It is conceptualized that 6G will bring a paradigm shift from connected things to connected intelligence, thus calling for AI/ML-based automation and configuration support for swifter and more effective decision making in the scheduling, control, and orchestration of network resources and end-to-end services [44].

As B5G networks are expected to support extremely diverse services and use cases (e.g., holographic communications, autonomous driving, remote surgery, real-time traffic control, unmanned aerial vehicle mobility control, real-time video surveillance, and smart factories) and highly rely on low-latency and autonomous intelligent decision making, the role of AI/ML in B5G edge networks is crucial for supporting more stringent KPIs and enabling several real-world applications [22]. AI/ML at B5G edge networks not only allows the execution of network functions at the edge, but also allows the performance of data analytics at the edge that is closer to where data is produced [44]. Analyzing data and developing solutions at the edge network using AI/ML techniques are referred to as edge analytics (EA) or edge intelligence (EI) [22]. EA and EI can be used to enable network operators to support ambitious performance targets, such as ultra-low latency on the order of a few milliseconds, nearly 100% reliability, and high availability. EA and EI also enable supporting a new diverse class of innovative mobile services [44].

6.4.2 AI/ML for B5G networks

AI and ML techniques are considered as enablers for B5G networks [45]. Currently, various AI and ML techniques are investigated and exploited in many 5G and B5G research projects under the umbrella of the 5G Public Private Partnership (PPP) [45]. In particular, neural networks, reinforcement learning, and deep reinforcement learning techniques are considered. Neural networks are nonlinear statistical data-modeling and decision-making tools that are used to find and model the relationships between input and output parameters of a complex system or to find patterns in data. Some of the types of neural networks are feedforward neural networks, deep neural networks, recurrent neural networks, and convolutional neural networks. Reinforcement learning deals with how intelligent agents interact with the environment and take actions in order to maximize a collective reward or to minimize the total cost. Deep reinforcement learning combines reinforcement learning with deep neural networks in order to operate on nonstructured data [45].

AI/ML techniques can be applied in three major areas of networking in B5G network deployments [45]: (1) network planning, (2) network diagnostics and insights, and (3) network optimization and control. Network planning mainly focuses on network element and function placement and service function chaining aspects. Network diagnostics and insights mainly focus on mobile traffic forecasting and tools that autonomously inspect the network state and trigger alarms when there is a need (e.g., anomaly detection and other network security-related aspects). Network optimization and control mainly focus on network resource allocation and management, traffic steering, and service orchestration.

6.4.3 Data analytics function in 3GPP 5GS architecture

A new, AI/ML-based CPF is introduced in the 3GPP 5GS architecture to make decisions based on the information derived or inferred from data analytics [26]. The AI/ML-based CPF is called the *network data analytics function* (NWDAF) [26, 46]. The NWDAF collects data from multiple other 5GC CPFs, such as the AMF, SMF, PCF, UDM, NEF, and AF. The collected data are analyzed by the NWDAF using AI/ML techniques, and then the derived results are notified to different 5GC CPFs [46]. Data collection and analytics reporting functions of the NWDAF can use a request/response or subscribe/notify communication model as the service consumer or producer. The NWDAF can be used to implement predictive data analysis that enables closed-loop automation based on the collected data. The NWDAF facilitates a standardized way of collecting data from multiple sources, analyzing the collected data using different AI/ML models, and exposing the analyzed insights to different consumers. The NWDAF can perform data analytics and provide insights to external authorized consumers as well. The NWDAF allows NOs to manage, automate, and optimize their network operations in an efficient way. The NWDAF leverages cloud-native and SBA features to enable probeless solutions and simplifies the collection and analysis of data from networks and services.

Analytics information is either statistical information of past events or predictive information of future events [46]. Currently, the data analytics results provided by the NWDAF are used by operators to monitor the quality of service (QoS), network resource usage, UE behavior and mobility, network slice load level, and congestion in the network. The role of the NWDAF will be more crucial in B5G and 6G networks. In order to meet the extreme and time-critical service requirements of different use cases, the NWDAF can leverage the features of advanced AI/ML techniques that support autonomous intelligent decision making. The NWDAF can be used to provide analytics services per use case by considering priority, requested accuracy, and targeted users. Some of the envisioned use cases are to anticipate local and global congestion situations to ensure perfect load balancing, prevent security issues on IoT deployments, and predict the user's location in order to allocate the optimal network resources [47]. A NWDAF-based analytics solution at a network edge enables the improvement of operational efficiency and users' QoE. Distributed (local NWDAF for providing analytics at the edge in real time, and central NWDAF for aggregation) and hierarchical NWDAF architectures can make analytics available where needed to meet the diverse latency requirements of industrial and societal use cases.

6.4.4 Distributed edge AI

Cloud computing–based centralized data centers are typically used for data-driven AI/ML techniques to train models and process high volumes of data, as ample amounts of computing and storage resources are available. However, processing and storing data at a distant centralized cloud increase latency and may not meet the stringent latency requirements of many real-time applications that require near-instantaneous communications. Also, since sensors, surveillance video cameras, unmanned aerial vehicles, autonomous ground vehicles, and other IoT devices have proliferated and are deployed at customer locations, they generate a large amount of data. The high volume of data generated from different sources needs to be processed at the edge of the network that is close to the source of data generation in order to minimize latency, bandwidth, source transmission power, and data privacy concerns. As resources available in edge clouds are limited compared to centralized core clouds, the large amount of data generated by different IoT devices and vehicles needs to be distributed to multiple edge clouds in an opportunistic manner to handle resource scarcity and low-latency requirements.

Distributed EC helps to avoid the need to move large amounts of data to a centralized cloud and provides the ability to process data near the source. AI at distributed edge clouds can be a game changer by helping to automate network operations and enabling new businesses. AI algorithms can be distributed with network edge nodes to provide low-latency and reliable results [22]. AI can also help to process only an optimal amount of data from the collected vast amount of data to derive insights and make intelligent decisions. This is because processing too much data can lead to more computing resource consumption and latency-related issues, and processing too little data may not help to find anomalies and derive meaningful insights.

Distributed edge clouds can coordinate with a centralized core cloud in different ways for training models and deriving inferences, as shown in Figure 6.10 [48]. The first possibility is that edge clouds pass their data to the centralized core cloud to train models and get back inferences (centralized AI). A second possibility is that edge clouds share data to the core cloud for a training model and then get the trained model from the core cloud for deriving inferences locally at edge clouds (the same model shared by the core cloud is used by all edge clouds for deriving inferences locally). A third possibility is that edge clouds train models locally using AI, share the locally trained models

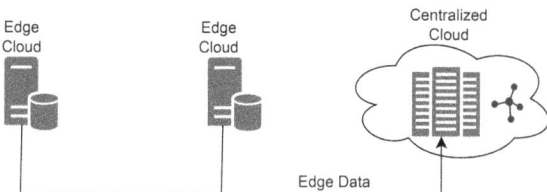

Train and infer from centralized cloud using edge data

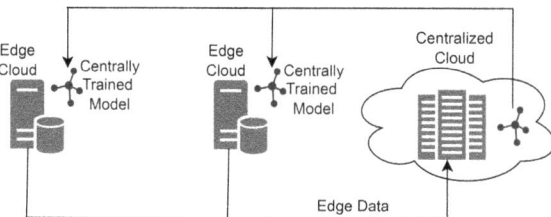

Train at centralized cloud using edge data and infer locally

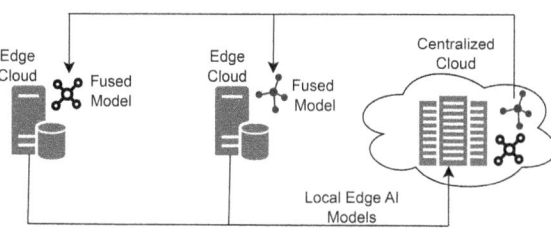

Federated learning and inferencing

Figure 6.10 Edge clouds and core cloud coordination possibilities for training models and deriving inferences.

to the core cloud to aggregate, and then get a fused model for deriving federated inferences locally at edge clouds (this is federated learning, or distributed edge AI). The data is moved to the algorithms for processing in centralized AI, whereas the algorithms are moved to the data locations in distributed edge AI.

6.4.5 Prospective use cases that can be enabled by AI at the B5G edge

It is expected that EC and AI/ML-based EI methods will enable network operators and service providers to offer novel services to multiple industry verticals and society in an efficient, safe, secure, and robust manner. Some of the prospective use cases that will be enabled by EI are as follows [22, 23]:

- *Autonomous driving*: There are five different levels of autonomous driving from simple driver-assisted driving to fully automated driving (e.g., vehicle platooning). As the autonomy level increases in autonomous driving, decision making is very crucial to make safe and secure decisions as human lives and properties are at risk. AI/ML techniques will help to process data in a nearby edge cloud co-located with roadside units or base stations and make intelligent decisions to disseminate data about road conditions, trajectories, the surrounding environment, and traffic-level details to other vehicles in a timely manner using different communication techniques (e.g., dedicated short-range communications and cellular vehicle-to-everything communications) and the available spectrum in a dynamic manner.
- *Real-time video surveillance*: Sensitive locations such as hospitals, airports, schools, colleges, smart factories, and stadiums can be monitored by closed-circuit television cameras and unmanned aerial vehicles (or drones) for safety, security, and entry access control purposes. Hence, processing large volumes of data in real time and providing access to authorized entities through facial and object recognition are very important. AI/ML techniques can be employed to perform these tasks in a nearby edge cloud and communicate the results in real time for further actions. AI/ML techniques can also be used to control drone mobility, control the amount of data being exchanged with ground computing facilities, and detect anomalies by data fusion.
- *Collaborative robots in smart factories*: In smart factories and manufacturing units, next-generation robots will collaborate with humans to perform many tasks such as monitoring of machine health, autonomous or semi-autonomous navigation and management of smart factory functions, switching from one task to another based on priority, and collaborating with other robots for fleeting and carrying goods. AI/ML-based EI methods will be employed to guide collaborative robots (cobots) to cooperate with humans and coordinate with back-end

private edge clouds in factories and manufacturing units for performing these tasks in a fine-grained controlled manner. As heterogeneous IoT devices and sensors are used in smart factories and manufacturing units, AI/ML-based techniques can be used to handle load variations and to detect faults and security-related issues.

- *Online cloud gaming and immersive experiences*: Online cloud gaming is gaining momentum in the gaming market. The gaming service runs on an edge node, and the rendered video is streamed to the players, which avoids the necessity to have high-performance equipment at the user end and enables meeting the delay requirement that is on the order of a few milliseconds. Similarly, extended reality (virtual reality, augmented reality, and mixed reality) techniques can be used to give immersive experiences to users. The next generation of games is based on AI/ML and extended reality to improve the QoE of users. As low latency and jitter are important for interactive extended reality–based gaming, the location of edge nodes and collaborative edge methods are important for service continuity and will support the online gaming use case. AI/ML techniques can also be used to access gaming and immersive services through different 3GPP and non-3GPP access technologies via dynamic traffic steering, switching, and splitting.

6.5 FUTURE RESEARCH DIRECTIONS AND CHALLENGES

6.5.1 Trust-related aspects in AI at the B5G edge

In recent years, deep learning (DL)-based techniques have been employed in edge networks to successfully handle hard, complex tasks that are beyond the limit of human operators. ML and DL techniques are applied for specific network functionalities, and the models either are pre-trained or adapt to the conditions at operation time [44]. However, DL-based models are considered as black boxes, and thus it is difficult to understand their underlying operations and the reasons why the models have taken certain complex actions and decisions [44]. This lack of transparency raises an issue of vulnerability to attacks and malicious data. To offer seamless and secure services, it is expected that AI/ML techniques should be explainable, robust, and verifiable. Otherwise, a small change in inputs to the system may cause catastrophic effects [44]. Hence, it is of paramount importance that AI/ML techniques are trustworthy (i.e., transparent, interpretable, and robust), and NOs should be able to understand the logic behind the models' decisions. To handle this issue, explainable ML and adversarial ML techniques are recommended, and they are considered as promising areas to explore for supporting critical tasks and making sensitive decisions with logical reasons [44].

6.5.2 Energy consumption–related aspects at the B5G edge

Adapting AI and ML techniques to support new use cases at B5G edge networks may consume more energy to train models, as AI/ML techniques (e.g., deep neural networks [DNNs]) often have large amounts of computational power and data requirements [22], which may cause global warming and climate change. Hence, the challenge of developing sustainable and environmentally friendly advanced AI/ML techniques and architectures needs to be considered. Also, developing new application-specific AI accelerators and integrating pre-trained AI/ML models with online learned models can be considered to reduce energy consumption and costs [22]. Another aspect to reduce energy consumption for training models is sharing AI/ML-trained models for different related applications with other edge nodes.

6.5.3 Edge federation aspects at the B5G edge

Edge federation allows horizontal scaling of the edge infrastructure, between the edge infrastructures of different operators. Other challenges include discovering suitable edge nodes for providing services to users, and migrating or relocating user context and application context from one edge node to another due to user mobility (e.g., traveling in a vehicle, or entering into a new region or service area) and/or application mobility (e.g., planned maintenance, load balancing, lack of resources, and failures) across different edge infrastructures, all while satisfying user requirements and maintaining service continuity [49]. Integrating telecommunications companies' edge networks with third-party hyperscale cloud providers is also possible as part of a federation to extend the coverage and user base [6, 49]. However, secure integration, privacy, and slice isolation need to be considered carefully to explore this option.

6.5.4 Reliability aspects at the B5G edge

It is expected that B5G edge networks support high reliability and low latency for URLLC use cases, such as autonomous driving and remote surgery [22]. Although NFV and SDN provide many benefits in terms of cost reduction and flexible management of resources to dynamically provide diverse services, they create avenues for reliability, availability, and latency-related issues, as they are more prone to software failures [50]. Hence, autonomous detection of failure of network functions and recovery are some aspects that need to be explored from a reliability point of view to ensure service continuity and improve the QoE of users [22]. Network monitoring can also help to detect security issues and service degradation as quickly as possible in order to mitigate the violation of service-level agreements and failure of network functions.

6.5.5 Resource allocation and mobility aspects at the B5G edge

Low-latency services context synchronization in mobility is important. MEC-based services coverage is limited to a particular geographical area or service area. When users are moving, the service functions context should be relocated or migrated from the source MEC application or EAS to the target MEC application or EAS in a new coverage area (a local breakout roaming scenario). Otherwise, a new route through a target network RAN to a source network RAN and to the source MEC application or EAS in the EDN should be determined to maintain service continuity (a home routed roaming scenario). If the overall latency to access services from the MEC application or EAS exceeds the actual latency requirements of the users, then it results in a violation of service-level agreements [18]. Hence, application context relocation or migration has some implications for service requirements and service-level agreements. AI/ML techniques can be used to predict the user's location and future traffic in order to allocate the optimal network resources and meet service-level agreements.

6.5.6 Security and privacy aspects at the B5G edge

EC environments are characterized as complex ones involving multi-vendor hardware and software devices, and they are heterogeneous in nature [19]. They also may be managed by multiple network operators. Hence, security, privacy, and trust in heterogeneous EC environments are key research topics, as they are a major concern for industry verticals and other customers. Furthermore, edge cloud federations and massive IoT environments impose additional challenges. Also, exposing EC capabilities and deployments through APIs may lead to security threats. Thus, it would require end-to-end security solutions [19]. Federated learning, blockchain-based smart contracts and distributed ledger mechanisms, privacy-preserving mechanisms, and zero-trust trust management are some of the potential areas to explore to address the security-related issues in B5G edge networks [45].

6.6 CONCLUSION

In this chapter, we first discussed the role of edge computing (EC) in beyond-5G (B5G) systems and the architectural aspects of integrating EC with B5G from a standardization point of view. We also discussed the key technology enablers for B5G edge networks. Then, we discussed the role of artificial intelligence (AI) and machine learning (ML) in B5G edge networks for enabling new use cases that require stringent or extreme service requirements to support multiple industry vertical applications in real time. Finally, we listed some of the potential research directions to explore further regarding the role of EC and AI/ML in B5G and 6G networks.

REFERENCES

1. 5G Americas, "5G & LTE Deployments." [Online]. Available: https://www.5gamericas.org/resources/deployments/
2. Global mobile Suppliers Association (GSA), "5G-Market Snapshot June 2022." [Online]. Available: https://gsacom.com/paper/5g-market-snapshot-june-2022/?utm=reports5g
3. NGMN, "5G White Paper," NGMN Alliance, White Paper, Feb. 2015.
4. 3GPP, "Release 15." [Online]. Available: https://www.3gpp.org/release-15
5. ——, "Release 16." [Online]. Available: https://www.3gpp.org/release-16
6. NGMN, "5G White Paper 2," NGMN Alliance, White Paper, July 2020.
7. 3GPP, "Release 17." [Online]. Available: https://www.3gpp.org/release-17
8. ——, "Release 18." [Online]. Available: https://www.3gpp.org/release18
9. University of Oulu, "6G Flagship." [Online]. Available: https://www.3gpp.org/news-events/2194-ran_webinar_2021
10. ATIS, "Next G Alliance." [Online]. Available: https://nextgalliance.org/
11. B5GPC, "Beyond 5G Promotion Consortium." [Online]. Available: https://b5g.jp/en/
12. "one6G." [Online]. Available: https://one6g.org/
13. NGMN, "6G Drivers and Vision," NGMN Alliance, White Paper, Apr. 2021.
14. 6G IA, "The 6G Smart Networks and Services Industry Association (6G-IA)." [Online]. Available: https://6g-ia.eu/
15. Sustainable Development Goals, "Take Action for the Sustainable Development Goals." [Online]. Available: https://www.un.org/sustainabledevelopment/sustainable-development-goals/
16. NGMN, "6G Use Cases and Analysis," NGMN Alliance, White Paper, Feb. 2022.
17. M. Patel et al., "Mobile-Edge Computing - Introductory Technical White Paper," 2014.
18. S. Kekki et al., "MEC in 5G Networks," *ETSI White Paper No. 28*, 2018.
19. D. Sabella et al., "MEC Security: Status of Standards Support and Future Evolutions," *ETSI White Paper No. 46*, 2021.
20. ETSI, "Multi-access Edge Computing (MEC)." [Online]. Available: https://www.etsi.org/technologies/multi-access-edge-computing
21. P. K. Thiruvasagam, A. Chakraborty, and C. S. R. Murthy, "Latency-aware and Survivable Mapping of VNFs in 5G Network Edge Cloud," in *17th International Conference on the Design of Reliable Communication Networks (DRCN)*, 2021, pp. 1–8.
22. E. Pletonen et al., "6G White Paper on Edge Intelligence," *6G Research Visions, No. 8, 6G Flagship, University of Oulu*, 2020. [Online]. Available: http://urn.fi/urn:isbn:9789526226774
23. A. Albanese et al., "D2.1 Use Cases, Requirements, and Preliminary System Architecture," *AI@EDGE, 5G PPP*, 2021. [Online]. Available: https://aiatedge.eu/wp-content/uploads/2021/09/AI@EDGE_D2.1_Use-cases-requirements-and-preliminary-system-architecture_v1.0-1.pdf
24. ETSI GS MEC 003, "Multi-access Edge Computing (MEC); Framework and Reference Architecture," *ETSI, Version 3.1.1*, 2022.
25. ETSI GS MEC 011, "Mobile Edge Computing (MEC); Mobile Edge Platform Application Enablement," *ETSI, Version 1.1.1*, 2017.
26. 3GPP TS 23.501, "System Architecture for the 5G System (5GS); Stage 2," *3GPP, Version 17.5.0*, June 2022.

27. 3GPP TS 23.548, "5G System Enhancements for Edge Computing; Stage 2," *3GPP, Version 17.3.0*, June 2022.
28. 3GPP TS 33.122, "Security aspects of Common API Framework (CAPIF) for 3GPP northbound APIs," *3GPP, Version 17.0.0*, Mar. 2022.
29. 3GPP TS 23.558, "Architecture for enabling Edge Applications," *3GPP, Version 17.4.0*, June 2022.
30. P. K. Thiruvasagam, A. Chakraborty, and C. S. R. Murthy, "Resilient and Latency-Aware Orchestration of Network Slices Using Multi-Connectivity in MEC-Enabled 5G Networks," *IEEE Transactions on Network and Service Management*, vol. 18, no. 3, pp. 2502–2514, 2021.
31. ETSI ISG NFV, "Network Functions Virtualization: An Introduction, Benefits, Enablers, Challenges and Call for Action," Oct. 2012.
32. ETSI GS NFV 002 V1.2.1, "Network Functions Virtualization; Architectural Framework," Dec. 2014.
33. F. Z. Yousaf, M. Bredel, S. Schaller, and F. Schneider, "NFV and SDN - Key Technology Enablers for 5G Networks," *IEEE Journal on Selected Areas in Communications*, vol. 35, no. 11, pp. 2468–2478, 2017.
34. P. K. Thiruvasagam, V. J. Kotagi, and C. S. R. Murthy, "A Reliability-Aware, Delay Guaranteed, and Resource Efficient Placement of Service Function Chains in Softwarized 5G Networks," in *IEEE Transactions on Cloud Computing*, vol. 10, no. 3, pp. 1515–1531, 2022.
35. N. Feamster, J. Rexford, and E. Zegura, "The Road to SDN: An Intellectual History of Programmable Networks," *ACM SIGCOMM Computer Communication Review*, vol. 44, no. 2, pp. 87–98, Apr. 2014.
36. N. McKeown, T. Anderson, H. Balakrishnan, G. Parulkar, L. Peterson, J. Rexford, S. Shenker, and J. Turner, "OpenFlow: Enabling Innovation in Campus Networks," *ACM SIGCOMM Computer Communication Review*, vol. 38, no. 2, pp. 69–74, Mar. 2008.
37. Open Networking Foundation, "Software-Defined Networking." [Online]. Available: https://opennetworking.org/sdn-definition/
38. ONF TR-502, "SDN Architecture," June 2014.
39. B. A. A. Nunes, M. Mendonca, X. N. Nguyen, K. Obraczka, and T. Turletti, "A Survey of Software-Defined Networking: Past, Present, and Future of Programmable Networks," *IEEE Communications Surveys & Tutorials*, vol. 16, no. 3, pp. 1617–1634, Sep. 2014.
40. J. Halpern, and C. Pignataro, "Service Function Chaining (SFC) Architecture," *RFC 7665*, Oct. 2015.
41. W. Haeffner, J. Napper, M. Stiemerling, D. Lopez, and J. Uttaro, "Service Function Chaining Use Cases in Mobile Networks," Internet Engineering Task Force, Internet-Draft draft-haeffner-sfc-use-case-mobility-09, Jan. 2019.
42. D. Z. G. L. L. T. M. Jalalitabar, E. Guler and X. Cao, "Embedding Dependence-Aware Service Function Chains," *IEEE/OSA Journal of Optical Communications and Networking*, vol. 10, no. 8, pp. 64–74, 2018.
43. 3GPP TR 23.700-18, "Study on System Enabler for Service Function Chaining," 3GPP, *Version 0.3.0*, May 2022.
44. C. Fiandrino, G. Attanasio, M. Fiore, and J. Widmer, "Toward Native Explainable and Robust AI in 6G Networks: Current State, Challenges and Road Ahead," *Computer Communications*, vol. 193, pp. 47–52, 2022.
45. 5G PPP, "AI and ML - Enablers for Beyond 5G Networks," *5G PPP Technology Board, Version 1.0*, 2021. [Online]. Available: http://doi.org/10.5281/zenodo.4299895

46. 3GPP TS 23.288, "Architecture Enhancements for 5G System (5GS) to Support Data Analytics Services," *3GPP, Version 17.5.0*, June 2022.
47. P. Rhude, "Using NWDAF to Create Value in 5G Use Cases." [Online]. Available: https://www.nokia.com/blog/using-nwdaf-to-create-value-in-5g-use-cases/
48. W Chong et al., "What is Distributed AI?" [Online]. Available: https://developer.ibm.com/learningpaths/get-started-distributed-ai-apis/what-is-distributed-ai/
49. GSMA, "Teleco Edge Cloud Value & Achievements." [Online]. Available: https://www.gsma.com/futurenetworks/wp-content/uploads/2022/03/GSMA-TEC-Value-Whitepaper-v13.pdf
50. P. Kaliyammal Thiruvasagam, V. J. Kotagi, and C. S. R. Murthy, "The More the Merrier: Enhancing Reliability of 5G Communication Services With Guaranteed Delay," *IEEE Networking Letters*, vol. 1, no. 2, pp. 52–55, 2019.

Chapter 7

AI in the wireless 5G core (5GC)

Vishal Murgai, Vasanth Kanakaraj,
and Issaac Kommineni
Samsung R&D Institute India-Bangalore
Bangalore, India

7.1 INTRODUCTION

The 5G core (5GC) is a virtualized functionality that runs on powerful ×86 servers with a huge amount of compute, memory, and network interface resources. 5GC is designed to deliver large volumes of data with low latency and high reliability. The 5G user plane function (UPF) [1] is a key component of 3GPP's New Radio (NR) mobile core system architecture (Figure 7.1).

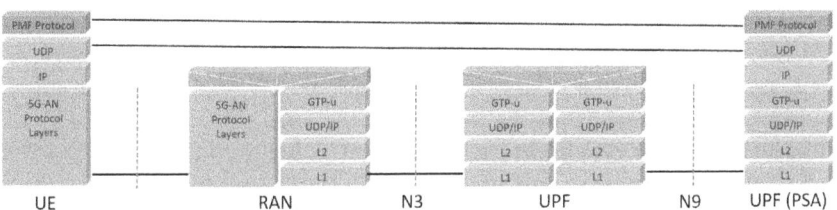

Figure 7.1 Protocol stack for the user plane.

By 2030, internet of things (IoT) devices will constitute the next billion wireless devices, according to a conservative estimate. The global adaptation of data-intensive technologies and the rapidly increasing number of wireless devices create a multitude of cascading problems. Among them, the problems of buffer bloat and congestion in the downlink are major factors that can impact the user experience. The UPF [1] is the backbone node in the 5GC network, as it serves as the route for all user traffic to the user equipment (UE) and internet servers. According to user traffic statistics, the majority of the data flows are download flows (i.e., from the internet server to 5G UE). A rapid increase in data-intensive applications such as augmented reality (AR), virtual reality (VR), content streaming, online gaming, and so on is leading to a rapid increase in volumes of elephant flows (long-term flows). Moreover, the mass deployment of IoT devices can lead to scenarios with bursty traffic conditions, creating a plethora of challenges for operators in traffic engineering.

Traditional solutions like the elective acknowledgment (ACK) option, proxying, and link-layer retransmissions between gNodeB (gNB) and the UE

DOI: 10.1201/9781003303527-8

are not enough to tackle the problems generated by next-generation wireless networks. The following sections of this chapter dive deep into how AI can be used to mitigate this congestion in downlink. Furthermore, we will also look at how flow classification using AI can help us with the prioritization and efficient management of resources in the core network.

Ever since 5G millimeter wave's (mmWave) commercialization, transport-layer protocols have been open to a multitude of challenges due to their high intermittence [2]. The extensively used transport-layer protocol called Transmission Control Protocol (TCP) is no exception to mmWave's extreme variance in channel quality [2]. Frequent handovers within densely deployed small cells, handovers from high-BDP (bandwidth-delay product) to low-BDP cells, and radio link control (RLC) configurations with large buffers call into question the credibility of TCP's congestion control (CC) algorithm's [2] reliable packet delivery. Furthermore, in this chapter, we explain the throughput issues experienced by UE moving from high-BDP to low-BDP cells, a common scenario often observed in deployments.

In this chapter, we also discuss implementing efficient flow control for TCP in the UPF by using AI methods. CC and fair flow control play key roles in the bandwidth performance of TCP, which is the most widely used transport-layer protocol. The majority of CC algorithms, based on packet loss or delay, work well in most cases, but they do not react optimally when congestion occurs suddenly in the network. With the advent of 5G UE with large memory, the end devices can advertise a large receive window (RWND) [2]. In the case of downlink flows (flows from the internet to the UE), the internet servers can send a large number of inflight packets to the UE due to a large RWND advertised by multiple devices. This phenomenon [2] can lead to buffering, packet loss, and congestion in the wireless network when multiple servers react simultaneously with traffic bursts. To address this problem, this chapter proposes using ML-based prediction to determine the optimal maximum receive window (maxRWND) size that can be advertised by the UE. The ML-based solution achieves better fair flow control for TCP in the core network, ensuring optimal utilization of resources and improved network throughput during peak and off-peak hours. First, the chapter presents the results of a fivefold cross-validation, which demonstrate that the trained model can accurately predict an optimal maxRWND per the UPF. Second, the chapter discusses a proactive feedback mechanism in TCP for CC. Delivering a seamless data experience in wireless networks presents challenges due to congestion in the access network caused by frequent handovers [3] between cells with different BDPs. To address this issue, a proposed solution called the smart bandwidth regulator (SBR) utilizes a handover prediction ML model, which can predict UE handover from a high-BDP to a low-BDP cell 800 ms in advance, allowing for graceful adaptation to the approaching congestion event. This approach results in 15% less packet loss and a 17% reduction in flow completion time (FCT). In addition, the UPF enables an explicit congestion notification (ECN) capability for UE-associated TCP and QUIC flows.

7.2 FAIR FLOW CONTROL FOR TCP
IN THE CORE USING ML

TCP is the most commonly used transport-layer protocol. A TCP sender uses CC algorithms and the advertised RWND to modulate data transmission rates [4]. The most commonly used CC algorithms are based on packet loss or packet delay (e.g., receiving the same ACK packet three consecutive times indicates that the associated transmitted packet has been lost, so that the sender can take appropriate action). These algorithms work well in most conditions, but they react suboptimally when a sudden congestion event happens in the network. Currently, most internet servers and 5G UE have a large memory. This leads to the advertisement of higher RWND by the UE during connection establishment [2]. A TCP sender at an internet server estimates congestion and regulates the number of inflight packets to UE using flow control. The RWND advertised by the UE is less than the server's estimated congestion window (CWND) due to good throughput and improved reliability in the 5G network (Figure 7.2) [4]. Hence, the TCP sender at the server transmits the data at the advertised RWND rate.

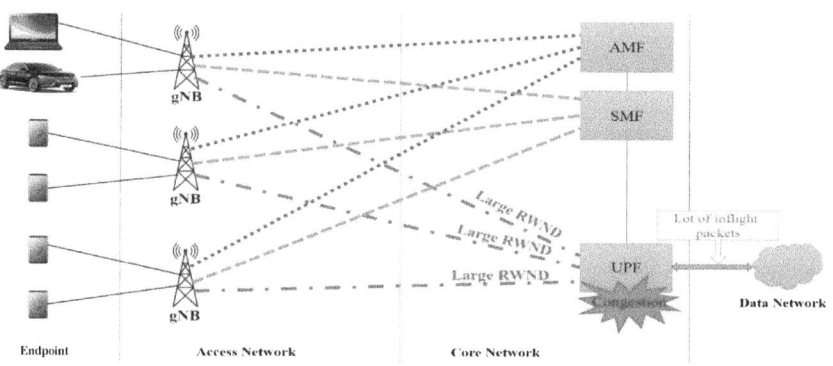

Figure 7.2 Necessity for intelligent TCP and QUIC flow control in the 5G core.

The operator network's fast path is overwhelmed with similar reactions from many other internet servers simultaneously with traffic bursts. This leads to packet buffering, packet loss, and congestion in the core network. To tackle this problem, ongoing work is focused on fixing an upper bound for the RWND size advertised by the UE. However, using a static upper bound on the RWND [4] will lead to non-optimal utilization of resources and can adversely affect the network throughput during off-peak hours, as the user traffic is dynamic in nature. An efficient method to determine the optimal maxRWND is using ML-based prediction. The predicted maxR-WND can be used for optimal bandwidth regulation in the UPF. The occurrence of sudden congestion events can be attributed to factors like a high

network processor load in the UPF due to traffic bursts, high queue utilization leading to packet loss, and high variation in round trip time (RTT).
Moreover, there is no well-defined pattern on the state transitions of active
and idle users. Such dynamic variations in traffic patterns with respect to
different parameters demonstrate the need for a ML-based prediction of an
optimal maxRWND per the TCP flow in the UPF. There are multiple UPFs
of varying bandwidth capacity that are managed by the session management
function (SMF) [1]. The SMF also performs a session-wise load balancing
across all UPFs (Figure 7.3) [1].

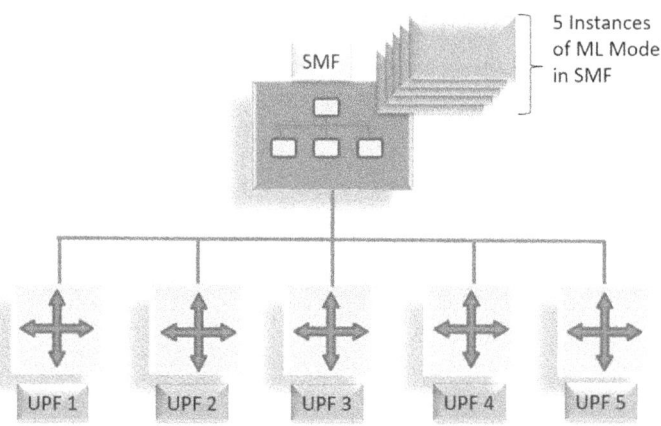

Figure 7.3 Analysis: Data traffic load versus active users.

The SMF has access to all of the management key performance indicators (KPIs) of the UPF. KPIs such as the total number of active versus idle
users (current, peak, and average), the load of the network processor (peak
and average) that performs the fast path function, and the user plane traffic
load (peak and average) influence the bandwidth capacity of the UPF. A ML
model is trained on an external node (AI server) [5] and later deployed on the
SMF for AI inference. The model on the SMF will begin to predict the maxR-
WND per the UPF. The predicted maxRWND will be communicated to the
UPF by the SMF. This communication will depend on the rate of change in
KPI values in the UPF. UPF is capable of intercepting and modifying layer 4
(Transport Layer) contents of all packets that are traversing through it. The
flow manager module in the UPF will monitor all TCP flows for the RWND
advertised by the UE and internet server. The flow manager in the UPF will
replace the advertised RWND value with the predicted maxRWND value,
and will recompute and modify the TCP checksum on the modified packet
before forwarding the packet in case the advertised RWND size is more
than the maxRWND. A reduced RWND (predicted maxRWND) becomes

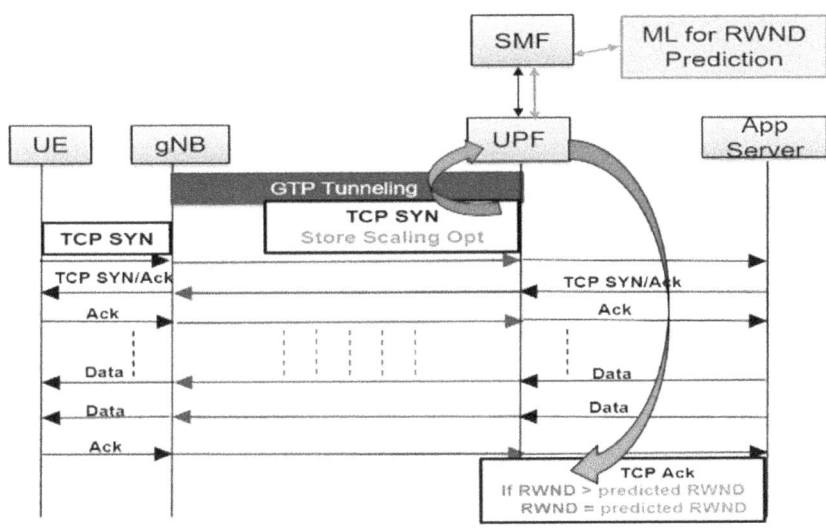

Figure 7.4 Flow diagram: ML-based TCP RWND regulation in a core network.

a limiting determinant for TCP senders when the CWND is higher than the received RWND (Figure 7.4).

Use a fivefold cross-validation for evaluating the performance of the maxRWND prediction model [5, 6]. The observed train and test loss values are 0.42 and 0.43, respectively. This shows that the trained model can accurately predict an optimal maxRWND per the UPF. The model is able to predict the maxRWND within 0.3~0.6 ms. The solution applies a uniform upper bound on the maxRWND for all TCP flows in the UPF at that instant, thus ensuring fairness for TCP flows in the UPF's bandwidth share. The solution achieved a better and fair flow control for TCP in a core network.

7.3 PROACTIVE FEEDBACK METHOD FOR CONGESTION CONTROL IN NETWORKS

In wireless networks, congestion occurs majorly at access networks (wireless medium). User mobility between cells with a large BDP difference in a heterogeneous network creates challenges in delivering a seamless data experience to the end user [2, 3]. Frequent handovers between cells with higher variance in their BDPs influence CC mechanisms [3], leading to packet queueing delays, packet drops, and finally a degraded user experience. Instead of reacting to a change in the BDP after the transition, it is better to proactively predict the transition and take corrective measures. An effective ML inference mechanism can predict a UE handover event from a high-BDP cell to a low-BDP cell based on the current load and the total load of source and target gNBs. In the current

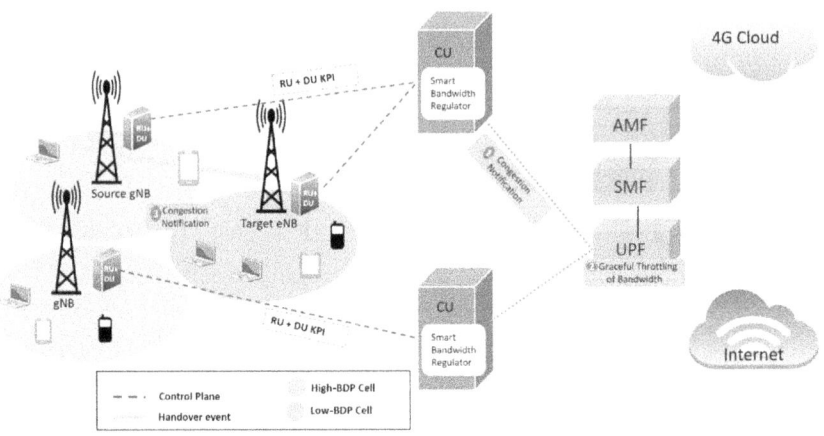

Figure 7.5 Analysis: Necessity for proactive congestion notification in 5G.

architecture, there is a limitation, as the core network is not aware of the pre-vailing or impending congestion at the access network (Figure 7.5).

A solution to mobile handovers from high-BDP to low-BDP cells is to intro-duce the smart bandwidth regulator (SBR) in a centralized unit (CU) of the 5G and Beyond access network, a TCP performance enhancement technique. The CU hosts a SBR, as it has access to the wireless network KPIs required to predict UE handover to a congested cell. The CU collates congestion KPIs and shares this among the neighboring CUs to provide collective intelligence on congestion in the access network. The CU also monitors user movement through UE measurement reports. The solution formulates a ML model that can be deployed at the SBR to predict user movement between cells with a high BDP difference and to cells with more congestion. The SBR predicts a UE handover to a congested cell through UE measurement reports and confirms whether the cell is congested through collated congestion data. The SBR noti-fies the core network's UPF with a congestion notification prior to actual UE handover as the ML module predicts the UE handover to a low-BDP cell. The UPF performs traffic shaping of buffers associated with the UE as it receives the congestion notification. As traffic shaping leads to measured packet loss per flow, the TCP endpoints proactively adapt to the packet losses as an indi-cation of congestion in the network. Thus, the SBR provides a proactive noti-fication of impending congestion event to CC algorithms in endpoints.

Among the KPIs identified to analyze and predict congestion at a cell, the average central processing unit (CPU) and memory utilization of the radio unit and distributed unit (RU+DU), the average queue utilization per quality of service (QoS), the packet loss rate, the Packet Data Convergence Protocol (PDCP) downlink packet discard rate, the load histogram, and the session setup success rate are the significant KPIs. A live commercial network was set up to analyze key metrics that cater to various traffic scenarios and introduce

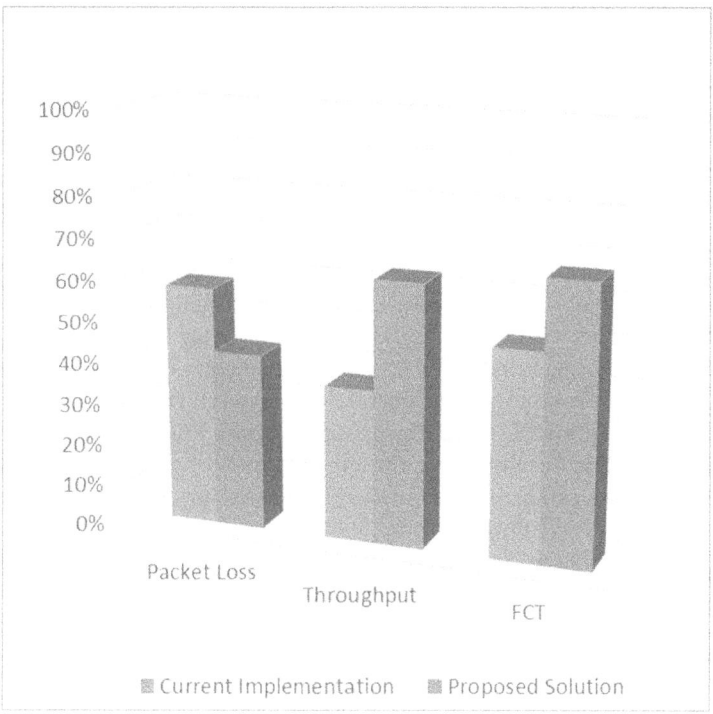

Figure 7.6 Results from the solution.

variations in the data. A trained neural network model on the prepared data-set is deployed into the SBR, and concurrently starts predicting UE handover to the congested cell and notifies the UPF through a congestion notification. Soon after receiving such packets, the UPF enables an ECN to UE-associated TCP flows [7]. To handle ECN bit failure cases, the UPF starts regulating the traffic of impacted flows through queue management techniques, allowing the endpoints to react accordingly (Figure 7.6).

The UE's TCP CC algorithm can suffer from a slow start due to switching from a high-BDP-capable cell to a low-BDP cell. The SBR's early prediction of UE handover to a low-BDP cell avoids this slow start and instead enters the congestion avoidance state. The 0.41 observed train loss value and 0.19 observed test loss value prove the efficiency of the handover prediction ML model. The UPF's traffic shaping gives TCP and QUIC endpoints ample time to react and regulate traffic sent to the network, since the prediction happens 800 ms earlier. UE applications now gracefully adapt to the approaching congestion event rather than engaging in reactive adjustment. The UE now experiences a smooth handover transition, even if it is to a low-BDP cell through the SBR. Enabling the SBR in the CU results in 15% less packet loss with a 17% reduction in flow completion time (FCT).

7.4 CONCLUSION

In this chapter about 5GC and AI, a robust method for enabling proactive congestion feedback is proposed. Experiments are performed over KPIs collected from a live air network. Statistics from the live network show that TCP makes 35–60% of the total traffic in the UPF. The proposed congestion feedback method delivers a consistent TCP bandwidth performance along with optimized link utilization. This method also enables optimal utilization of UPF resources, since the predicted maxRWND is based on the real-time KPIs. Proactive prediction of a UE handover from a high-BDP cell to a low-BDP cell in a radio access network (RAN), and marking packets with an ECN bit when congestion builds up, help TCP's CC to scale linearly to the available bandwidth. We can observe a negative correlation between the data traffic pattern, network processor's CPU load (that runs fast-path software), and predicted maxRWND. These results prove the effectiveness of the proposed solution. In conclusion, the rapid increase in data-intensive applications and the massive deployment of IoT devices in the 5G network have created a multitude of challenges for operators, such as congestion and buffer bloat in the downlink. As the demand for high-speed connectivity and low-latency services increases, the need for intelligent network management and optimization becomes more evident, making AI an essential tool for the future of the 5G network.

REFERENCES

1. System Architecture for the 5G System. 3GPP TS 23.501 version 15.2.0 Release 15, 2018.
2. M. Zhang, M. Polese, M. Mezzavilla, J. Zhu, S. Rangan, S. Panwar, and M. Zorzi. "Will TCP work in mmwave 5g cellular networks?" IEEE Communications Magazine, vol. 57, no. 1, pp. 65–71, 2019.
3. R. Mondal, A. Biswas, and S. Bhaskar. Effect of mobility and receive window on TCP in device to device communication. International Conference on Research in Computational Intelligence and Communication Networks, 2018.
4. F. Ciaccia, O. Arcas-Abella, D. Montero, I. Romero, R. Milito, R. Serral-Gracià, and M. Nemirovsky. Improving TCP performance and reducing self-induced congestion with receive window modulation. International Conference on Computer Communication and Networks, 2019.
5. D. P. Kingma and J. Ba. "Adam: A method for stochastic optimization." [Online]. Available: https://arxiv.org/abs/1412.6980
6. J. D. Rodriguez, A. Perez, and J. A. Lozano. "Sensitivity analysis of k-fold cross validation in prediction error estimation," IEEE Transactions on Pattern Analysis and Machine Intelligence, vol. 32, no. 3, pp. 569–575, 2010.
7. L. Kalampoukas, A. Varma, and K. Ramakrishnan. "Explicit window adaptation: a method to enhance TCP performance," in Proceedings. IEEE INFOCOM '98, the Conference on Computer Communications. Seventeenth Annual Joint Conference of the IEEE Computer and Communications Societies. Gateway to the 21st Century (Cat. No.98, vol. 1, 1998, pp. 242–251).

Chapter 8

AI as a service
AI for application service providers

Ralf Tönjes, Marten Fischer, and Frank Nordemann
University of Applied Sciences
Osnabrück, Germany

8.1 THE BENEFITS OF USING AI AS A SERVICE

Using artificial intelligence (AI) in commercial products is challenging. Applying AI techniques for analyzing and processing speech, text, or images requires a high level of technical expertise about the creation, training, and fine-tuning of models, and it is a time-consuming process. Models may have to be adapted during their use, especially if incoming datasets vary or objectives of the AI analysis change over time.

Training and testing data must be prepared for supervised learning. The required data may be well structured (e.g., CSV files), but often it is semi-structured or unstructured and buried in e-mails, log files, or Word or Excel documents. The quality of the datasets directly affects the quality of the results identified by the model, and usually a large amount of high-quality datasets is required for the creation, training, and fine-tuning of models. However, preparing datasets is often a recurring and time-consuming process and not straightforward for personnel without AI expertise. Relevant data may be missing, or its identification may demand large efforts.

Besides technical expertise, hardware is required for training and executing AI models. In general, most hardware resources are needed for the training and verification of models. However, the execution of models also may require certain hardware capabilities depending on the task. For example, the analysis of video streams on mobile devices such as cell phones may not be possible in real time due to limited hardware resources. While increasing the hardware capabilities of products may work for some AI analyses, it may not be an option considering the economic impacts. Many companies are not capable of spending high budgets on AI personnel, as well as the necessary tools and hardware for a useful integration of AI into their products. This is especially true for small and medium-sized enterprises (SMEs). For AI tasks requiring powerful hardware, external computation in server farms is a sensible decision.

A solution addressing the outlined challenges is offered by *artificial intelligence as a service* (AIaaS). In the concept of "something as a service," any hard- or software can be used across a network because it relies on cloud computing. Mostly the software is available off-the-shelf, bought by third-party

DOI: 10.1201/9781003303527-9

vendors. When AIaaS is offered as a commercial solution by companies with AI expertise, different types of AI are offered to customers in the form of services. While a variety of services applying different layers of abstraction exists, some provide ready-to-use AI functionality without the need of creating and training models. For instance, a company may use a speech-processing service mapping speech-to-text and analyze the text using a text-processing service afterward. Another example is an image recognition service, assisting in the identification of imperfections of products. As an advantage, there is no need for customers to invest in the creation and configuration of fundamental AI algorithms. Hosting of hardware, including aspects such as availability and scalability, is taken care of by the service providers. Payment is done only for the algorithms and hardware resources required for the defined task on a pay-per-use principle.

In summary, for a long time, AI was cost-prohibitive to most companies due to the following reasons:

- The machines were massive and expensive.
- The programmers who worked on such machines were in short supply (which meant they demanded high payments).
- Many companies didn't have sufficient data to study.

This is where AIaaS comes in. With cloud services having become incredibly accessible, AI, in the form of AIaaS, is more accessible [1].

8.2 TYPES OF AI

AI systems can be classified in two ways (Figure 8.1). In a more technical approach, the classifications are artificial narrow intelligence (ANI), artificial general intelligence (AGI), and artificial superintelligence (ASI). All AI systems that have been developed to date, even the most complex ones, fall in the ANI class. These AI systems are designed to solve *one* specific problem or task. "The systems can do nothing more than what they have been programmed to do" [2]. AGI, in contrast, is able to learn new skills and perform increasingly complex tasks (up to a certain difficulty), like a human being. These systems will be able

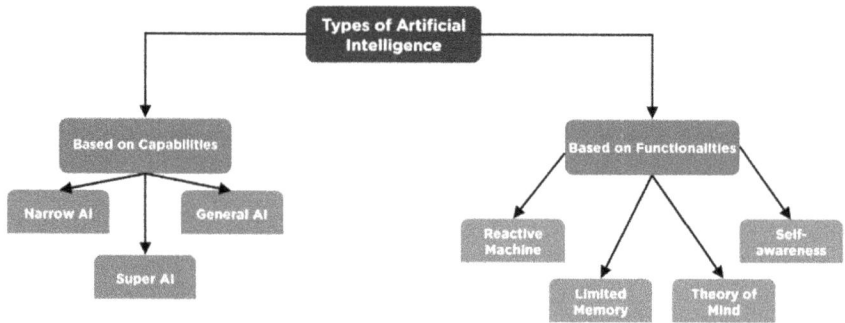

Figure 8.1 Classifications of artificial intelligence.

to transfer learned knowledge to new situations and derive new solutions. The last class, ASI, is expected to be the pinnacle in AI research. These systems will be able to replicate the multifaceted intelligence of human beings combined with a superior memory and faster data-processing and learning speeds.

The second way to classify AI systems is based on their functionalities [3] and the ability of the AI to learn and think [4]. The first class is *reactive* systems. These systems have no memory and thus are not able to learn from previous "experience" or improve their performance. In other words, when faced with the same stimuli, these systems always produce the same output. They can also be used for a very limited number of inputs. IBM's Deep Blue, which beat chess grandmaster Garry Kasparov in 1997, is an example of such a reactive system. The next class in this classification system is named *limited memory*, and with memory it can learn and improve. Today's AI machines can be grouped in this class. This class corresponds to the ANI class mentioned before. The next class is named *theory of mind*, which describes AI systems that are able to really understand the objects they interact with. Here it is worth mentioning that all current assistant systems and chatbots belong to the limited-memory class. They are not able to empathize with the users and don't understand their needs or emotions. In contrast, machines in the theory of mind class would be able to do so. In the last class, *self-aware*, the AI not only is able to understand the user's emotions but also has developed self-awareness. This class forms the final development in AI evolution, and its realization is probably decades or even centuries away.

8.3 AI TECHNOLOGIES AND USAGE

AI has a high potential to improve a vast number of processes in almost every domain. However, the use of AI tools requires some background knowledge about the algorithms used. Figure 8.2 presents an overview of these algorithms. AI must not be confused with machine learning (ML), although most of the AI algorithms currently used employ ML. AI is not limited to ML, but also includes logic programming systems, like Prolog, and knowledge-based systems. Logic programming is based on formal logic represented by declarative clauses that a solver interprets to derive the conclusion. Knowledge-based systems employ an inference engine that controls the execution of if-then rules, changing a fact base stepwise to evolve to a conclusion. The stepwise derivation of the conclusion can be either data-driven (forward chaining) or goal-driven (backward chaining). The knowledge in logic programming systems (i.e., the logic clauses) and knowledge-based systems (i.e., the rules) is designed by humans and uses explicit knowledge representations. In contrast, ML systems learn their behavior from datasets. Supervised learning uses pre-classified data to teach the algorithm in a training phase before using the algorithm in the operational phase. Unsupervised learning exploits the similarity to group patterns to cluster. In reinforcement learning, an agent performs

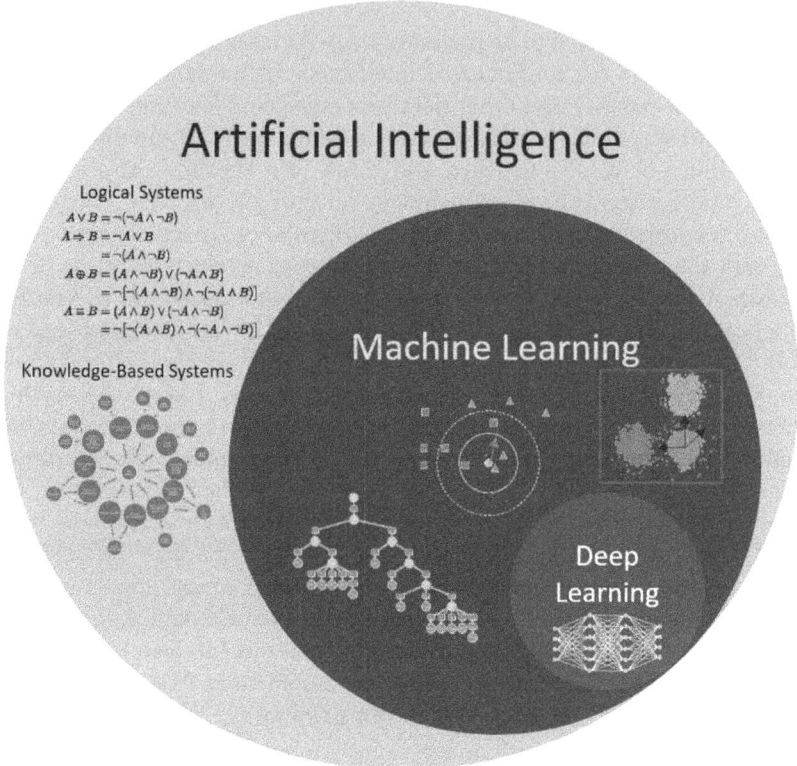

Figure 8.2 Machine learning and deep learning are just subsets of artificial intelligence [6].

actions to complete a certain task and afterward receives a reward (which also can be negative) depending on the result. With small variations, the agent then tries to maximize the reward and thus consequently learns new and better strategies. This way, the agent will learn from experience made in prior iterations. Examples of ML are K-means clustering, Q-learning, decision trees, random forest, artificial neural networks (ANNs), and deep learning (DL). K-means clustering [5] is an unsupervised algorithm that allows the classification of objects in a predefined number of groups, where the median between each group is as small as possible. Q-learning is well suited for supervised and reinforcement learning by optimizing a quality function ($\rightarrow$ Q-learning) of a model. Decision trees and random forest, which are extensions for multiple decision trees, are well suited for classification when no calculation of attribute values is possible. They allow for explainable AI, which may be mandated by regulation and certain user groups. An algorithm selects the best attribute for a decision at each branch fork. A typical ANN is composed of a few, usually three, layers of neurons, each layer executing a matrix multiplication followed by a nonlinear (sigmoid) function applied to the resulting vector values. A backpropagation algorithm learns the weights of the matrices in the training phase. ANNs work well as classifiers but usually need to be fed with good feature values extracted from labeled datasets. The training dataset should also be diverse for unimportant features, as there is a risk of overfitting. As an example, if an ANN is being trained to classify pictures of cats and dogs, and the cat pictures always have a blue background, there is a high risk that the ANN learns to classify background colors instead. DL tries to integrate feature extraction by concatenating multiple neural network layers and inserting convolutional layers in between. However, to learn the many parameters, DL requires large learning datasets.

8.4 PRINCIPLES OF AI SERVICES

A variety of different types of AI services is available on the market. Distinctions can be made based on the level of abstracting technical details during AI operations. Some services may require less or no AI expertise to be used. This section elaborates the different types of AI services and their basic principles.

As a general principle of AIaaS, service providers offer hosted AI algorithms, models, platforms, and tools, and customers are billed for using them. Many offered services act as black boxes, where no technical insights about algorithms and models are provided. Hosting, including availability and scalability, is managed by the provider depending on the customer's needs. Depending on the level of abstraction regarding AI algorithms and models, AIaaS is split into the terms *AI software services*, *AI developer services*, and *AI infrastructure services* [7]. Figure 8.3 illustrates the terms, their abstraction level, and their relation to cloud computing.

AIaaS Stack

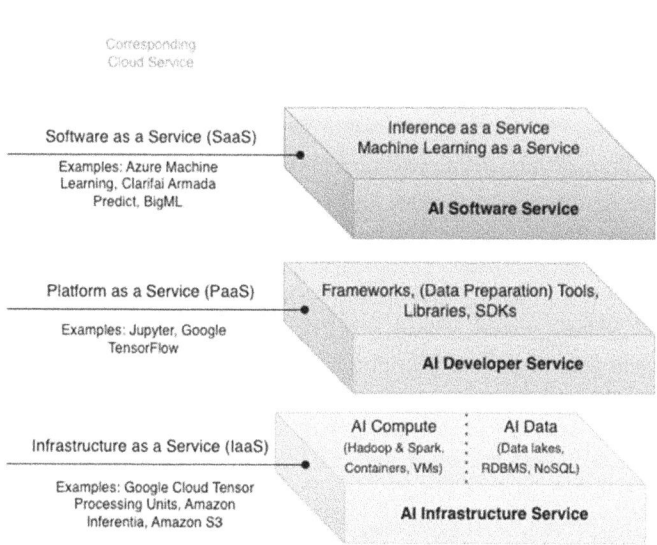

Figure 8.3 The AIaaS stack.

The *AI software services* layer corresponds to the software as a service (SaaS) principle, widely used across cloud computing: AI services are provided ready-to-use for specific tasks. Related terms in the literature are *inherence as a service* and *machine learning as a service*, which differ in their level of abstraction. Usually, inherence as a service provides pre-trained algorithms and models working fully automated as black boxes, requiring no or minimal knowledge about how to apply AI techniques. Typically, these services are lacking customization options. Widespread examples are text-to-speech translation services and text-processing and image recognition services. With ML as a service, many providers offer existing AI algorithms and models as customizable templates. For instance, this allows a customer to adapt an image recognition service to identify custom labels or objects. Many services provide guidance in customizing models by assisting in dataset preparation, the selection of features, the fine-tuning of classifiers, and the choosing of performance metrics.

Less abstracted products are offered on the *AI developer services* layer. This layer basically includes frameworks, (data preparation) tools, software libraries, and software development kits (SDKs), helping developers to develop and integrate AI functionalities into their products. This includes frameworks and pre-built examples, reducing the user's effort in implementing and training models.

The least abstracted level is represented by the *AI infrastructure services* layer, corresponding to the infrastructure as a service (IaaS) principle known from cloud computing. This basically represents the computational power for building and training models (e.g., the central processing unit [CPU] and graphics processing unit [GPU]) and network storage and sharing capabilities for datasets. Typical implementations are containers, virtual machines, and data warehouses or data lakes.

8.5 AIAAS IN PRACTICE

Based on the close relation between AIaaS and cloud computing, and due to the immense computing resources and memory required, many cloud computing companies offer AI services using the AIaaS principle. Major activities are carried out by Amazon AWS, Google Cloud [8], Microsoft Azure [9], and IBM Watson. Table 8.1 illustrates AI functionalities for different application areas, such as natural language processing (NLP), text translation, text analysis, chatbots and customer care, and computer vision. Furthermore, environments for AI development and AI infrastructure services are provided as well.

To use an AI service, application programming interfaces (APIs) are provided. These APIs can be used via HTTP/REST requests or a remote procedure call (RPC) in combination with, most times, a JavaScript Object Notation (JSON) encoded payload. SDKs or libraries for different programming languages are usually available. In addition, some sort of graphical

Table 8.1 Selected examples of Artificial Intelligence as a service provided by Amazon, Google, Microsoft

Service type or application area	Level of abstraction	Provider	Product name (and description)
Speech processing	AI software services	Google	Speech-to-text (map speech to text)
		Microsoft	Speech-to-text (map speech to text)
Text processing	AI software services	Amazon	Textract (text analysis)
		Amazon	Polly (text-to-speech)
		Google	Translation AI (real-time translation of text)
		Microsoft	Azure Bot Service (build chatbots)
		OpenAI	Text summary, creation, analysis (chatbot ChatGPT)
Computer vision and image processing	AI software services	Amazon	Recognition (analysis of images and videos)
		Amazon	Lookout for vision (quality control)
		Amazon	Lookout for equipment (abnormal machine status detection)
		Amazon	AWS Panorama (computer vision at edge clouds and on premises)
		Microsoft	Azure Computer Vision (analyze images and videos)
		Microsoft	Face API (detect and tag faces in images)
Machine learning and deep learning	AI developer services	Amazon	SageMaker (implement, train, and deploy machine learning models)
		Google	AutoML (develop customized machine learning models)
		Google	Vertex AI (create machine learning models)
		Microsoft	Azure Machine Learning (implement, train, and deploy machine learning models)
Infrastructure	AI infrastructure services	Google	Cloud Infrastructure (tensor processing units, GPUs, and CPUs)

(Continued)

Table 8.1 Selected examples of Artificial Intelligence as a service provided by Amazon, Google, Microsoft *(Continued)*

Service type or application area	Level of abstraction	Provider	Product name (and description)
		Google	Deep Learning Container (pre-configured containers for deep learning)
		Google	Deep Learning VM Image (pre-configured virtual machines for deep learning applications)
		Microsoft	Data Science Virtual Machines (pre-configured virtual machines)

interface or console is typically available. Most APIs offer a limited number of free requests to test and develop a product using them before a paid plan is necessary. Consequently, an authentication mechanism is needed. This may require the generation of a key file or access tokens beforehand. Prices are graduated (i.e., the more requests that are done in total, the cheaper a single request gets). Detailed prices and plans vary between different service providers and over time; hence, specifics are left out at this point. Another business model provides a certain amount of starting budget that can be used to test the AI services. Next to pure online AIaaS, which is used over the internet, are solutions such as the computer vision AI service AWS Panorama [10], a hardware device that can be deployed on premise. These solutions can be used in environments with limited network bandwidth or by companies with very strict data governance rules.

Depending on the use case, a combination of different AI services can increase the efficiency of an application significantly. A combination of cloud and edge services allows developers to fuse the benefits of both paradigms. For example, in a voice-controlled assistant system, one AI service can be deployed on an edge device that is responsible for converting the spoken command into text (speech-to-text), while a second AI service located in the cloud processes the command. This way, only the textual presentation of the command needs to be uploaded to the cloud, reducing the latency and reaction time. In contrast, in a use case scenario for a music identification service, the entire audio sample may need to be transferred to the cloud [11].

For common tasks, pre-trained models are available. The performance may vary between the different service providers. If a custom service for ML needs to be created, automated machine learning (AutoML) may serve as an option for people with no or little AI expertise. AutoML assists in the end-to-end implementation of ML models, beginning with dataset preparation, then feature selection and extraction, followed by model creation, training, verification, and deployment. With AutoML, the user only needs to provide labeled training datasets to the service. The service will then learn to identify and extract the relevant features itself, without the need to write any code by hand. The results may be less accurate than those by specifically designed models, but AutoML offers an easy entry point into AIaaS.

In conclusion, a wide range of AIaaS services and service providers exists. The usage can be done by accessing the API endpoints directly or, more simply, by using one of the libraries, if available. The APIs are well documented, and for services by big service providers, tutorial videos can be found on well-known video portals such as YouTube. In general, the field of AIaaS providers can be described as very dynamic. New services are added, or the prices are adjusted—the reader is referred to the corresponding product websites.

8.6 ENERGY CONSUMPTION AND AIAAS

Another important aspect of using AI is its relatively high energy consumption and the resulting CO_2 footprint. This accounts not only for the time when an AI model is in operation but especially for the training process. Often, small increases in an accuracy score require a substantial amount of computing time. In 2019, Strubell et al. [12] gave an example in which increasing the BiLingual Evaluation Understudy (BLEU) score by just 0.1 for a NLP model came "at the cost of at least \$150k in on-demand compute time and non-trivial carbon emissions." Also, the training of a single deep learning NLP can lead to approximately 600,000 pounds of CO_2. According to Ref. [13], the training of Google's AlphaGo AI emits 96 tons of CO_2 in a period of just 40 days. This compares to an airplane traveling for 1,000 hours! And it is pretty much to allow a computer to play games. For this reason, Tamburrini [14] proposed a shift in the idea of what has to count as a "good" result in AI research, and recommended that the gained improvements in accuracy should be viewed in light of how computationally expensive the training of a model was. In a more recent (2022) work by Petterson et al. [15], the authors pointed out that early works on the prediction of carbon emissions by AI were overestimated. Using highly energy-efficient data centers instead of on-premise data centers, which have been built properly for other purposes, reduces energy costs by a factor up to 2. Moreover, a significant reduction of carbon emissions can be achieved by AIaaS and cloud data centers using renewable energy sources. Here, Petterson et al. saw a reduction by a factor between 5 and 10. Dodge et al. [16] further indicated that a data center's location and the time when training have important impacts on carbon emissions during the training of an AI model. Figure 8.4 shows an experiment they have done fine-tuning the same model (BERT-small [17]) on eight V100 GPUs for 36 hours in data centers in different regions and at different times. As can be seen, the CO_2 emissions can vary between 10 and 28 kilograms, a difference by almost a factor of 3. This can be explained by the different

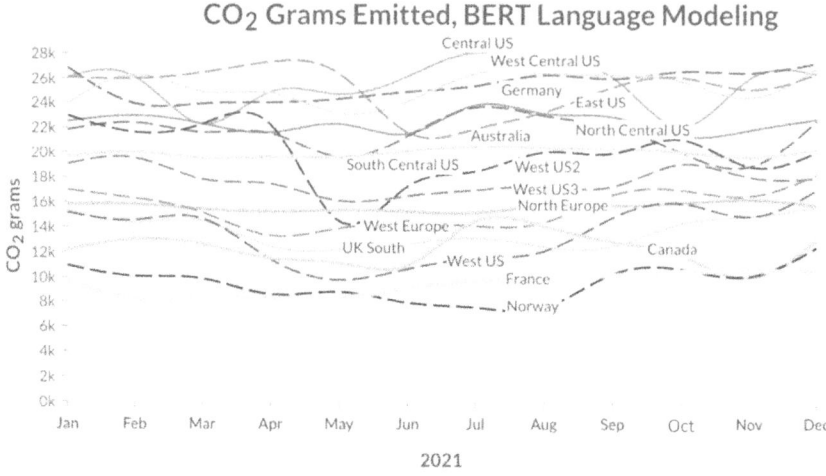

CO₂ Grams Emitted, BERT Language Modeling

Figure 8.4 Carbon emissions in different data center locations [16].

energy mix (e.g., solar, wind, and coal) that is available in different regions. It must be noted that these numbers are only estimates and consider only GPU energy consumption. Also, the measurements and estimations were done prior to the energy crisis in Europe in 2022, and changes in the energy mix in some states have happened due to the shortage of petroleum gas. Other aspects that have limited the growth of CO_2 emissions in past years are the development and use of more efficient hardware for AI, such as GPUs optimized for ML (not graphics) and tensor processing units (TPUs) [15]. For example, current versions of the NVIDIA A100 TPU with Multi-Instance GPU (MIG) make the GPU available for up to seven instances, allowing more of the workload to be executed simultaneously. "The NVIDIA A100 GPU is architected to not only accelerate large complex workloads, but also efficiently accelerate many smaller workloads" [18]. This is an especially useful feature for AIaaS service providers, which suffer from an unpredictable workload in the form of on-demand service requests.

In summary, AI has a noticeable effect on energy consumption and carbon emissions. Recent advances and developments in hardware as well as best-practice approaches for training setups have mitigated this development. However, it can be expected that AI will continue to be deployed in more and more domains, requiring an increasing amount of energy. Here, using AIaaS can provide a solution, as available resources are used more efficiently and shared. In addition, if renewable energy sources are used, a significant improvement of carbon emissions can be achieved. AIaaS service providers are often located near renewable power plants or operate one on their own. Thus, choosing the right region is also important. Clear predictions of how much CO_2 could be saved are hard to make, as the energy sources are volatile and depend on external factors such as the weather, electricity demand, and so on.

8.7 DATA PROTECTION AND PRIVACY

When working with datasets to train an AI model that contains privacy-related data, you may have to anonymize the data in order to comply with rules such as the European Union's General Data Protection Regulation (GDPR). Hence, it is worth knowing which anonymization techniques exist and how anonymity can be determined. The overall goal of anonymization is to remove as little detail as necessary from the data to make it impossible to link an entry in the dataset to a specific person. In other words, details are removed to form groups in such a way that a known detail about a person matches all group members. This includes the case of combining the dataset with different datasets or collaborating with third parties. This also means there is a risk that a dataset does not remain anonymous as new data gets published over time.

In principle, there are four different methods to anonymize a dataset, but all of them can be combined to achieve greater anonymity: masking, generalization, swapping, and perturbation. In masking, information, or pieces of it, is removed to reduce the detail in the dataset. A well-known example is zip codes, where lower significant digits are removed. In the resulting dataset, it is still possible to make statements about the broader region or home state of an entity, but not about specific cities. Generalization describes a method where entries in the dataset are mapped to more general groups. For example, the age of a person can be mapped to groups of 10-year intervals, such as 1–10 years, 11–20 years, 21–30 years, and so on.

Tables 8.2 and 8.3 depict examples [19] of masking and generalization methods (the asterisk * marks the sensitive attributes, i.e. information that must not be assignable to a single person, because otherwise privacy would be impaired, possibly even with severe negative consequences.). Here, the zip codes have been masked using the character 'x', where each x replaces a digit in the zip code. The birth dates have been generalized. As can be seen, the masking can be variable: For the

Table 8.2 Database example without anonymization

Birth date	Insurance	Zip code	Diagnosis*
08.01.1953	ABC	76131	Stroke
13.01.1953	ABC	76135	Cardiac Infarction
21.02.1949	ABC	76149	Cardiac Infarction
03.03.1949	ABC	76149	Cardiac Infarction

Table 8.3 Database example with 2-anonymity

Birth date	Insurance	Zip code	Diagnosis*
1953	ABC	7613x	Stroke
1953	ABC	7613x	Cardiac Infarction
1949	ABC	761xx	Cardiac Infarction
1949	ABC	761xx	Cardiac Infarction

latter two entries, two digits have been removed, while in the former two entries only one digit was removed. The birth dates have been generalized by removing the information about day and month. The anonymized dataset has two groups.

Swapping is a method in which entries in the dataset are interchanged with each other. Afterwards, it is still possible to make statements, such as how often an entry appears in the dataset, but no linkage to a specific person can be done anymore. The last anonymization method, perturbation, is interference with the data for the purpose of removing details from the dataset. For example, this can be the addition of a noisy, random disturb signal to a series of measurements, rounding of data, and so on. The term *pseudomization* is also often mentioned in the context of anonymization and describes the replacement of an identifier with a (pseudo-)random identifier or hash value. However, as there is a 1:1 relationship with the identifier and its replacement and as the pseudomization might be reversible, legally this is no anonymization method! Anonymization requires irreversibility.

The degree of anonymity can be expressed by the k-anonymity metric. It describes the size of the smallest group, and therefore, in a worst-case scenario, a specific person can be identified within one group. In Table 8.3, the smallest number of entries in a group determines the k value (here, two for both groups); therefore, the example has 2-anonymity. k-anonymity does not ensure that all sensitive attributes in a group are different. In Table 8.3, for example, someone who knows that a person was born in 1949 also knows that the diagnosis was cardiac infarction. The anonymity metric l-diversity [20] extends k-anonymity, so that in each group, at least l different sensitive attributes are present. In case one of the sensitive attributes is statistically significantly more present than others, the anonymity metric t-closeness [21] can help by enforcing a statistically more even distribution.

Depending on the scenario, privacy-preserving techniques must be applied during the collection of data. An example of such a technique is homomorphic encryption (HE), which allows performing mathematic computations on the encrypted data without the need to decrypt it beforehand. This way, data can be processed by third parties without revealing the sensitive contents. HE schemes are categorized depending on the number of operations that are supported. In contrast to the above-mentioned group-based anonymization, HE does not remove any details in the dataset. Like any other encryption scheme, HE can be undone using the correct decryption key. The difference is that the decrypting party can only see the result of the computations. An ideal use case is the aggregation of values within a network.

8.8 SUMMARY AND OUTLOOK

This chapter gave an overview of the different types of AI systems that can be classified in general, and also different technologies that form subsets of AI. Widely used technologies like ML and DL are just small pieces of AI. Starting to use AI may require expert knowledge and special hardware, which might be challenging, especially for SMEs. AIaaS tries to mitigate this problem by providing AI services with different abstraction levels focused on easy usability. Pre-trained models for common tasks are available. Analogous to cloud computing, AI services are provided on different abstraction levels, namely, AI software services, AI developer services, and AI infrastructure services. For each level of abstraction, several service providers are available on the market, most noticeably the same companies with a big market share in cloud computing. Using AIaaS instead of on-premise computing resources is more energy efficient and leads to a smaller CO_2 footprint. Although there have been significant advances in AI research and development, currently used AI solutions belong to the more primitive types of AI, which are designed to perform specific tasks. As such, AI is still in its infancy. However, it is reasonable to assume that AI solutions will be deployed in more and more domains with an increasing number of abilities and at the same time become even more complex. AIaaS will continue to play an important role by providing affordable yet powerful AI capabilities to start-ups and SMEs, allowing them to build new and innovative solutions on top of them. In the future, we will probably see the use of even more powerful AI chips that mimic the function of a human brain more efficiently, like stimulated neural networks (SNNs) or even chips that contain brain tissue [22].

REFERENCES

1. BMC Blogs. "What Is AIaaS? AI as a Service Explained". Zugegriffen 2. November 2022. https://www.bmc.com/blogs/ai-as-a-service-aiaas/.
2. Joshi, Naveen. "7 Types of Artificial Intelligence". Forbes. Zugegriffen 6. October 2022. https://www.forbes.com/sites/cognitiveworld/2019/06/19/7-types-of-artificial-intelligence/.
3. Biswal, Avijeet. "7 Types of Artificial Intelligence That You Should Know in 2022". Simplilearn.com. Zugegriffen 6. October 2022. https://www.simplilearn.com/tutorials/artificial-intelligence-tutorial/types-of-artificial-intelligence.
4. Marr, Bernard. "Understanding the 4 Types of Artificial Intelligence (AI)". Zugegriffen 6. October 2022. https://www.linkedin.com/pulse/understanding-4-types-artificial-intelligence-ai-bernard-marr.
5. MacQueen, J. B. Some Methods for classification and Analysis of Multivariate Observations. Proceedings of 5th Berkeley Symposium on Mathematical Statistics and Probability. Vol. 1. University of California Press. 1967.
6. Aunkofer, Benjamin. "Machine Learning vs Deep Learning - Wo liegt der Unterschied? - Data Science Blog". Zugegriffen 12. October 2022. https://data-science-blog.com/blog/2018/05/14/machine-learning-vs-deep-learning-wo-liegt-der-unterschied/.
7. Lins, Sebastian, Konstantin D. Pandl, Heiner Teigeler, Scott Thiebes, Calvin Bayer, und Ali Sunyaev. "Artificial Intelligence as a Service". Business & Information Systems Engineering 63, Issue 4 (1. August 2021): 441–56. https://doi.org/10.1007/s12599-021-00708-w.
8. Ravulavaru, Arvind. Google Cloud AI Services Quick Start Guide: Build Intelligent Applications with Google Cloud AI Services. Packt Publishing Ltd, 2018.
9. Jeffme. "What Are Azure Applied AI Services? - Azure Applied AI Services". Zugegriffen 5. October 2022. https://learn.microsoft.com/en-us/azure/applied-ai-services/what-are-applied-ai-services.

10. Stormacq, Sébastien. "Computer Vision at the Edge with AWS Panorama | AWS News Blog". 20. October 2021. https://aws.amazon.com/blogs/aws/computer-vision-at-the-edge-with-aws-panorama/.
11. Wang, Avery Li-Chun, Shazam Entertainment, Ltd. "An Industrial-Strength Audio Search Algorithm". last accessed 7. October 2022. https://www.ee.columbia.edu/~dpwe/papers/Wang03-shazam.pdf.
12. Strubell, Emma, Ananya Ganesh, und Andrew McCallum. "Energy and Policy Considerations for Deep Learning in NLP". arXiv, 5. June 2019. https://doi.org/10.48550/arXiv.1906.02243.
13. Wynsberghe, Aimee van. "Sustainable AI: AI for Sustainability and the Sustainability of AI". AI and Ethics 1, Issue 3 (1. August 2021): 213–18. https://doi.org/10.1007/s43681-021-00043-6.
14. Tamburrini, Guglielmo. "The AI Carbon Footprint and Responsibilities of AI Scientists". Philosophies 7, Issue 1 (February 2022): 4. https://doi.org/10.3390/philosophies7010004.
15. Patterson, David, Joseph Gonzalez, Urs Hölzle, Quoc Le, Chen Liang, Lluis-Miquel Munguia, Daniel Rothchild, David R. So, Maud Texier, und Jeff Dean. "The Carbon Footprint of Machine Learning Training Will Plateau, Then Shrink". Computer 55, Issue 7 (July 2022): 18–28. https://doi.org/10.1109/MC.2022.3148714.
16. Dodge, Jesse, Taylor Prewitt, Remi Tachet des Combes, Erika Odmark, Roy Schwartz, Emma Strubell, Alexandra Sasha Luccioni, Noah A. Smith, Nicole DeCario, und Will Buchanan. "Measuring the Carbon Intensity of AI in Cloud Instances". In 2022 ACM Conference on Fairness, Accountability, and Transparency, 1877–94. FAccT '22. New York, NY, USA: Association for Computing Machinery, 2022. https://doi.org/10.1145/3531146.3533234.
17. Devlin, Jacob, Ming-Wei Chang, Kenton Lee, und Kristina Toutanova. "BERT: Pre-training of Deep Bidirectional Transformers for Language Understanding". arXiv, 24. May 2019. https://doi.org/10.48550/arXiv.1810.04805.
18. NVIDIA. "Mehr-Instanzen-Grafikprozessor (MIG) von NVIDIA". Accessed 29. September 2022. https://www.nvidia.com/de-de/technologies/multi-instance-gpu/.
19. Jörn Müller-Quade, Dirk Achenbach. "Leitfaden: Anonymisierungstechniken". Begleitforschung Smart Data Programm des Bundesministerium für Wirtschaft und Energie. 2018. https://www.digitale-technologien.de/DT/Redaktion/DE/Downloads/Publikation/2018_10_18_Smart_Data_Leitfaden_Anonymisierung.pdf?__blob=publicationFile&v=5 (last visit 09.2023)
20. Aggarwal, Charu C., und Philip S. Yu. "A General Survey of Privacy-Preserving Data Mining Models and Algorithms". In Privacy-Preserving Data Mining, herausgegeben von Charu C. Aggarwal und Philip S. Yu, 34:11–52. Advances in Database Systems. Boston, MA: Springer US, 2008. https://doi.org/10.1007/978-0-387-70992-5_2.
21. Li, Ninghui, Tiancheng Li, und Suresh Venkatasubramanian. "t-Closeness: Privacy Beyond k-Anonymity and l-Diversity". In 2007 IEEE 23rd International Conference on Data Engineering, 106–15, 2007. https://doi.org/10.1109/ICDE.2007.367856.
22. Kagan, Brett J., Andy C. Kitchen, Nhi T. Tran, Forough Habibollahi, Moein Khajehnejad, Bradyn J. Parker, Anjali Bhat, Ben Rollo, Adeel Razi, und Karl J. Friston. "In Vitro Neurons Learn and Exhibit Sentience When Embodied in a Simulated Game-World". Neuron 12, (October 2022). https://doi.org/10.1016/j.neuron.2022.09.001.

Chapter 9

Digital twins for beyond 5G

Caglar Tunc, Tuyen X. Tran, and Kaustubh Joshi
AT&T Labs Research
Bedminster, New Jersey

9.1 INTRODUCTION

In recent years, the 5G rollout has started to ramp up, and mobile and connected devices are enjoying the high data rates that 5G provides. As new services utilize 5G networks to enable use cases and applications with diverse requirements, it is crucial to optimally design, operate, and maintain the network. Theoretical analyses and simulations at limited scales can only provide insights to some extent with limited capability and accuracy. Moreover, these orthodox techniques can fail to closely characterize the complex nature of large-scale networks with a variety of technologies and devices being deployed.

An alternative to the conventional tools to model and analyze the physical network is to build a virtual replica of the system. An emulated software replica of a 5G physical network is referred to as a digital twin, and it allows for continuous prototyping, testing, assuring, and self-optimization of the living network [1]. Hardly a new concept, digital twins have a history of prior usage in aeronautics [2], manufacturing [3, 4], and building design [5] to help simulate complex systems. But for beyond-5G (B5G), which, as compared to 5G, has an even more complicated nature and a more diverse set of services to provide [6], the digital twin is still a relatively recent development that's unquestionably groundbreaking. Although a real-life twin does not always perform and respond in the same ways as its counterpart, this one does. That consistency allows continuous prototyping, modeling, and research, and probably makes it one of the best and most reliable B5G R&D tutors ever. Through the digital twin's multiple emulation processes, traffic and signal generation functions work in harmony to mirror the actual 5G network in every way. Consequently, the physical system's behavior can be tested, analyzed, and then accurately predicted under a nearly infinite set of "what if" possibilities. Better yet, all of this can be accomplished quickly, at a low cost, and whenever needed.

The possibilities and benefits brought by digital twins to 5G and B5G networks are multifold. First, digital twins allow for designing, testing, and optimizing future network deployments, technologies, and control policies without the need to implement and conduct the studies in the actual network. This helps avoid the expensive costs associated with physical experiments and the risk of causing performance degradation. Second, a closed-loop process

DOI: 10.1201/9781003303527-10

established between the physical network and its digital twin can enable continuous monitoring of the network status and triggering adaptations when needed to ensure the performance, availability, and resiliency of the network. Another benefit of digital twins is their ability to process vast amounts of available data and integrate complex tools and algorithms such as machine learning (ML) and artificial intelligence (AI) to improve network performance.

In this chapter, we lay out the vision of digital twins for B5G and describe the architectural design requirements as well as the challenges in keeping consistency between digital twins and the physical networks. We further explain the benefits of the digital twin for B5G networks, along with potential use cases from several physical domains that are closely coupled with the envisioned digital twin framework.

The remainder of this chapter is organized as follows. In Section 9.2, we present the envisioned architecture of the digital twin framework, which consists of three main components: the physical domain or subsystem of interest, the radio access network (RAN) digital twin, and the digital twin engine. In Section 9.3, we discuss the applications of digital twins with an emphasis on their capabilities and the performance metrics that can be gauged by digital twins, and we introduce some exemplary use cases from different domains with diverse performance requirements. We describe the design objectives to be considered while building the digital twins in Section 9.4. In Section 9.5, we discuss different players in the digital twin ecosystem and propose strategies for collaboration to overcome the challenges of building a unified digital twin ecosystem. Finally, in Section 9.6, we conclude the chapter with some final remarks.

9.2 DIGITAL TWIN ARCHITECTURE

In this section, we describe how the proposed digital twin approach can be split into horizontal layers according to their functionalities. The envisioned digital twin, as illustrated in Figure 9.1, is a unified framework that

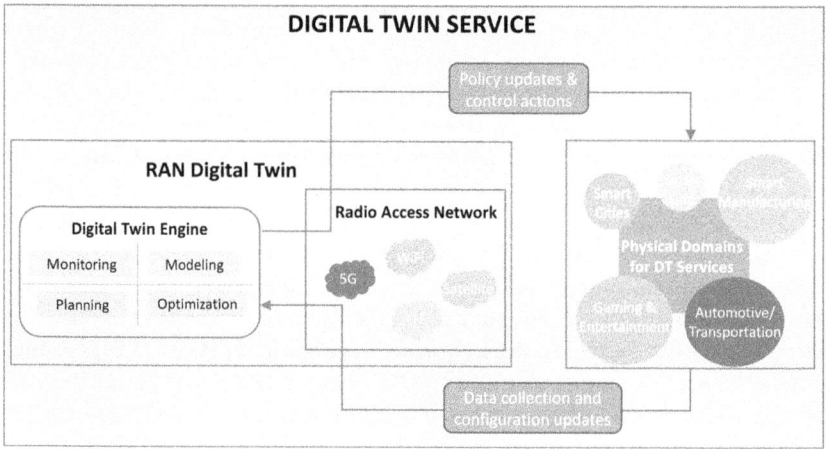

Figure 9.1 Overview of digital twin architecture.

encompasses (1) the physical domain or subsystem of interest, such as gaming, automotive, manufacturing, and energy grids; (2) the RAN digital twin, which takes the data and signaling generated by the physical domain as inputs and is responsible for generating the consumable data; and (3) the digital twin engine that models and represents the physical environment to monitor and optimize its operation. Regardless of the domain of interest, the workflow of the digital twin framework is as follows: (1) Gather data from the physical network, (2) plan the deployment/operational policies for the network, (3) exchange policy and parameter updates with the physical network, and (4) continuously monitor and optimize its operation. The first step utilizes the underlying communication technology of the network (cellular, fixed-access, WiFi, satellite, etc.) to generate, carry, and collect signaling and network data. After domain and service-aware data analytics, this data is fed to the RAN digital twin as the input, where the collected data, together with the twins of the network nodes and user devices, is used to obtain the virtual representation of the physical environment. Finally, the engine of the digital twin is responsible for accurately modeling the physical network and optimizing the desired policies and parameters. This engine usually takes the form of an ML model. The process of monitoring, optimization, and update continues as the digital twin keeps improving its modeling and optimization engine and also adapts to the changing network and service dynamics.

9.2.1 Physical domains for digital twin services

In this subsection, we will list several physical domains that can employ the underlying 5G/B5G network for sharing the data generated by the network components, and discuss how these domains can benefit from the digital twin.

9.2.1.1 Automotive and transportation networks

As the deployment of 5G ramps up, the amount of data that vehicles transmit over cellular networks increases at a drastic rate. Vehicle-to-everything (V2X) communication technology enables vehicles to share information with the network, which is used to improve the security, performance, and reliability of a vehicular ecosystem. Data shared among vehicles, and between vehicles and the network, can include information on the speed, location, and trajectory of the vehicles, and also cellular data traffic from the vehicular users and/or pedestrians. The type and amount of data, as well as the performance requirements that need to be satisfied, depend strictly on the specific use case of interest, such as cooperative driving/maneuvering, autonomous vehicles, vehicle platooning, vulnerable road user detection and protection, and so on. The requirements of these use cases can be assessed by the digital twin, which can provide an accurate representation of the convoluted transportation networks by ingesting the generated data and obtaining virtual models of the network components [7].

9.2.1.2 Gaming and entertainment

The deployment of reliable and high-data rate connections enabled a variety of new interactive and real-time use cases and technologies, such as online gaming, interactive video streaming, virtual reality (VR), and augmented reality (AR). These use cases involve rendering large amounts of data to be displayed on the device of an end user. For example, a user in a venue, such as a sports game or a concert, can enjoy interactive live streams and additional content via fast and reliable connections to the network. This can lead to a vast amount of data traffic from thousands of users to be handled by the network. On the other hand, with the increasing computational powers of CPUs and GPUs, the image quality, the bitrate requirements, and the amount of data processing required for such services grow exponentially, which can surpass the rendering capabilities of the end devices, such as AR/VR headsets and online consoles. Considering this limitation, end devices can share the data with cloud computing resources, where the data is processed and the output data is sent back to the end device to be displayed to the user. These services also need to satisfy very stringent delay, data rate, and reliability constraints, to provide the users with a good quality of experience (QoE). Therefore, the gaming and entertainment domain can benefit significantly from digital twins to process the available data, understand the challenges, and assess strategies to overcome these challenges.

9.2.1.3 Smart manufacturing

Monitoring production lines, demand levels, products, and equipment to minimize cost and maximize revenue is of great interest to any manufacturer in any industry. In order to minimize human monitoring, input, and decision making, smart manufacturing aims to digitalize and automate the entire process of gathering raw materials, production, delivery to the customer, and maintenance of the product [4]. Moreover, uncertainties in demand and supply, due to competitive markets, economic instabilities, and supply chain issues caused by pandemics and other unexpected incidents, bolster the need to develop a digitalized, complex, and accurate framework to control and optimize the entire manufacturing process. A digital twin for a smart manufacturing ecosystem can undertake significant roles in equipment testing, calibrating, and tracking, as well as optimizing the production line and design production layout, which will increase revenue and eliminate unexpected costs.

9.2.1.4 Smart power grids

As communication technologies evolve, more buildings and other infrastructures get connected to the network via Internet of Things (IoT) devices. This can open up new horizons for the *smart grid* concept, which aims to provide more efficient, dynamic, and digitalized power delivery to cities [8]. Moreover, due to the dynamic nature and instability of the demand and cost of energy delivery, increasing sources and amounts of data collected from customers, as well as the new technologies emerging to provide more efficient energy resources, the design and operation of power grids remain a salient research problem. A digital twin of a smart grid can be used for various use cases, including but not limited to optimizing the design of the power grid, detecting power grid anomalies and faults, creating virtual power plants to test and calibrate new equipment, and intelligent monitoring of existing equipment [9].

9.2.1.5 Smart buildings and cities

Connectivity inside homes and buildings keeps expanding with the massive deployment of IoT devices. These devices can be used to collect sensory data to monitor any desired quantity and take necessary actions. With the help of IoT devices and the data collected by them, it is possible to build a digital twin of a home or building. This digital twin environment can then be used for optimizing the operation and maintenance of the home or building. On a larger scale, large and accurate maps of buildings and terrain are available publicly, making it possible to build a digital twin of smart cities by integrating the available urban maps with the data available from connected devices in the city and inside the buildings [10]. Such a unified approach is useful not only for maintaining homes, buildings, and other structures, but also for integrating them with other domains, such as smart power grids and traffic networks, to optimize urban planning, operation, energy delivery, and traffic management [11].

9.2.2 RAN network

In this subsection, we will discuss the components of the digital twin for a RAN, which represents the B5G radio network as a central part of the digital twin ecosystem that provides connectivity to different physical domains discussed in the previous subsection. This is not an attempt to describe in detail all components of the physical radio network but, rather, an introduction of the high-level functional blocks of the digital twin where important considerations need to be taken into account. To this end, our discussion will focus on three main blocks: (1) the radio environment, (2) the RAN system, and (3) the RAN intelligent controller.

9.2.2.1 Radio environment

The virtual radio environment in a digital twin is built with a realistic representation of the physical environment where the signal propagates and with channel models that accurately characterize the signal propagation effects. Besides, it is also important for the digital twin to model new radiofrequency (RF) environments, for example with the deployment of terahertz (THz) bands, which do not exist widely in the field today.

The radio signals, when propagating over the air, experience a complex set of physical effects that are dependent on not only the distance between the transmitter and the receiver, but also the RF at which the signal is carried and any obstacles in the surrounding environment such as buildings, trees, and moving objects like human and cars. To realistically represent the radio environment, it is important for the digital twin to utilize accurate geospatial maps of physical objects such as buildings, roads, trees, and the like and continuously reflect changes such as seasonal variation of foliage, weather conditions, new buildings, and so on.

Wireless signal propagation behavior can be modeled using channel models that typically account for three main effects: large-scale pathloss, shadowing, and small-scale (or multipath) fading. There are several methods for generating the channel models. The first approach is to use statistical models that are built from a combination of theoretical models and empirical measurement samples. From past measurement campaigns, for example, in certain morphologies such as urban, suburban, and rural areas and at different carrier frequencies, the observations on signal power attenuation and delay are collected and generalized in closed-form formulations. The second approach is to use machine techniques to train prediction models on a large collection of real-world measurement data. Due to the sensitivity of channel effects on the surrounding environment, which is constantly changing, it is very important for the channel models to be updated with the most accurate data. However, keeping the model updated is a challenging task due to the complexity of the model generation process and the laborious and costly task of data collection. Another alternative is to utilize measurement data that is being generated by the network and users today as part of their normal operations. For example, the base station (BS) periodically collects channel measurements from its connected users in order to make appropriate scheduling and mobility management decisions. If this data can be correlated with other features, such as the locations of the users, the height of the BS antenna, the clutter information, and so on, and then archived in a database, it will become a valuable dataset for channel-modeling purposes.

9.2.2.1.1 Channel models at new frequency bands

Wireless communications technologies at new frequency bands (such as millimeter-wave [mmWave] and THz bands) are being constantly explored. The deployment of commercial mmWave cellular systems is still limited, although it is expected to grow in the coming years, while THz communications are still mainly conducted in lab environments. This results in a lack of measurement data in the field and consequently makes it challenging to build a virtual radio environment at these frequency bands. One of the important features of the digital twin is its ability to constantly incorporate new findings and observations to refine the channel models and to evolve as new communications technologies mature.

9.2.2.1.2 Model of new RF scenarios

Another important feature of a virtual radio environment model in the digital twin is the ability to make accurate predictions of channel characteristics in new network deployment scenarios that do not exist today, such as the estimation of coverage maps for new cell sites and new carrier bands, or new configurations of existing antennas such as those that transmit power and orientation. This capability is crucial for network planning and optimization processes, which often require many trial-and-error iterations.

9.2.2.2 RAN system

The digital twin of a RAN system simulates RAN components, such as the BSs (e.g, long-term evolution [LTE] eNodeBs and New Radio [NR] gNodeBs), the user equipment (UE), and the protocol stacks, based on which the BSs and UE operate. In the remainder of this subsection, we will describe the creation, configuration, and functional features of their virtual counterparts in a digital twin.

9.2.2.2.1 Network topology

Network topology refers to the placement of BSs over a geographical area under study. Depending on the use case, the size of the area under study can vary from a cluster of several BSs with a radius of a few miles, to a wider area spanning a city or even a country. When the virtual BSs are created as objects within the digital twin environment, they should be positioned in a similar topology as that of the actual network and be overlaid on the corresponding radio environment representing the area under study. This allows accurate characterization of the radio condition, for example, to conduct downlink and uplink channel measurements in this region.

9.2.2.2.2 Network configuration

After being deployed in the digital twin environment, the cell sites should be parameterized to reflect the various configurations of the actual cell sites. The main configuration parameters of the cell sites can include the following:

- *Antenna configuration*: This includes the number of transmitting and receiving antennas, 3D orientation (azimuth and elevation angles), antenna gain and directivity pattern, transmit power, cable loss, number of antenna elements and array configuration, and so on
- *Carrier configuration*: This includes uplink and downlink frequency, bandwidth, multiplexing mode, subcarrier spacing, and slot configuration (if using TDD)
- *Mobility management configuration*: This includes conditions on received signal strength and quality that are used in the decision making

of cell reselection when UEs are in idle mode and cell handover when UEs are in connected mode
- *Traffic management configuration*: This includes the triggering and de-triggering conditions of various traffic offloading and equalization mechanisms in order to alleviate network congestion and improve spectral efficiency

9.2.2.2.3 Network functions

The RAN network today is a very complex system that operates on rich sets of features at different network layers of the 4G and 5G protocol stacks. The BSs in a digital twin environment should be programmed to support similar functionalities as those in actual network. These include the functionalities defined by 3rd Generation Partnership Project (3GPP) standards, for example, beamforming codebooks, UE admission procedures, mobility management, and so on. For functionalities where specific implementations are not specified by the standards—for example, message authentication code (MAC) scheduling algorithms, traffic load balancing, and so on—the digital twin models should support the incorporation of different variants that can be contributed by different network vendors or the research community.

In addition to having feature parity with the currently deployed physical network, the digital twin framework should be easily extensible and evolvable as new standards are defined. These characteristics might include supporting new functional splitting options or incorporating advanced algorithms in existing functional blocks, such as advanced beamforming, application-aware scheduling, and network slicing, among others.

9.2.2.2.4 User distribution and mobility pattern

The locations of users in the network and their mobility patterns play big roles in many aspects of network operations and significantly impact the connection performance. Therefore, the placement of virtual users in the digital twin should reflect how frequently the users are present at different locations in the network and their mobility patterns. Such placement and mobility events could be derived from a geodistribution map of the users that is built from historical network measurements or is shared by the users themselves via crowdsourcing. The user distribution map might contain multiple snapshots to emulate the geographical and temporal movements of users, such as indoor versus outdoor, office versus residential areas, weekdays versus weekends, and so on.

9.2.2.2.5 User traffic

Traffic demands vary greatly across different users, and collectively differ across geographical areas and times of day. To realistically generate user traffic, the traffic generator model in the digital twin should emulate the aggregated traffic patterns of users in the network, which can be represented by the arrival pattern and traffic volume. In addition, the digital twin should utilize information where possible to represent the traffic patterns of individual users, such as their uplink and downlink usage patterns, and the traffic classes (such as voice, video, and data) associated with the applications running on the users' devices. It is also important for the traffic models to support new types of traffic and applications such as extended reality (XR), V2X, live videos, and so on that have very different arrival patterns and QoE requirements compared to traditional traffic.

9.2.2.2.6 User capability

The user population consists of a heterogeneous set of devices with various capabilities. They range from low-power IoT devices with limited cellular capability, to the latest smartphones with advanced RF chains that support very high data rates and multiple frequency bands. Many network management functions are only applicable to certain classes of users, for example, advanced massive MIMO (multiple-input and multiple-output) beamforming, carrier aggregation (CA), dual connectivity (EN-DC), and so on that require UEs to have compatible receiver capability. A realistic representation of user capability in the population will have a considerable impact on ensuring the accuracy of simulation models and the assessment of network performance overall.

9.2.2.3 RAN intelligent controller

Along with the advances in radio technologies, the RAN is evolving toward a new architecture that is more agile, open, and interoperable than the current monolithic paradigm. This new open RAN (O-RAN) architecture paradigm is realized via the decoupling of the control plane from the user plane in the RAN protocol stack, allowing for innovation at the control plane to happen at a faster pace and to fuel the use of AI/ML techniques that leverage near-real-time fine-grained RAN data for more effective RAN management, automation, and optimization. As illustrated in Figure 9.2, the O-RAN architecture is mainly

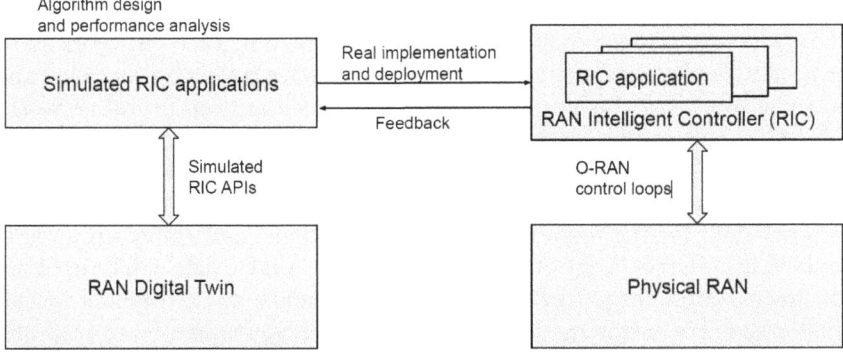

Figure 9.2 Simulation of O-RAN RIC applications in a digital twin environment.

constituted of three components: (1) the RAN Intelligent Controller (RIC) platform, (2) the open interfaces connecting the RAN to the RIC to facilitate RAN data collection and RIC control loops, and (3) the RIC applications (often referred to as the *xApps* for near-real-time RICs and *rApps* for non-real-time RICs) that perform RAN data analytics and make intelligent control decisions that can be applied to the RAN via O-RAN standardized interfaces.

Despite the many potentials of O-RAN, it is still a very challenging task to realistically assess the effectiveness of RIC applications before deploying them in actual systems. First, this is due to the lack of RAN implementations, both commercially and experimentally, that are fully compatible with O-RAN in terms of measurement reporting and control service models. Second, the realization of O-RAN today is still at a very limited scale, mostly consisting of a few BSs in a lab environment or in a commercial trialing zone. Hence, it is difficult to fully assess the value of O-RAN data feeds and control loops, as well as the impact of RIC applications on large-scale networks.

With the simulated RIC application programming interfaces (APIs) built into the digital twin, we will be able to implement simulated RIC applications that interact with the RAN digital twin to access fine-grained RAN state information and make control actions in similar ways as the actual O-RAN RIC would enable. This can be facilitated through an extensible set of RIC APIs based on the O-RAN standard in a digital twin environment that allows accessing RAN information at a fast timescale and fine-grained control capabilities applicable to individual UEs and traffic bearers. By carrying out performance analysis of RIC applications in a digital twin environment, their potential gains in large-scale network scenarios can be projected and used as a measure to improve RIC control algorithms.

9.2.3 Digital twin engine

The engine of the digital twin is, in general, a mathematical model that represents the physical RAN. With a massive number of connected devices, an increased number of supported services and use cases, and a wide range of sources and types of data, B5G networks are quite complex to be modeled accurately. The vast amount and variety of data generated in a B5G network show the need to deploy computationally efficient and powerful data processing and modeling tools. For this purpose, ML models, such as deep neural networks (DNNs) and generative adversarial networks (GANs), are strong candidates to represent the physical environment in a B5G network. These models can ingest vast amounts of data for training, which are available from a B5G network. Network data for the topology, node configurations, and traffic are usually available at different layers of the network. This available data can be used not only to create and train the RAN digital twin, but also to do different "what-if" analyses. For instance, the RAN digital twin engine can be trained and fine-tuned to provide insights on the impacts of deploying a new BS, enabling a new frequency band, or changing cell configurations or parameters. Given the highly dynamic nature of radio access technologies, this will bolster the efforts to investigate future generations of RANs in a more cost-effective and time-efficient manner. Another important feature of the RAN digital twin is its flexibility in processing and representing data collected from different domains. For the specific service of interest, the RAN digital twin engine uses domain knowledge and data analytics to process and ingest the data as required by the domain characteristics. This data is then consumed by the digital twin engine to predict and optimize service-specific outputs.

9.3 APPLICATIONS OF DIGITAL TWINS

In this section, we first outline the main operational capabilities of digital twins. These capabilities prove the usefulness of the digital twin approach in terms of various key performance indicators (KPIs), which we discuss next. Finally, we list several use cases from different domains in Section 9.3.3, and describe how digital twins can be utilized for these use cases in terms of control actions and KPIs.

9.3.1 Capabilities of digital twins

9.3.1.1 Planning and building

At the first level of capability, a digital twin can be used during the planning and building of the physical network to identify potential challenges and propose design insights to overcome them. The digital twin's capability of modeling and reflecting the characteristics of the physical environment enables optimal planning of the network, which provides a cost- and time-efficient planning phase. Specifically, the digital twin can utilize the available data from prior deployments or similar networks to optimize the planning of the current physical deployment. Moreover, the digital twin can provide insights on new technologies, use cases, services, and KPIs during the planning phase, since it can make predictions on how different network components and designs will perform for the particular physical environment. For instance, in a vehicular network, design considerations and KPIs for vehicular anomaly detection are quite different than those of autonomous driving, which requires significantly low latency and high data rates with high reliability. A digital twin of the vehicular network can utilize the domain knowledge and data available for deployed and modeled use cases to predict the challenges of others with much more stringent requirements, and make planning recommendations accordingly.

9.3.1.2 Monitoring and optimization

Once the network is deployed and operational, the digital twin continuously monitors the network by collecting data from all available data sources. This process covers a wide spectrum of data sources and data types, which are then used for optimizing the operation of the network in terms of different KPIs. As an example, network traffic data is collected and used for optimizing the network resources, configuration, and algorithms, such as bandwidth and physical resource provisioning, handover control, and user scheduling. On the other hand, in a smart city ecosystem, satellite data can be used to monitor high-traffic-volume areas and control and optimize traffic flow by adjusting the traffic light cycles and traffic routing to avoid congestion.

9.3.1.3 Maintenance and troubleshooting

Another responsibility of the digital twin is to use the monitored data to detect anomalies and faults in the physical environment that can occur in time. For example, sensory and visual data can be used to monitor the static and/or dynamic changes in the physical environment, such as a faulty power grid element or a physically damaged cell tower. Then, the digital twin can either react to these changes by interacting with external processes—for instance, by adjusting the resource routing in the power grid and offloading the traffic to active cell towers—or alert and provide a maintenance plan for human operators, if physical intervention is required.

9.3.2 Digital twin performance metrics

The digital twin makes use of several key performance metrics while planning, gauging, and optimizing the network. Different metrics and specific KPIs can be more prominent for the digital twin framework, depending on the particular physical domain and the use case of interest. Although these categories are usually correlated and used jointly to assess the network, we divide the performance metrics into the following categories and discuss each of them in detail below: (1) performance, (2) resiliency, (3) energy efficiency, and (4) security and privacy.

9.3.2.1 Performance

Although performance can be used as a more general term to evaluate a network, in this section, we mainly consider data rate, latency, and quality as the performance-related metrics. In physical domains and corresponding use cases, peak, average, and/or minimum performance guarantees are provided to the users, which are used by the digital twin for planning and optimization. For example, for a given use case, increasing the peak or average data rate of UEs can be the main objective to maximize the total data rate, whereas for some other use cases, the goal can be to prevent the data rate from dropping below a minimum value. Similarly, keeping jitter, or the average and/or maximum latency experienced by the UEs, below certain thresholds can be desirable. Finally, QoE is a metric that is used to simultaneously consider data rate and latency requirements.

9.3.2.2 Resiliency

The first deployments of telecom networks introduced the first means of resiliency requirements. Initially, for voice calls, the most important criteria included (1) availability (i.e., the proportion of time the service is accessible) and (2) retainability (i.e., the proportion of time voice calls do not drop). However, as new services and use cases that mostly carry data traffic come out, resiliency requirements have taken more general forms to measure how accessible and reliable the services are. For example, for voice traffic, accessibility and retainability are measured by the probability of making a successful voice call. On the other hand, for data traffic over an LTE network, the accessibility and retainability can gauge both the time on LTE and the time the connection falls back to 3G, which does not necessarily result in connection drops. A related and more general metric, referred to as *reliability*, quantifies the proportion of packets that satisfy a given data rate and/or latency requirement.

9.3.2.3 Energy efficiency

With the variety of systems that run on different sources of energy deployed at larger scales, the energy efficiency of networks and end devices has gained significant importance. The goal to improve the energy efficiency of systems can be investigated from two perspectives. First, energy resource limitations and emission requirements highlight the need for more efficient power delivery to all connected devices in a network compared to the conventional energy delivery mechanisms [12]. On the other hand, with the number of connected devices increasing at a drastic rate, the cost of energy delivery to devices such as servers, BSs, and the massive number of IoT devices and other smart equipment has become a major factor. Moreover, the energy and/or battery limitations of end devices, such as smartphones, tablets, laptops, connected cars, XR goggles and devices, and so on, deem the analysis of energy efficiency crucial for the networks deploying such devices. The digital twin of the network can provide insights on the energy usage and efficiency of new network components and optimize the network operation to improve energy efficiency.

9.3.2.4 Security and privacy

As the connectivity across the network increases with the deployment of more smart devices and systems, more data is generated and shared within the network. This can jeopardize the security and privacy of the network by (1) exposing the data to unintended and potentially malicious users and devices, and (2) providing the malicious nodes with more potential points of attack as the network becomes more heterogeneous and distributed, which limits monitoring and control over fraudulent activities. With an accurate representation of the network topology and the data generated, the digital twin can help identify the security risks and provide means to improve the security of the network [13–15]. Moreover, as a more online approach, the digital twin can monitor real-time data and the behavior of the nodes to detect network anomalies and fraudulent activities [16].

9.3.3 Digital twin use cases

9.3.3.1 RAN design and configuration

RAN design engineers must consider and analyze several factors while designing the locations and the density of BSs and cell towers, including but not limited to signal strength measured at different UE locations, interference caused by neighboring cells, indoor and outdoor UE penetrations, static and dynamic physical characteristics of the cell sites, and so on. Moreover, when a new frequency band is deployed at a cell site, careful planning and analysis are required due to the different propagation characteristics of the new frequency band and the interaction/interference among the co-band cells. By using the data available from other cell sites and frequency bands, the digital twin of the RAN can serve as the cell and site planner to optimize UE performance, in terms of coverage, data rate, latency, and quality, while also focusing on the resiliency of the network. This will reduce the cost to test and deploy new RAN elements, which can bolster the efforts to improve coverage in B5G networks. Similarly, for cloud and virtual RAN architectures, server and resource pooling and traffic provisioning contribute significantly to the energy and cost efficiency of the network. An effective framework for RAN planning, provisioning, and optimization is the digital twin, which can help analyze the limitations and provide resiliency insights for the network of interest.

9.3.3.2 Cloud gaming and cloud XR

Interactive real-time applications, such as online gaming and AR/VR, require high data rates and extremely low latency to provide users with a seamless experience. For example, in the cloud-gaming scenario, the images and videos of the game are rendered in the cloud with powerful processors, and the rendered frames are sent back to the users [17]. With the high frame rates of 720–1080p that such games support, the network must satisfy stringent latency, throughput, and reliability constraints. On the other hand, mobile edge computing will be another key enabler for remote-rendered applications, where potentially mobile end devices, such as XR headsets, offload the computationally heavy tasks to the edge server, with an end-to-end latency requirement of around 20–30 ms. As the variety of end devices and access technologies expands quite rapidly for such applications, it is crucial to gauge the limitations to provide customers with good experiences and performance guarantees. A digital twin can play an important role in modeling the physical network responsible for carrying gaming and/or XR traffic, which can be used to assess the performance limitations for these applications.

9.3.3.3 Connected and autonomous vehicles

A key player in the 5G ecosystem is connected vehicles, which are empowered by the underlying 5G infrastructure and the extended connectivity it provides to vehicular networks. Connectivity of different vehicular network components, such as vehicles, pedestrians, traffic lights, and so on, enables constant data exchange among these components to provide the entire network with increased safety and performance. This constant connectivity of vehicles allows the concept of *connected and autonomous vehicles* (CAVs) to be investigated as a potential enabler of autonomous vehicular networks, in which human interaction and control are at the minimum level [18]. Some use cases that can be supported through the CAV vision are vehicle platooning, remote or autonomous driving, vulnerable road users, and extended sensors. All of these use cases require various levels of data rate (1–1000 Mbps), latency (3–1000 ms), reliability (90–99.999%), and communication range (50–1000 m) guarantees [19]. A potential solution to model this diverse set of use cases and requirements in a single ecosystem is through the digital twin, which can provide a unified modeling and optimization framework for the vehicular network.

9.3.3.4 Production planning and control

Across different industries, one of the main goals of today's companies is to increase the production volume per unit time, while maintaining the quality and reliability of the products, in a time-, cost-, energy-, and workload-efficient manner. By modeling the production line, the digital twin can provide performance guarantees for the production process and suggestions for new mechanisms and components to improve network performance. Energy and cost efficiency of the production process can also be improved by using sale, storage, and delivery statistics and by optimizing the production timeline accordingly [4]. Moreover, the reliability of the entire production process is key to reducing costs and avoiding unexpected delays. Digital twins can be responsible for the reliability of the system by monitoring the lifecycle of production line components and detecting production anomalies when new components and/or production mechanisms are deployed.

9.3.3.5 Power grid anomaly detection

Anomalies in a power grid can be caused by several internal and external factors, including but not limited to cyberattacks, physical attacks and damage, and component malfunctioning. Providing the required levels of security for the smart grid is critical for the safety and performance of the network. Virtualization of the physical network enables digital twins to identify subsystems of the power grid with high-security risk and monitor potential threats in real-time [8]. Moreover, capturing component malfunctions and similar anomalies in the power grid by human monitoring can be a challenging task due to the complex nature of these systems. For such scenarios, digital twins can provide the required levels of reliability and performance by detecting such anomalies in the virtual environment [20].

9.4 DIGITAL TWIN DESIGN OBJECTIVES

It is expected that the digital twin for B5G will be highly compute- and data-intensive. In this section, we discuss important design objectives for the digital twin to realize its promise as being a continuously evolving mirror of large-scale and highly complex physical B5G networks.

9.4.1 Accuracy

The digital twin is responsible for generating responses or outputs that can be used by human (e.g., network operators, engineers and researchers) or other external processes (e.g., an automated process that makes online reconfigurations on an actual network based on analysis done in the digital twin). In all cases, it is very critical for the outputs from the digital twin to be accurate, which necessitates the accuracy both of the input data and of the underlying models in the digital twin engine.

9.4.1.1 Accuracy of input data

The digital twin relies on various sources of input data, which can be majorly categorized into offline data and online data. Offline data includes configuration information that is infrequently changed, such as network topology, frequency bands, and antenna configuration as well as historical statistics of UE distribution and their traffic demand. Online data refers to information that is continuously updated and is streamed in real-time or near-real time from the live network. Online data might include instantaneous locations of the UEs, their channel conditions, buffer status, and so on. In practical data pipelines, there could be many reasons that can cause data inaccuracy. For example, a UE measurement record might be reported at a wrong location or a wrong time-stamp. The accumulation of these incorrect reports will cause significant skewness in the modeling of the digital twin. Due to the number of data sources, and differences in their formats and ingestion protocols, it is clearly a challenging yet very important task to ensure the quality of the input data, which might require various filtering and quality control mechanisms to be implemented.

9.4.1.2 Accuracy of underlying models

Residing at the heart of the digital twin engine are the simulation models that mimic the processes in a real network. These models could be implemented as 1-to-1 replicas of the actual protocols or decision logics, or sometimes can be abstracted at a higher level to reduce the complexity by relying on statistical models. In the former case, it is important for the replicated functions to have accurate implementation while continuously evolving with the actual counterparts in the real network—for example, when certain software features in the BSs are upgraded or extended with new functionalities. In the latter case, statistical models are often built based on historical measurement data whose distribution can be shifted over time. An example of model shift is the change of radio channel characteristics due to seasonal foliage or new buildings being built. In this case, it is important for these statistical models to be updated frequently and calibrated with the new dataset to ensure their accuracy.

9.4.2 Scalability

As the physical network becomes more complex and continues to grow in multiple dimensions (including the network infrastructures, surrounding environment, the number and types of UE devices, as well as their traffic volume), there should be reasonable ways for the digital twin to cope with the increase in scale.

The architecture of a digital twin that operates at a large scale is usually highly specific to the use case. There is hardly a generic, one-size-fits-all scalable architecture that models all layers of the network and the involved subsystems at the same level of granularity. The problem may stem from the almost infinite number of possible configuration options (e.g., channel models, beamforming and scheduling choices, etc.), as is often considered in Monte Carlo simulations that require parallelization of the computation. It could also be the scale of the network in terms of the number of cell sites and UEs that reflect the scope of the network under study. For example, a digital twin that is designed to represent a private 5G network in the context of a manufacturing floor with a few hundred UE devices with light traffic might look very different from a macrocellular network with millions of devices.

A digital twin that scales well for a particular network is built around assumptions of what types of UE devices (regular smartphones, IoT or XR devices, etc.) and applications will be present (the *complexity* factor), as well as the number of each type (the *load* factor). Although the digital twin for B5G will typically be built from common building blocks (e.g., a network protocol stack, a device, and radio environment maps), the design choice for each block can be customized. For example, the computational load for a given block will depend on how much abstraction is considered appropriate. Also, depending on whether the operations of the network elements need to be synchronized, parallelization of the simulations might not be possible.

9.4.3 Reliability

The digital twin is becoming more integrated into the operation of live networks in which there is real-time information exchange between the twins and the decision making in the live network depends upon the computation and analysis done in the digital twin. As much as we would expect reliability from the live network, which provides services to millions of users and critical operations in many other domains, the digital twin needs to be highly reliable as well. This means that the digital twin needs to be provisioned to run and provide its service with high availability, be able to tolerate hardware and software failures, and be robust to human errors. Therefore, running digital twin services on a cloud-native environment would be a compelling choice; however, the specific deployment—whether it is in a centralized cloud or edge cloud—will need to factor in the various requirements for compute, bandwidth, and storage resources as well as latency and data privacy.

9.4.4 Maintainability

The maintainability of the digital twin relates to the aspects of operability, simplicity, and evolvability. In essence, the digital twin should be designed with a simple yet flexible interface that can be operated effectively by users with different backgrounds. Depending on the use cases at hand, users might not be required to learn all aspects and features of the digital twin and can focus on the functionalities relevant to their analysis. Furthermore, the digital twin architecture should not be overspecialized to the current protocol stacks (such as LTE and 5G), but rather kept as an easily extendable framework that allows the incorporation of new technologies, or new alternatives of current functional blocks. For example, the implementation of the simulated protocol stack can be modularized so that different blocks (e.g., the MAC scheduler) can be easily switched between implementations or algorithms provided by different contributors.

9.5 DIGITAL TWIN ECOSYSTEM COLLABORATION

The digital twin is undoubtedly a promising enabler for 5G and B5G networks. However, the realization of such a digital twin is a very challenging task due to its complexity and the interdependency of multiple subsystems. In this section, we discuss how network operators, industry partners, the research community, and end users can join forces to collaboratively create a scalable and interoperable digital twin for B5G.

Although physical cellular networks today are owned and operated by mobile operators, they are constructed from multiple components, including software and hardware that are created by different network vendors. Similarly, user devices (e.g., smartphones, tablets, IoT devices, etc.) are created by different manufacturers, and each user runs a diverse set of applications that interact with different application service providers. This mixed set of stakeholders at various levels of the network makes it very challenging to collect and combine the information needed to accurately build the digital twin engine that is representative of the actual network. As such, we strongly believe that it will be highly important for these stakeholders to collaborate through data sharing and integration of the respective digital twin subsystems. On the one hand, network operators will be able to utilize the digital twin to better plan and optimize their networks in order to minimize cost and improve the performance of the end users. On the other hand, equipment vendors and application service providers can benefit from being able to run experiments of their new technologies in the digital twin environment and utilize its feedback to improve their products and services.

Practically, there are many challenges and barriers related to data sharing and end-to-end integration across different stakeholders. These include non-sharing of proprietary information and technologies, user privacy protection, and business objectives, among others. In the following, we lay out several solutions and provide some discussion on how they can help address these challenges and facilitate a stronger collaboration culture among the network stakeholders.

9.5.1 Crowd-sourced data collection

Crowd-sourced data collection has been widely utilized in the research community, where end users volunteer themselves to participate in data collection campaigns and contribute these measurements to create large and statistically meaningful datasets. Many of the network-related metrics can only be accurately measured at the end user's devices. For example, downlink radio channel quality measurements, video quality, and user perceptions of the QoE are measured from the UEs. Although some subsets of these measurements are reported back to the serving BSs and/or the service providers, they can only be used for limited purposes and are bounded by privacy policies. Therefore, the contribution of measurement reports directly from the end users through crowdsourcing will help create valuable datasets that can be shared among different stakeholders to build the digital twin.

9.5.2 Anonymized data sharing

To ensure user data privacy is protected, it is important to employ anonymization mechanisms such as identity removal, encryption, and randomization and to robustly follow all the privacy guidelines. This will create a safe environment and mechanisms by which crowd-sourced and production data can be shared without exposing sensitive information about the network, users, and applications. For example, if users' location data can be made available without revealing the identity of the users, the digital twin can generate accurate placement of users on the geographical map over time, which will then create realistic user distributions and mobility patterns. Many of the network design decisions today, such as where to deploy the BSs and how much bandwidth should be provisioned to each BS, are made without complete knowledge about user distribution. Having an accurate representation of the user population in the digital twin environment can therefore enable effective evaluation of different network deployment plans and allow the decision making to be done in a faster and more accurate manner.

Another example area where anonymized user data can be useful is application-level QoE scores. These scores can vary depending on the specific applications (e.g., bitrate and starting time for video-streaming applications, latency and jitter for online gaming, etc.) and are mainly measured either by the application clients running on the end users' devices or by the application servers. These emerging applications, such as live videos, online gaming, XR, and so on, are growing very quickly and carry the majority of traffic volume in cellular networks. Therefore, application-level QoE scores are becoming important metrics for network design and optimization, in addition to traditional metrics such as spectral and energy efficiency. Application metrics today are associated with the end users; however, it is possible to anonymize these metrics and make them available for digital twin modeling.

9.5.3 Digital twin model sharing

In certain scenarios, direct sharing of user data or network measurements is not possible, which could be due to data privacy or data volume. For example, it would be very costly or even impossible to store all the channel feedback from all the users, since these feedbacks are reported very frequently with intervals ranging from a few milliseconds to a few hundred milliseconds. One effective approach to handle these scenarios is to build abstraction models based on sample sets of data, such as link-level channel models or models of user behavioral profiles that encapsulate their real-world characteristics. These abstraction models can be lightweight and contain no identifiable information about the users, and therefore they can be easily packaged and shared across different stakeholders. Model sharing can also enable the decoupling of a digital twin system at different layers, allowing them to be designed and implemented in a modularized manner and making it easier to scale and maintain the system.

9.5.4 Digital twin as a service

To enable extensibility and scalability, the digital twin can also be decoupled into multiple subsystems, as described previously in this chapter. Each digital twin subsystem focuses on the virtual implementation of one specific domain and might contain proprietary data and technologies that are not directly shareable with other entities. For example, RAN equipment vendors need to protect the advanced signal-processing and traffic-scheduling algorithms that are running on their BSs, while application service providers cannot reveal the core implementation of their services. In order to enable interoperability between different digital twin subsystems, it is important to define the APIs based on which these subsystems can interact with each other. With standardized APIs, different network stakeholders can build their own respective digital twin subsystems and provide them as a service to others, forming an extensible and interoperable digital twin ecosystem.

The combination of multiple digital twin subsystems will provide a new venue on which new cross-domain technologies can be developed and experimented. For example, the current approach for verifying a new feature (e.g., advanced beamforming) in a BS today is to implement the feature in the actual

BS product, followed by a sequence of testing in a lab environment and then in the production network of a mobile operator. In the future, this feature development and verification process can be done in a digital twin system combining both the digital twin subsystems representing the RAN equipment vendor's BS and the mobile operator's network, respectively. This will accelerate technology development for B5G in a much more systematic and cost-efficient manner.

9.6 CONCLUSION

With the rapid progression of mobile cellular networks in terms of technology features, scale, and user heterogeneity, the need for computer-aided tools to design, manage, and optimize networks is becoming extremely pressing. In this chapter, we have laid out the vision of the digital twin, a software framework that models and mimics the behavior of the physical network. We discussed the architecture design, benefits, and applications of digital twins in reducing cost and risk, and accelerating network innovations for B5G. We have also elaborated on the interplay of different subsystems in the network ecosystem and how their corresponding virtual models and services can interface with each other to form a holistic digital twin. The realization of the envisioned digital twin is going to be a multiphase process; however, we believe that this chapter has provided insightful motivation and directions for further research and development efforts on this important topic.

REFERENCES

1. L. U. Khan, Z. Han, W. Saad, E. Hossain, M. Guizani, and C. S. Hong, "Digital twin of wireless systems: Overview, taxonomy, challenges, and opportunities," *IEEE Communications Surveys & Tutorials*, vol. 24, no. 4, pp. 2230–2254, Fourthquarter 2022, doi: 10.1109/COMST.2022.3198273.
2. E. Glaessgen, and D. Stargel, *The Digital Twin Paradigm for Future NASA and U.S. Air Force Vehicles*. [Online]. Available: https://arc.aiaa.org/doi/abs/ 10.2514/6.2012-1818
3. B. Schleich, N. Anwer, L. Mathieu, and S. Wartzack, "Shaping the digital twin for design and production engineering," *CIRP Annals*, vol. 66, no. 1, pp. 141–144, 2017. [Online]. Available: https://www.sciencedirect.com/science/article/pii/ S0007850617300409
4. W. Kritzinger, M. Karner, G. Traar, J. Henjes, and W. Sihn, "Digital twin in manufacturing: A categorical literature review and classification," *IFAC-PapersOnLine*, vol. 51, no. 11, pp. 1016–1022, 2018, 16th IFAC Symposium on Information Control Problems in Manufacturing INCOM 2018. [Online]. Available: https:// www.sciencedirect.com/science/article/pii/S2405896318316021
5. C. Boje, A. Guerriero, S. Kubicki, and Y. Rezgui, "Towards a semantic construction digital twin: Directions for future research," *Automation in Construction*, vol. 114, p. 103179, 2020. [Online]. Available: https://www.sciencedirect.com/ science/article/pii/S0926580519314785

6. A. Dogra, R. K. Jha, and S. Jain, "A survey on beyond 5g network with the advent of 6g: Architecture and emerging technologies," *IEEE Access*, vol. 9, pp. 67 512–67 547, 2021.

7. K. Zhang, J. Cao, and Y. Zhang, "Adaptive digital twin and multiagent deep reinforcement learning for vehicular edge computing and networks," *IEEE Transactions on Industrial Informatics*, vol. 18, no. 2, pp. 1405–1413, 2022.

8. J. Lopez, J. E. Rubio, and C. Alcaraz, "Digital twins for intelligent authorization in the B5G-enabled smart grid," *IEEE Wireless Communications*, vol. 28, no. 2, pp. 48–55, 2021.

9. H. Pan, Z. Dou, Y. Cai, W. Li, X. Lei, and D. Han, "Digital twin and its application in power system," in *2020 5th International Conference on Power and Renewable Energy (ICPRE)*, 2020, pp. 21–26.

10. G. White, A. Zink, L. Codecá, and S. Clarke, "A digital twin smart city for citizen feedback," *Cities*, vol. 110, p. 103064, 2021. [Online]. Available: https://www.sciencedirect.com/science/article/pii/S0264275120314128

11. A. Fuller, Z. Fan, C. Day, and C. Barlow, "Digital twin: Enabling technologies, challenges and open research," *IEEE Access*, vol. 8, pp. 108 952–108 971, 2020.

12. Y. Wang, X. Kang, and Z. Chen, "A survey of digital twin techniques in smart manufacturing and management of energy applications," *Green Energy and Intelligent Transportation*, 2022, vol. 1, no. 2.

13. V. Damjanovic-Behrendt, "A digital twin-based privacy enhancement mechanism for the automotive industry," in *2018 International Conference on Intelligent Systems (IS)*, 2018, pp. 272–279.

14. G. P. Sellitto, M. Masi, T. Pavleska, and H. Aranha, "A Cyber Security Digital Twin for Critical Infrastructure Protection: The Intelligent Transport System Use Case," in *The Practice of Enterprise Modeling*, E. Serral, J. Stirna, J. Ralyté, and J. Grabis, Eds. Cham: Springer International Publishing, 2021, pp. 230–244.

15. R. Faleiro, L. Pan, S. R. Pokhrel, and R. Doss, "Digital Twin for Cybersecurity: Towards Enhancing Cyber Resilience," in *Broadband Communications, Networks, and Systems*, W. Xiang, F. Han, and T. K. Phan, Eds. Cham: Springer International Publishing, 2022, pp. 57–76.

16. C. López, "Real-time event-based platform for the development of digital twin applications," *The International Journal of Advanced Manufacturing Technology*, vol. 116, p. 835–845, 2020.

17. M. Carrascosa, and B. Bellalta, "Cloud-Gaming: Analysis of Google Stadia traffic," *arXiv preprint arXiv:2009.09786*, 2020.

18. A. Talebpour, and H. S. Mahmassani, "Influence of connected and autonomous vehicles on traffic flow stability and throughput," *Transportation Research Part C: Emerging Technologies*, vol. 71, pp. 143–163, 2016. [Online]. Available: https://www.sciencedirect.com/science/article/pii/S0968090X16301140

19. A. Gohar, and G. Nencioni, "The role of 5g technologies in a smart city: The case for intelligent transportation system," *Sustainability*, vol. 13, no. 9, 2021. [Online]. Available: https://www.mdpi.com/2071-1050/13/9/5188

20. W. Danilczyk, Y. L. Sun, and H. He, "Smart grid anomaly detection using a deep learning digital twin," in *2020 52nd North American Power Symposium (NAPS)*, 2021, pp. 1–6.

Index

Pages in *italics* refer to figures and pages in **bold** refer to tables.

Milton Keynes UK
Ingram Content Group UK Ltd.
UKHW031132141024
449569UK00006B/248